Frontispiece—See page 13.

A SPILL IN THE RIVER

Storm and Stampede
on the Chisholm

HUBERT E. COLLINS

Foreword by Hamlin Garland

ILLUSTRATED BY PAUL BROWN

INTRODUCTION TO THE BISON BOOKS EDITION
BY ROBERT R. DYKSTRA

UNIVERSITY OF NEBRASKA PRESS
LINCOLN AND LONDON

☉ The paper in this book meets the minimum requirements of American
National Standard for Information Sciences—Permanence of Paper for
Printed Library Materials, ANSI Z39.48-1984.

First Bison Books printing: 1998
Most recent printing indicated by the last digit below:
10   9   8   7   6   5   4   3   2   1

Library of Congress Cataloging-in-Publication Data
Collins, Hubert E. (Hubert Edwin), 1872–1932.
[Warpath & cattle trail]
Storm and stampede on the Chisholm / Hubert E. Collins; foreword by
Hamlin Garland; illustrated by Paul Brown; introduction to the Bison books
edition by Robert R. Dykstra.
p. cm.
Originally published as: Warpath & cattle trail. New York: William Morrow,
1928.
ISBN 0-8032-6386-4 (pbk.: alk. paper)
1. Frontier and pioneer life—Oklahoma.   2. Collins, Hubert E. (Hubert
Edwin), 1872–1932—Childhood and youth.   3. Cheyenne Indians—
Oklahoma—History—19th century.   4. Arapaho Indians—Oklahoma—
History—19th century.   5. Ranching—Oklahoma—History—19th century.
6. Chisholm Trail.   I. Title.
F697.C73   1998
976.6'04'092—dc21
[B]
97-32941   CIP

To the memory of ❧

My father, Rev. M. D. Collins, D.D., M.D., —a pioneer of Iowa in the '40s, Colorado in the '50s and early '60s, then back to Iowa, where he reared his family. Hunter, scout, trapper, guide, minister of the gospel and medical doctor.

And my mother, Keturah Williams Collins,— pioneer girl, wife and mother, and companion.

INTRODUCTION TO THE BISON BOOKS EDITION

Robert R. Dykstra

What was it like to live in the Old West?

Hundreds of memoirs, their writers conscious of having experienced a historic time and place, tried to convey that experience—with varying degrees of success. Of the many published, comparatively few are worth making permanently available to a wide modern readership. Such a memoir is Hubert Collins's recollections of fifteen months' residence in the Indian Territory, now the State of Oklahoma, in 1883–84. He was eleven and twelve years old at the time (not the ten years given in the introduction). Some forty years later, annoyed by Hollywood screenwriters' depictions of frontier life and encouraged by the famous novelist Hamlin Garland, Collins spent four years recovering boyhood recollections of his territorial sojourn and writing them for publication.

Hubert Edwin Collins had been born in Iowa on March 27, 1872, the son of a Methodist preacher active in several locations in the Hawkeye State. In 1883, during the family's itinerancy at Corning, young Collins persuaded his father to let him drop out of school in order to join his twenty-five-year-old brother Ralph at Red Fork Ranch in the Indian Territory.

Red Fork Ranch was a very prominent landmark on the famous Chisholm Trail. It lay just within the "Unassigned Lands" or "Oklahoma" proper—that is, in the heart of the Indian Territory about two-thirds of the distance between Texas and Kansas, at a strategic juncture where the original Chisholm Trail continued north to Caldwell while the so-called Eastern Trail veered northwestward toward Dodge City. Here, on the left bank of the Cimarron River, where today a town named Dover occupies the site, Red Fork Ranch had been established in 1876 by a frontiersman named Reynolds. That pioneer entrepreneur recognized the spot as an ideal location for what was known in the Old West as a "road ranch," where money could be made providing necessary supplies and services to the crews of northward-bound cattle herds, and where one's own potentially valuable herd might be assembled from footsore animals discarded by passing outfits.

Reynolds operated the ranch for a year or two before selling out to a noted border character, Dan W. Jones. What Reynolds sold to Jones, let it be understood, were only the improvements—a sod-roofed cabin and a horse corral. The land itself would remain strictly public domain, under title of the United States government, until the late eighties. Dan Jones, after two or three years, sold out in 1879, moving to Caldwell to become that new cattle town's assistant city marshal. The buyer, one Hood, two years later sold Red Fork Ranch to Ralph Collins and his cousin Fred. The cousins added a larger store with a second-floor sleeping area and an enormous circular corral to facilitate the branding and tallying of any cattle being sold in advance of their arrival at Caldwell or Dodge City. The establishment of a freight and stagecoach route adjacent to the Chisholm Trail only increased the value of their enterprise.

Who was Cousin Fred? Collins does not give us his full name, but he is, he tells us, from the Quaker side of the family. The Society of Friends had been a presence in Iowa since its early territorial period. In 1869, when the administration of President Ulysses S. Grant decided to reform a corrupt and unnecessarily violent federal policy toward the Indians, it accepted the Society's offer to nominate from its ranks pacifists of proven honesty as Indian agents. That settled, the Society then chose its first nominees from among the faithful living in sufficient numbers closest to the Plains—the Iowa Quakers. Such men as Laurie Tatum and Thomas C. Battey (both of whom left interesting memoirs) and Collins's uncle Brinton Darlington were given what the government considered the toughest assignment: managing the still warlike—and warring—Kiowa, Comanche, Southern Cheyenne, and Southern Arapaho nations, all of which had recently been uneasily relocated on Indian Territory reservations. In 1870 Darlington, a member of the Collinses' extended kin network, finally found an acceptable site for the new Cheyenne-Arapaho Agency (that is, the reservation headquarters), which, after its founder's death, continued to be called the Darlington Agency in his honor. Located some twenty-five miles south of Red Fork Ranch, the agency lay on the left bank of the North Canadian River adjacent to the "western cutoff" of the Chisholm Trail. A protective military post, Fort Reno, lay on the opposite side of the river.

Darlington called on trusted Iowa relatives to take jobs at the agency. He first recruited Cousin Fred, and then Ralph Collins, who, if not a Quaker, was at least a bona fide churchgoer with progressive views toward native Americans. Also originally employed by Darlington was

Ben Williams, the Uncle Ben of Collins's narrative. In 1874, after much lobbying by Darlington's Quaker successor, John D. Miles, Williams began serving as one of the territory's two deputy United States marshals. Their job was to stamp out illegal sales of liquor and firearms to the reservation tribes, to end the slaughter by whites of buffalo grazing on reservation lands, and to stop the wholesale theft of Indian ponies by well-organized white gangs. During his boyhood stay in the territory, Hubert would divide his time between Red Fork Ranch and the Darlington Agency.

It is good that before putting pen to paper the middle-aged Collins spent time checking his memories with those of his brother, his cousin Sarah Covington (Brinton's daughter), and authorities at the Oklahoma Historical Society. After all, his own recollections were those of a preteenager, and however intellectually curious a youngster he may have been, he must have recalled things with some degree of abbreviated accuracy. Perhaps most important of all, he relies on a good deal of "as-told-to" material. In other words, Collins did not personally witness many things he describes. Some of what he tells us must of course be regarded as only a version of historical truth, which in the best of documented circumstances is not always easy to establish.

For example, the author tells us, summarizing his brother's words, that Jesse Chisholm had not only laid out the trail that bore his name but also guided the first cattle herds up that route to Abilene in 1867. In fact, Chisholm, a half-Cherokee trader living in Kansas during the Civil War, had established the trail only as far as the present-day city of Wichita. The first Texas herds did not follow it until 1868, when they were induced to do so by word spread by the Abilene cattle broker, Joseph G. McCoy. But this is not a terribly serious error; other early accounts fallaciously attribute the trail to John S. Chisum, the famous Texas rancher.

Several historical characters encountered by Hubert Collins and/or his informants appear in these pages. "Celebrities" encountered at one time or another at Red Fork Ranch ranged from Jesse and Frank James to an English baronet meriting the courtesy title of Lord Wilson. Another notable was the army scout, horse trader, and trail-boss Theodore Baughman, a large, unkempt know-it-all given to telling dirty stories, recalls Collins, that nobody but he himself laughed at. Interested readers may wish to consult Baughman's considerably more flattering account of himself, a memoir modestly titled *Baughman, the Oklahoma*

Scout, published in 1886. As for the outlaw Collins refers to as "Wild Bill," he was most probably William ("Hurricane Bill") Martin, leader of a notorious band of cutthroats who headquartered on the Cimarron River, regularly stealing horses in the territory, taking them to Kansas for sale, and returning south with illegal cargoes of whiskey for surreptitious sale to the Indians.

Two of the many interesting characters who passed through Red Fork Ranch are described but not named. The first was a bad-tempered horse-breaker who spent a week at the ranch and employed all his free time practicing with both six-shooter and throwing knife. His intention was to ride north to Caldwell, says Collins, locate a man who had done him wrong, and kill him. But the bronco-buster was himself killed by his intended victim.

Who was this man? Three persons died violently in Caldwell during Collins's sojourn on the Cimarron. One was a housewife, killed by a drunken husband. Another was a visiting Pawnee Indian whom City Marshal Henry N. Brown shot for loitering and resisting arrest. (The Indian was feeling for a concealed weapon, Brown later testified.) The third victim was evidently Collins's horse-breaker.

His name was Newt Boyce. He was in town in December 1883 not to stalk an enemy but because he lived there in the off-season. Having been paid for his recent labors, he was in a mood to relax. The newspaper calls him a gambler, but that was a generic cattle-town term for any adult male who hung out in bars playing cards for money every afternoon and evening. The night before his demise, in a minor saloon brawl, Boyce had pulled a knife on a soldier and one of the proprietors of the place; Assistant Marshal Ben Wheeler disarmed him and told him to go home to his wife. But soon Boyce was on the street again, rearmed. Marshal Brown arrested him, locked him up for the night, and marched him to police court in the morning. In the afternoon, Boyce began to nurse a grudge against both lawmen. That evening, presumably drunk, Boyce threatened the marshal. Taking him seriously, Brown made his Saturday night rounds carrying a Winchester rifle. When he and Wheeler later spied Boyce on the street, Brown confronted him and fired twice. (The man was feeling for a concealed weapon, Brown later testified.) One bullet shattered Boyce's arm and lodged in his chest. He died a few hours later from loss of blood. His wife—perhaps relieved to be rid of him?—had him shipped back to his father in Texas.

Newt Boyce, as it turned out, was Marshal Henry Brown's last legal victim. Four months later he and Assistant Marshal Wheeler were captured after perpetrating a fatal bank heist at nearby Medicine Lodge, Kansas. That town's outraged citizens promptly executed Brown, Wheeler, and their two accomplices.

Less dramatic, if more mysterious, is Collins's story of the obstreperous black army officer passing through on his way to Fort Reno. The man was, says Collins, "the only negro graduate of West Point ever to reach the western territory." This appears to be a reference to Lieutenant Henry O. Flipper, class of 1877, the first African American to graduate from the U.S. Military Academy and the army's *only* black officer in the early 1880s. But there are three problems with this identification.

First, Cadet Flipper survived four years of harrassment meted out by the other cadets by displaying almost superhuman stoicism and much Christian forbearance. That such a seasoned racial diplomat could have been the profane, out-of-control young officer described by Collins is impossible to credit, even though Collins saw with his own eyes at least the tail end of the encounter.

Second, Lieutenant Flipper was never assigned to Fort Reno. Instead, he spent his time in the territory with the famous 10th Cavalry at Fort Sill before that all-black regiment was transferred to Texas in 1879. (He, too, left a memoir of his adventures in the West.)

Third, by the time Hubert Collins got to Red Fork Ranch, Flipper had been a civilian for almost a year, having been unfairly cashiered for "conduct unbecoming an officer" by a racially prejudiced post commander in June 1882. And there would not be another African American graduate of West Point until 1887.

If there is any reasonable explanation for this misidentification, it may have been that the officer in question—perhaps a darkly complected young man—was on his way to join the white officer corps of another famous "buffalo soldier" regiment, the 9th Cavalry, which did indeed have a detachment at Fort Reno from late 1881 until 1885. By the 1920s Collins's memory confused the association of the (white) officer with black troops and ended up supposing him to have been the celebrated Lieutenant Flipper.

Most of the last half of Collins's memoir is devoted to his observations about the Darlington Agency's Indians. A great deal of history had of course preceded Hubert to the Cheyenne-Arapaho Reservation.

Tribal elders, archaeologists, cultural anthropologists, and historians have carefully reconstructed the migrations of the two tribes. Both were members of the great Algonquian linguistic family, although their languages were (and are) very distinct. In the 1680s the components that later came together to form the two nations lived in present-day Minnesota, hunting, gathering, and farming—the Arapahos along the Red River to the west, the Cheyennes to the east around the headwaters of the Mississippi. But when the French and their Indian trading partners abruptly extended their fur-trapping operations westward from Lake Superior in the 1690s, the well-armed and numerically stronger Ojibwas began driving these groups south and west in order to monopolize the areas of beaver production. By the 1750s the two peoples—Arapahos ahead, the Cheyennes just behind—extended along a three-hundred-mile, southwestward-facing front, its lower end still in the forests, its upper end out on the Great Plains.

Soon the Arapahos had retreated as far west as present-day Wyoming. The Cheyennes, caught geographically between the warring Ojibwas and Sioux, allied themselves with the latter—which simply subjected them to the ferocity not only of the Ojibwas but also of the Ojibwas' Assiniboin and Cree allies. The Cheyennes finally escaped by slipping west through their Sioux allies and establishing fortified villages on the Missouri River. But the equally beleaguered Sioux retreated in turn, violently ousting the Cheyennes from their riverside lodges and herding them southwestward. The Arapahos and Cheyennes, in turn, collaborated in forcibly clearing the Kiowas and Kiowa-Apaches from the Black Hills. When first encountered by whites, the two tribes were hunting together on the northern Plains, both having completed the transition from relatively sedentary farming to a migratory economy based on the horse and the buffalo.

By the 1830s the Arapahos and Cheyennes were scattered some six hundred miles down the western half of the Great Plains. In 1851 the United States government acknowledged the tribes' possession of this enormous territory. But no sooner had it done so than it began to implement plans to lay out wagon roads through the heart of these lands. The Pike's Peak Gold Rush then brought thousands of whites swarming into central Colorado. These incursions began to split the tribes into what came to be known as their northern divisions, living mainly in Wyoming and closely allied with the Sioux, and the southern divisions living mainly in Colorado and closely associated with the Kiowas, Kiowa-Apaches, and Comanches.

Just before the Civil War the federal government managed to win a new treaty from the southern tribes by which they accepted a much diminished reservation. But the increasingly large and influential *Hotametaneo* band of the Cheyennes, the famous Dog Soldiers, refused to agree to the cession. The belief of Colorado's governor that a good Indian scare might compel Washington to clear the tribes' claims to his territory, opening it to complete white settlement and statehood, helped sabotage peace on the central Plains. Sporadic clashes eventually led in 1864 to the Sand Creek Massacre. This surprise attack by Colorado militia on the encampment of the leading Southern Cheyenne "peace chief," Black Kettle, resulted in the deaths of 120 Indians. The victims included Left Hand, a leading Arapaho chief, but the great majority happened to be women and children whose bodies were scalped and otherwise mutilated by the militiamen. Leading war chiefs assumed control in both tribes, and in 1864 and 1865 the Southern Arapahos and Southern Cheyennes scourged the frontier with death and destruction.

While the somewhat less militant Arapahos soon proved receptive to peace feelers from the federal government, the 1865 treaty supposedly ending hostilities was signed by only a small minority of the Cheyennes. For the next four years the Dog Soldiers continued to raid transportation routes and white settlements on the central Plains, undermining and coercing the peace chiefs and opposing any voluntary accommodation to reservation life. Full-scale war raged again in 1868, culminating in a second surprise attack on a camp of Black Kettle, this time by Colonel George Custer's cavalry. Black Kettle himself died in the so-called Battle of the Washita, along with some fifteen warriors and thirty women and children. But not until the Dog Soldiers' destruction as a major Cheyenne political unit at the Battle of Summit Springs in 1869 did the unconditional surrender of the Southern Cheyennes and Arapahos result in a lasting peace.

Only two last outbreaks occurred. The first, the Red River War of 1874, saw most of the Southern Cheyennes, together with a large body of Comanches, escape their reservations under the influence of a charismatic young Comanche warrior who convinced his followers that they would be magically protected from white men's guns. The army gradually wore down the group's fighting spirit, forcing their surrender in 1875. One lasting effect, however, was a permanent rift between the Southern Cheyennes and their Arapaho neighbors, whom the former never forgave for the latter's refusal to join in the 1874 uprising. The

Cheyennes would not let their children attend the same schools with Arapaho youngsters, for example.

The second outbreak, the so-called Dull Knife raid, was almost a sideshow. In 1877 Washington began moving the Northern Cheyennes south to the Indian Territory reservation, where many immediately expressed themselves unhappy with their new situation. In 1878 a group of nearly 350, led by Dull Knife, left the reservation and headed north, determined to fight their way back to their old hunting grounds. After finally being run to ground by the army, seventy-four of the northerners were brutally killed while in custody. When the Southern Cheyennes and their agent both expressed themselves as happily rid of these discontented tribespeople, Washington agreed to settle the surviving escapees on a new northern reservation of their own. To this tract about half the Northern Cheyennes still in the south were allowed to relocate in the early eighties. Today, the Northern Cheyennes live in Montana, their old Northern Arapaho allies on a Wyoming reservation.

By the time of Hubert Collins's months at Red Fork Ranch some 1,300 Southern Arapahos and 2,200 Southern Cheyennes lived in various settlements on their joint reservation. Two very prestigious chiefs, Powder Face of the Arapahos and Little Robe of the Cheyennes, had located their followers in the Cantonment District on the North Canadian River about thirty-five miles due west of the ranch. From that relatively close proximity the two old warriors became fairly regular visitors to the Collins brothers.

The saber-scarred Powder Face was a leading participant in the war that followed the Sand Creek Massacre. But by 1868 he had renounced violent resistance to the government, personally assuring the authorities that he wanted no part in the hostilities of that year. In 1869 he became a leading Arapaho chief. When the Red River War broke out five years later Powder Face organized Arapaho protection of the Darlington Agency from a possible Cheyenne attack. In 1876 he was described as one of the most "progressive" leaders of either tribe, having used income from the sale of buffalo robes to start a cattle herd. By 1880 he was breeding cows to blooded bulls, and in 1883 was among the Arapaho chiefs with substantial herds of improved stock whose settlements were surrounded by cornfields and vegetable gardens, the produce of which was sold to the whites at Fort Reno and the Darlington Agency. In the eighties he encouraged his son Clarence to attend the famous Indian school at Carlisle, Pennsylvania.

As for Little Robe of the Southern Cheyennes, he was a Dog Soldier whose father had been killed at Sand Creek. After the massacre the Cheyennes chose Little Robe as one of two war leaders to replace the temporarily discredited Black Kettle. Not until 1866 did Little Robe and his followers sign the treaty ending hostilities, but thereafter he and Black Kettle jointly became the tribe's most prominent advocates of nonviolence. Not even Black Kettle's death at the hands of Custer deterred Little Robe from remaining at peace, and he helped negotiate the surrender of the Cheyenne hostiles in 1869. He was one of the first Cheyenne leaders to cooperate with Brinton Darlington in establishing the agency on the North Canadian River, and the following year he was instrumental in helping keep the Southern Cheyennes from joining the Kiowas in a new uprising. In 1873 he was temporarily deposed as a chief but was back in control of the peace faction during the Red River War. By this time he was using the surviving Dog Soldiers to enforce his peace policy among the young men of the tribe.

At the moment of Hubert Collins's excursions among them, things were starting to go badly for the Arapahos and Cheyennes. First, Agent Miles had rented out too much of the reservation to several big cattle companies. While this provided a welcome reservation income, the company herds, especially in the Cantonment District, began to crowd onto the tribal settlements, causing much turmoil and complaint. In March 1884, Miles felt obliged to resign. He was replaced by D. B. Dyer, a brusque and demanding administrator who was determined to force his charges to become conventional farmers. He quickly alienated old Cheyenne war chiefs like Little Robe, whose Dog Soldiers, their animosities inflamed, began stealing cattle from company herds, threatening those Cheyennes who had begun farming, and pressuring Cheyenne graduates of Carlisle to return to tribal ways. From a "progressive" leader, Little Robe had become a leading traditionalist; Agent Dyer termed him an "outlaw." In contrast to Powder Face, Little Robe was one of the last chiefs on the Cheyenne-Arapaho Reservation to send his children to school.

Powder Face continued to be a progressive. When the argument between Indians and cattlemen became heated in late 1884, the leaders of the tribes threatened a boycott of the reservation schools unless permitted to visit Washington to make their grievances known. Dyer gave in. Powder Face was one of a delegation sent to complain to the secretary of the interior, and his words made the tribes' dissatisfaction with the cattle leases clear. In 1885, following a congressional investigation,

President Grover Cleveland fired Dyer and ordered the cattle companies to vacate the reservation.

But this was a short-run victory for the tribes. The cancellation of
cattle leases helped encourage white demands for agricultural settlement of the "unused" portions of the reservation. The Oklahoma Boomers
described by Collins were only the vanguard of the white population
avalanche of the 1890s. In 1892 the Cheyennes and Arapahos were
virtually forced by Congress to accept family land allotments, and the
reservation was dissolved.

Meanwhile, Hubert Collins had graduated from high school back in
Iowa, spent a few years as a cowboy in Colorado and New Mexico, and
then took up the profession of engineering. Between 1891 and 1902 he
worked for companies in New York State and then was employed on
various engineering projects as an internationally respected consultant.
He wrote a nine-volume series on various practical engineering problems, and one year taught a course on power plant design at Columbia
University. He finally retired to Utica, in upstate New York, where he
composed this book. It was originally published in 1928. Collins died
four years later, one of the last surviving Americans to have experienced the Old West "up close and personal."

This is his story of that encounter.

CONTENTS

LIST OF ILLUSTRATIONS

FOREWORD

THE growing interest in America's beginnings and especially in its pioneer phase, evidences a deepening sense of historical values. We are getting perspective not only on the lives of our forefathers, but on certain vast movements of men from east to west, and the transformations of landscape which they have effected since the Civil War. Some of us were not only spectators, we were participants in this prodigious drama of settlement. As sons of pioneers we were schooled in the processes of mid-western settlement and its upbuilding.

Mr. Hubert Collins, the author of this book, though born ten years later than I, has seen much more of the actual wild west changes. By a singular, almost unaccountable decision on the part of his father, he passed when a boy of ten from the quiet round of village life in Iowa to his brother's cattle ranch on the bank of a river in Oklahoma territory, and there lived for a year or more surrounded by cow-boys, redmen, bandits and other dramatic and discordant types of the border.

Ten is an impressionable age, as I am able to bear witness, for many of my own books are based on what I saw and felt from my ninth to my thirteenth year, and Hubert Collins shows himself to have been both camera and graphophone. Everything he saw and heard during his stay in Oklahoma, he registered. The fact that ranch life was entirely new to him, rendered him the more sensitive to its every detail. I have no doubt that his boyish inquisitiveness, his wish to see and hear all that went on, was irritating even to the best-natured of his

Foreword

older companions, but of that he was happily unaware. It was all a glorious vacation for him. This book is the result of his constant interest.

Later, when he was nineteen, Collins served as cow-boy on the range in New Mexico and Colorado and later still as an engineer on the Amazon River—which he explored for hundreds of miles. In truth, his life is as adventurous as any romantic novelist could imagine, and yet it is only recently, in the intervals of his engineering projects, that he has been able to set himself the task of recording his experiences.

My own connection with his work has been that of instigator. Perceiving the value of his material I repeatedly urged him to proceed, and I am writing this brief introduction to his book because I know the scene and some of the characters with which he deals. As a farmer in Oklahoma (I still have land there), I knew the Washitay Country very well. I knew the Cheyennes and Arapahoes, who were my neighbors in Seger's Colony.

Some of the incidents of Collins' book I have heard Seger tell. It is history but it is more than that. It is a gusty record of joyous adventure—a series of youthful experiences upon which the gray-haired engineer of to-day dwells wistfully. It was a rough life, but it did the boy no harm, and it forms the basis of an interesting and valuable book.

Presenting as it does an intimate view of life on a ranch and at an Indian Agency some fifty years ago, I commend it to those who share the increasing interest in *Americana*. In it will be found red men and red women, quite different from those "fiends" and "demons" with which our border literature is filled. Here will be found fathers and sons as well as hunters and warriors. Hubert Collins, as a small and inconspicuous observer, studied the Cheyenne and Arapahoe way of life from a boyish angle.

Foreword

It remains to say that only a small part of young Collins' adventurous life is set forth in these pages. He has much more to give and I hope that the success of this book will lure him from his transit in order that other books of his adventures may appear.

HAMLIN GARLAND

New York City.

INTRODUCTION

A CERTAIN river of the Western Plains rises in the foot-hills of a spur of the Rocky Mountains in Northern New Mexico, and flowing east by south across the old buffalo range, finally loses its identity in a larger stream. The Indians called this the Buffalo and the larger one the Big River. In the Cheyenne tongue they were known as the Ho-to-oa-oa and the Mitsun respectively.

The first white men in the country named the Big River "Arkansas" and the sonorous name Ho-to-oa-oa they changed to "The Red Fork of the Arkansas." Later still, the Red Fork was known as the Cimarron River, which name it bears to-day. All the old cattlemen knew the Red Fork only as a stream which they forded on the cattle trail north from Texas to Kansas. In 1876, when a cattle ranch was located on both sides of the river, it was natural to name it Red Fork Ranch, and by this name it was known to all the old cattle country.

Chisholm Trail was in its ninth year when Red Fork Ranch was opened. Both operated for twelve years longer, then passed from view for all time. With their passing, they became a memory which grows more dim as the years go on.

It is to make those days at the old ranch and along the trail live again that the writer wishes to recall in this book scenes and incidents from the impressionable years of boyhood he spent there.

Present day denizens cannot properly know their country until they know the forces that have shaped it. The general public also has an erroneous conception of the old West, and it is hoped that these pen pictures will help to change it.

Introduction

Indians always have been, and still are, human beings who act, talk, and think as well as any other race on earth. Old-time cow-boys and cattlemen were, on the whole, law-abiding; many of them became leading citizens in communities after free range had passed. As for the gun-toting, loving, loved, lovely cow-girl of the present day rodeo and screen,—she never existed in the days of which I write. There are few people now living who can tell about this section of the old West.

A few years ago my brother Ralph and I met for the first time in many years, at Utica, N. Y. Here, far removed from the scene, we fell to talking of the old days and our part in them. We realized anew the great changes which have occurred in the United States of America during our own lifetime, and felt that our combined recollections might be of interest and value. During four years we have checked and re-checked the facts. They are as nearly correct in statement as it is possible to make them.

Scenes and incidents depicted here were in the old Indian Territory, now embraced within the boundaries of the prosperous and growing State of Oklahoma. The experiences related are mostly those in which one or both of us took part. As to other events, we have the best authority from first hand narratives of participants: Ben Williams, Deputy United States Marshal, an uncle; Little Robe, War Chief of the Southern Cheyenne, a close personal friend.

During the years of work on this record there has been much correspondence with the Oklahoma Historical Society, and much exchange of information. A real friendship has grown up between the author and Mr. J. B. Thoburn, the former Secretary, now Research Director of the Society, and a courteous, capable, hard-working guardian of the historical archives of that State. He has been an aid and an inspiration. The

Introduction

author acknowledges the source of the Wanamaker story within these pages as coming from Mr. Thoburn.

Sarah Darlington Covington, daughter of Brinton Darlington, Cheyenne and Arapahoe Indian Agent, 1868-1873, kinswoman of the author, has given enthusiastic assistance with her recollections. Mr. Hamlin Garland has taken a kindly interest, resulting in advice and counsel which have been invaluable. Without his aid and inspiration the author would not have persevered to complete accomplishment.

HUBERT E. COLLINS

Utica, N. Y.

WARPATH
and
CATTLE TRAIL

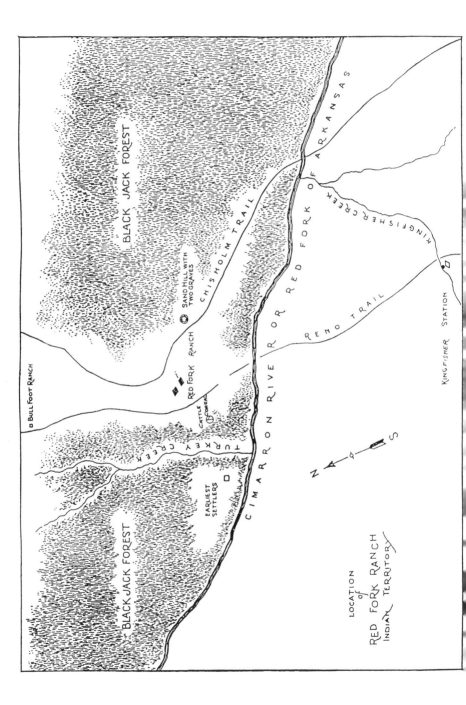

BLACK JACK FOREST

BLACK JACK FOREST

CHISHOLM TRAIL

SAND HILL WITH
TWO GRAVES

RED FORK RANCH

CATTLE
CORRAL

RED FORK RANCH

□ BULL FOOT RANCH

TURKEY CREEK

EARLIEST
SETTLERS

CIMARRON RIVER OR RED FORK OF ARKANSAS

KINGFISHER CREEK

RENO TRAIL

KINGFISHER STATION

N
S

LOCATION
of
RED FORK RANCH
INDIAN TERRITORY

Chapter I

W HAT is a shorthorn?

Look at that steer with two horns just showing on his head. Not only are his horns short, but they have no rings. When he is a year older the horns will be longer, and you will see a ring near the base of each. With each succeeding year of life, the horns will be larger and longer, and an added ring will appear for each twelve months.

When he has four rings, that steer will probably go up the trail to a slaughter house. A wild one may live to have five, six, seven,—yes, even ten rings for adornment. More knowledge of the ways of life has come with each ring. By the time four have been acquired, the wearer has learned all he needs for practical purposes. If he lives to add more than four, greater knowledge of life and some superfluities have been acquired.

Rings on horns, not size and length, show age, with consequent experience.

Look at the steer carrying a stub showing where one horn was, and a whole one with seven rings. A lesson was taught him when he lost that horn, and with only one left to defend his interests, the acquisition of life's knowledge has been proportionately greater for each succeeding year. Bet again. He is the best fighter of his weight in the herd.

Every ring on a bovine horn signifies experience to the wearer, equaling ten years of human experience. Some men with twenty years of life are not entitled to the one-ring knowledge of the cow. A newcomer to the cattle country and its life, no matter what his age, is a shorthorn, a tenderfoot.

I had the fortune to go into the cattle country of unfenced range when I had just passed the age equaling one ring on a range steer's horns. It was soon after my eleventh birthday that I reached the heart of the cattle country at Red Fork Ranch on the Chisholm Trail,—that legendary highway acclaimed in song and story as most celebrated of the old West's premier cow-land.

My experiences on the first journey out and during the two years after my arrival at Red Fork Ranch were sufficient for development of the first ring, and I passed from the shorthorn class. My enthusiasm for the experience was the logical outcome of our family life. Let me explain.

In the year 1868, great-uncle Brinton Darlington had been made United States Commissioner to the war-like tribes of the Comanches, Kiowas, Cheyennes and Arapahoes. He had accompanied and lived with the two latter tribes when they settled on their first reservation, ending their untrammeled freedom of the West. After establishing the first Agency, afterwards named in his memory, Uncle Brinton had called several other relatives to his aid, and their names were listed among the Agency employees in a variety of interesting capacities. My brother Ralph was among the later additions to the Agency forces.

Periodic visits from these relatives to our home in Iowa, bringing tales of the stirring events witnessed on the border and the life stories of red and white heroes, added to a continual exchange of letters, were no doubt responsible for building up a legendary Empire in my mind. Before I was ten years old, this was my great land of romance. No doubt I had heard of places named New York, Boston, and Chicago, but they meant nothing to me. Darlington Agency and Red

Fork Ranch were the only places worth consideration. When word came from Ralph that he was leaving the Agency and becoming part owner of the ranch, my parents had no rest from my importunities to be allowed to join him. I was big enough to be a cow-boy; I could work; in fact the prospect of going out to Red Fork Ranch became an obsession.

Frontier dangers had indeed been the lot of all my elders. Father was brought to Iowa Territory as a child, and he had grown to manhood fighting his way on the frontiers of Iowa, across the plains, in Colorado and Mexico,—as scout, hunter and trapper. Mother had been with him through many of his early experiences. The incidents of such a life were commonplace to them. With conditions settled in Iowa, father had entered the ministry. The tenets of Methodism had won his allegiance, as was the case with so many ex-frontiersmen. A pioneer in Iowa itinerancy, he was stationed at Corning at the time I was pleading for consent to embark on my youthful venture. Before giving final sanction, mother demanded that I must travel in company with some older person. This difficulty was overcome by means of a resident of our town.

Jim Owsley was a six-foot, broad-shouldered, mulatto-colored resident of Corning, whose son was in my class at school. Jim's business was that of horse trader, dealing in half-wild mustangs from the prairies of Texas. Each season he traveled by rail to Caldwell, Kansas, took the Chisholm Trail there and rode into the Lone Star State for his stock in trade. Driving them up the trail to Caldwell he would ship them from there by rail into Corning. My playmates of those days must recall Jim and his herds. They combined to make excitement for us as they tore along our streets to the railroad cattle corrals, with a roar of hoofs mingled with yells of men and squeals of frightened beasts, all hidden in a cloud of dust. I knew Jim, and had him enshrined as one of my heroes,

3

and was therefore pleased when father asked him to take me on his next trip down the trail and leave me at Red Fork. He consented, and I lost no time in acquainting all my chums of my good fortune. I became the hero of the day within my circle. This was in the month of May, 1883.

Two trains per day stopped at Corning for passengers going east, and two for west-bound traffic. I was to take the morning train east for Creston, where I would change for a train going south and west. I learned I was to go through St. Joseph, in Missouri, Atchison, Newton and Wichita, in Kansas, to Caldwell. The day being set, I appeared at the station with father and some playmates, after bidding good-by at the house to mother, sisters Mabel and Nell, and baby brother Roy. Jim was not there to meet me, nor did he appear until the incoming train whistled for brakes. Then he came dashing up on his mustang and announced that he could not go.

Here was a catastrophe indeed! I began to weep and beg father not to change his mind. At first he refused, then gave in, in time for me to scramble aboard the moving train with my carpet bag. I was off on my adventure, but hardly looked the part of a brave, dashing cow-boy. Before I realized it, I had forgotten my temporary sorrow over leaving home and worry over my lost escort. No boy of that age could long remain in low spirits, taking his first journey from home on such wonderful railroad coaches as those were.

No automatic air-brakes stopped our train. The engineer "blowed his whistle for brakes" at every station, and at the sound brakemen hastened to platforms and worked with might and main on the hand-wheel brakes. Before long I had recognized this signal and had adopted the brakemen's profession for my own. I answered the summons speedily, in fact was the first to set to work on my platform. But it seemed that I was an unwelcome co-worker. My ears were soundly boxed,

4

and I found myself in a heap. Just the same I did admire those brawny brakemen. Gee whiz! they sure did make those old brake shoes squeal.

Looking from the car window after leaving St. Joe, I beheld miles and miles, as far as the eye could reach, of yellow, muddy water. Soon we had water on both sides as we rolled along the railroad embankment. Then the boiling, sullen, roaring flood could be seen ahead as it passed beneath the railroad bridge. The surface seemed to reach the level of the bridge. The moving train was brought to a stop while a trainman went forward to investigate. It was decided to cross, and we moved out over the center of the flood at a snail's pace. As we crept along, the bridge and its load swayed and trembled, and we passengers were on our feet gazing in awe at the scene. Bodies of animals came to the surface at times, wrecks of houses and fences floated with them, desolation was everywhere in sight. At intervals, a tree with extra long roots would float under us and scrape the woodwork below the rails. It seemed hours before we proceeded on our way, after safely crossing one of the greatest floods in the Missouri Valley, so the records state, for twenty years before or after. Thus I first viewed Big Muddy.

Any one can guess that meals were very important to a growing, healthy boy, and so I register the memory of our noon-day repast on the first day of this trip. After leaving Topeka, while out on the prairie with no town or settlement in sight, the engineer signaled for brakes. The train was brought to a stop, without my assistance this time, and I followed the others. We were going to eat, but where? Away off, nearly a mile distant, was a farm house. Toward this the conductor led his flock streaming across virgin land. We ate in relays at a farmer's table. As this was my first meal away from home, I may have over-rated its quality. My boyish verdict was that we had a very sumptuous repast. There was an abundance of meat, potatoes, turnips, bread and coffee. In a common white dish, placed in the center of the table, were some oranges. These were the first I had ever seen and I did not know how to go about eating them. Some-one showed me how to peel one and part it into sections. This was the greatest treat I had ever experienced. I had another to take with me, and for that meal I paid twenty-five cents.

Proceeding on its way after the noon-day feast, our train reached Newton toward evening. Here we had news of high water ahead in the Arkansas River Valley. All passengers debarked and hunted up the one hotel in town for night lodging, for the train would not start until the following morning. This was my first experience in a public hotel. I spent the evening before dark strutting up and down in front of the hostelry, passing some boys of my age in order that they might feast their eyes on a real traveler, unaccompanied by a guardian. I put the idea over successfully, and in an effort to offset my advantage, one of the strangers offered to bet he could spit farther than I. I did not bet, but entered the contest. Standing on the edge of the board sidewalk for a mark, we expectorated into the dirt street. I won the contest, after which there was no other recourse for the defeated party but to offer to fight me. He made a perfectly amiable proposition which I was too modest to accept. It must have been that, for I was always in trouble at home over fighting.

When I boarded the train next morning, it was to find the greatest treat of the journey by rail. My eyes opened in astonishment at the unexpected sight of a large delegation of Cheyenne Indians filling a coach which had come into town during the night and had been attached to our train. The trainman ushered me into a coach ahead of the Indians, but my interest lay behind, and soon I was back in the coach with them.

Shorthorn Hits the Trail

Although it was my first sight of wild, red warriors, they seemed to be a natural part of life, the effect of all I had heard from their white friends, my relatives. They proved to be the Cheyenne located in the very country for which I was bound. I even recognized the names of Little Whirlwind, Little Big Jake, and Red Lodge, of whom I had often heard. These three, with several other bucks and two squaws, filled the coach. They made up a delegation returning to Darlington Agency from a first visit to the Great White Father in Washington.

I walked up and down the aisle of the car, feasting my eyes on the strange sights, delightedly listening to the strange tongue. Here in flesh and blood were the heroes of my dreams. My excitement attracted Red Lodge. Once when I was passing him he reached out, grasped me and pulled me to a seat beside him. I was delighted with the attention.

He set to work to amuse the white boy. Taking a new bandanna handkerchief from about his neck, and placing it over our heads as he bent to meet mine, he murmured over and over again, the words, "My papoose! My papoose!" I was a proud boy just then, and wished the boys back home were there to witness my great honor. I was adopted by an Indian brave.

Next he set out to teach me his language. Taking his turkey wing fan, he waved it before our faces to illustrate its use, after which he made me give the name in English while he pronounced the Cheyenne word. He pulled his stone pipe from a tobacco bag, filled and lit it Indian fashion, never touching the bowl during the process. Then he gave it to me for a puff. Never having smoked before, I choked on the cloud which I drew into my lungs. Laughing at my inexperience, he nevertheless signified that he was satisfied at my gesture of agreement, and said "Good!" He next stood up in the

7

aisle of the car, dropped his blanket from his shoulders and exhibited all the articles of Indian apparel which he wore, naming each in his native tongue. Drawing his scalping knife, he illustrated its use in pantomime. He had his "Medicine Bag" with him and showed me some of the potent charms contained therein. I learned more of these things later, but did that day acquire several words of the Cheyenne tongue under his tutelage. I was soon addressed as *Vehucus*, the equivalent of "Little White Boy."

Red Lodge was a six-foot specimen of athletic Cheyenne manhood, had been on the warpath only four years previously, yet showed all the traits of any man interested in and liking boys. We afterwards became better acquainted, as I shall relate. With his aid the journey to Caldwell passed all too soon. There I parted from my Indian friends and they joined a party of fellow tribesmen, to go on their way together, while I hunted up Amick Covington to direct me to the stage coach. Here I was at the end of the Iron Trail, where I met the Chisholm Trail of my dreams.

I was in Caldwell, cow-town terminus of the Chisholm Trail for a great many years. At that time the cattle business was at its peak. All cattle passing over this trail from Texas, after the rail-head was established, came by or into this town. The stock herds passed by, those for the market were entrained on the spot. Before shipping, some of the herds were held on the surrounding prairies for fattening. The inhabitants were all supported by the cattle business in one way or another. They were housed in a collection of frame houses, mostly rough shacks of various types, strung out an eighth of a mile along one street, which ran south, a continuation of the stage road named Reno Trail. There were no sidewalks. The railroad station—a shack—stood by the cattle pens at one end of the street, which ran parallel to the Chisholm and a quarter mile west. A rough, two-storied board structure, standing half-way down the street on the west side, served as a hotel. The town pump, with a half-hogshead watering trough and hitching rack, stood in front of the hotel, making of the spot a town center. Here the stage coaches discharged and assumed the care of passengers and mail. Two or three trading stores, many saloons and gambling houses, flanked the Leland House on either side. More saloons and the livery stables sprawled out on the opposite side of the road. Hogs, chickens, dogs, roamed at will. Garbage, tin cans, litter of the trail lay about, all thickly coated with dust. I do not recall a single shade tree or a tree of any size along that street or about the houses. Memory places the only fence about the dwelling of Amick Covington, the last on the stage road toward the Indian Territory. This house and fence seem also to have been the only places painted. Cousin Sarah had planted lilacs in the yard, making the only spot of color in town.

Here I found Amick and Sarah expecting me. They gave me a noon-day meal, after which I took the stage for Red Fork Ranch.

After parting with the Indians at the railroad terminal I had been on the lookout for my first view of cow-boys. The driving season was not yet in full flood, the herds were still on the trail, and as a consequence I saw few cow-men those first hours in cow-land. I was thus permitted to center all my thoughts on the coming stage coach and the journey ahead. I saw the outfit coming down the road toward the house soon after I had eaten my meal.

An old-time Concord stage coach, drawn by four horses coming at a fast trot, was brought to a sudden stop in front of us on the stage road. I was proud of the fact that this grand turnout was thus halted for me, on orders already transmitted. Adopted by an Indian in the morning, here I was again the center of attraction as the stage driver called out my name and greeted me. Who could expect higher honors? I asked no more of kind fate, yet was raised to a seventh heaven of bliss as I was invited and assisted to a seat beside the driver. From this vantage point, six feet or more from the ground, I was to have my first views of my empire.

We left the town behind us at a gallop which soon settled into a trot, the usual gait. Bluff Creek was soon reached where the trail led down one bank and up the other. The team kept a fast pace down the incline, until the driver set his foot on the brake lever rod and slackened speed just enough to keep traces taut. My, how strong that driver was; so I thought. With whip lash he flicked the leaders' rumps and the wheelers' ears to enthuse them all for the climb to level ground again. Under his guidance and whip urge, every beast settled into the collar, drew us up as the harness squeaked, wheels rattled, brake gear clattered. Never was there so grand a vehicle, one that swayed so charmingly, with strong horses that never paused and a wonderful driver who knew so much. The driver certainly felt that way about it, for he was soon relating his prowess to his audience of one. With the team settled into a regular, steady trot on the level prairie, the driver's tale covered many exploits of the road.

He had made many trips averaging twelve miles per hour,— we were going from six to eight. Never had he failed to make a trip, even in time of Indian trouble. Spoke his mind to the boss, never spoke to station tenders except to give orders. His orders were obeyed or there was trouble. He swore at the team almost constantly in an amiable manner, relating the good qualities of each member of it meanwhile.

In spite of his braggadocio there was a genuine desire on his part to please the boy, and much of my first information of the country came from him as we rolled along. It was he who first pointed out antelope as they bounded away in the distance, turning to look at us, then taking up their flight again. Animals of gray, others of yellow-brownish hue raced away from us. I was told the first was wolf, the second coyote. Golden eagles soared from level prairies until they appeared as specks floating in the clear atmosphere overhead. Other specks came out of the sky and settled to the ground. These were identified as turkey buzzards attracted by some dead or dying animal. Quail and prairie hens, doves, yellow-hammers, flushed from our path at almost every mile, and the driver told me the names. A bird the size of a chicken, having dark plumage and a long tail streaked with white, ran in front of our team for several miles. He held to a distance of twenty feet or more ahead of the leaders, which did not reduce at any time. No matter what rate of speed we made, his distance remained the same. As he paced along, one could see his legs work like piston rods, as he turned his head and seemed to say, "Come, catch me if you can." Finally dashing to the side of the trail, he stood jerking his head and tail in unison. His manner and actions plainly said, "I thought so. You never could catch me in a thousand years. I'm tired of fooling with you." My informant said the bird was a road-runner. With not a human habitation in sight anywhere during that afternoon ride, the boundless expanses of spring verdure teemed with wild life.

Spring flowers of the prairie land were in full bloom. With our six or seven miles of horizon from the top of that coach, there were times when the entire view in color range was tinged with yellow, white and blue. The day was balmy and nature was coming to full fruition when I first viewed that fairyland.

At one time during the afternoon I saw a low-lying cloud of dust almost straight ahead. As we neared, it was seen to be coming on a line east of us. Within a half mile a herd of ponies dashed from the dust cloud and passed us at a trot. An hour later came another larger cloud which disclosed some two thousand head of cattle, with riders here and there along the side and bringing up the rear. We had met the advance guard of the season's herds. They were being urged along late in the day, and would soon be allowed to spread out for feeding before bedding down for the night. There I beheld my first trailers.

As the sun began to near the western horizon, a grove of trees came into view ahead. Coming nearer we could make out buildings in the grove, and soon after we arrived at the stage station which marked the headquarters of Pond Creek Ranch. With a flourish of whip and curses directed at the team, we came to a stop in front of the largest building. There we were to have our supper served to us while the attendants changed the team to a fresh one for the night journey ahead. A tall, gaunt man seemed to be in charge here, whom the driver addressed as Miner.

Two other passengers, men of government position, had been with us on the trip from Caldwell, riding inside the coach. We were ushered into the ground floor of a two-story log house, built stockade fashion. There at a plain, pine table was spread the meal of fried bacon, hot biscuit and coffee.

There was no service aside from the placing of pans filled with the viands on the table. It was first grab, first served. With an appetite never satiated, I was not backward in self-service. I filled my tin plate with fried pork and biscuit as often as any one else did. Eating was a business, the meal progressed in silence and haste. By the close of the meal, dusk was falling over the land. It was hastened by dark clouds which betokened the coming of a storm.

Before starting on that night trip, I was placed inside the

coach with the other passengers. The vehicle swayed and
tossed as the team was urged to its best pace along the trail
toward the crossing of the Salt Fork. As we bowled along,
there came flashes of lightning and premonitory gusts of wind.
The storm reached us with a rush and a roar. We proceeded
at a walk as the rain pelted down and lightning flashed and
rolled along the surface of the prairies about us. The night
had become inky black, relieved only by these flashes.

I was still awake from the strangeness of the experience, and
the snores of the other passengers, when there came a cry from
the driver, followed immediately by the lurching of the stage
coach, as it settled over on its side and we three inside piled
one on the other. There was some scrambling to get out of
the wreck, and soon we all were standing in water more than
knee deep. The driver had miscalculated his way down the
bank at the river crossing. There we were, completely over-
turned, in the midst of a storm. What drenching we missed
from immersion was completed by the elements. Fortunately
the team remained quiet, and not one of the passengers suffered
hurt. With distant flashes of lightning to aid us we were able
to appraise our condition. Under the driver's direction and
with the aid of all hands, myself included, and much cursing
on the part of the men, we finally righted the coach. A pry
made of the wagon tongue also helped us. Finally we were
again aboard and proceeded on our way. It is a significant
fact that the driver apologized to the boy for the accident. I
had felt some surprise that so superior a being should allow
such a mishap.

There was no more sleep that night, as we were all soaked,
and so was the inside of the coach. We suffered no ill effects,
however, and landed in the morning at Bull Foot Ranch, a
change station on the route. There we ate a morning meal
while the horses were changed again. I could not do myself

justice this time, for I knew the next place of call was to be Red Fork Ranch. I was duly excited, and rode again with the driver as we galloped away from Bull Foot.

Soon we were passing through sand hills, and I noticed a curious structure close on our right. It was a rectangular enclosure of stakes driven into the ground and surmounted by a platform of other stakes. About the enclosure were many stones seemingly thrown there. There, the driver told me, lay the remains of Pat Hennessey, a former freighter, killed in an Indian fight only a few years before. Having exhausted my questions, and no doubt my companion, in reference to Pat and why he was buried thus, my thought again centered on the approaching haven of my desires. The trail soon emerged into the open at the top of a rise, and at that point could be seen a group of buildings some miles distant, which the driver pointed out as Red Fork Ranch.

These buildings were out in the open, plain and drab, with no trees about them. A half mile or more to the right were woods which evidently hid a stream. Beyond the buildings to the south was more forest. I was informed that the Cimarron River lay across our path beyond the forest, while the woods to the right bordered Turkey Creek. From the top of the stage coach, at the apex of the trail elevation, the scene embraced (to my mind) a fairyland. There lay the center of my legendary Empire. My mind leaped ahead of the team which had been urged into a gallop the last eighth of a mile. We came up to the buildings after swinging from the trail, and stopped in a cloud of dust, through which I saw brother Ralph standing in the door awaiting me with a welcoming smile.

(My brother Ralph was a young man of twenty-five at the time of my arrival at Red Fork Ranch. It was he who really backed my trip by providing the finances. A real brother in every way, he felt, with his fourteen years seniority, more like a father. He helped shape my character, and has been an influence throughout my life.)

Chapter II

IT had been growing all the way from home. In wealth of information concerning the ranch and its history, coupled with the first day's and night's personal experiences, that day ranks as the greatest of my years in the land. My brother was my mentor and guide, my bureau of information.

The accident of the preceding night had delayed our arrival. It was near noon when Ralph greeted me and told me to make myself at home. He immediately prepared a noon-day meal for us, and it was soon consumed; I was too anxious to inspect the new and strange sights about me to waste much time eating.

Ralph first conducted me to the horse corral and showed me a fine bay pony, which he informed me was to be mine as soon as I learned to ride. I gazed on the animal with the pride of full possession. Brotherly regard had also provided me with all the necessary gear for riding. I was shown a new stock saddle with flat pommel, bridle and lariat. Surely this was as good a brother as any boy could desire.

Prairie dogs barked all about us, and next demanded my attention. These little marmots lived in colonies of thousands about the ranch buildings. Their burrows and mounds seemed everywhere. Trying to catch one led me toward Turkey Creek, and Ralph joined me. He laughed at my efforts, and pointed out other denizens of the colony, screech owls. Some of them sat blinking in the sunlight, by convenient openings in the ground. The prairie dogs were such saucy, yet friendly animals that it seemed to me there was a chance to capture one. Failing in pursuit, I tried to dig one out. Ralph provided me with a shovel and I went about the task. It was no use, the ground was too hard, the channel ran too deep. I never did catch one that way.

Our walk continued toward the banks of Turkey Creek. The bottom land was covered with grass already knee high. From this cover we flushed prairie chicken and quail, and I was startled by a great noise as wild turkeys rushed away and rose in their short flight. A mother deer trotted before us with a baby wabbling beside her. We were within fifty feet of them and I could note the red bodies and the white spots on the fawn before the two disappeared into the woods ahead. The creek seemed to have found summer's quietude. Its waters were calm and clear. In the depths of pools I saw many catfish lying near the bottom, their working gills showing the only evidence of life. Returning to the house, we passed mulberry trees with ripened fruit, and stopped to sate our appetites. My questions were interminable, my brother patient with answers. Evening drew on to end this perfect day. Ralph shot a trio of prairie chicken for our supper.

The evening meal was to be a feast in celebration of my coming to Red Fork Ranch. Ralph skinned the fowls and cut them for the frying pan. He made biscuit and put them in the oven, and as he prepared the meal he talked of other days. He said, "A few years ago Grandfather Williams took me on a trip out of northwest Iowa and we traveled into the Sioux country until soldiers told us that we must go no farther. Almost every day we had prairie chicken for dinner, and grandfather told me the very nicest part of a prairie chicken was the neck. You know it is different from the necks of ordinary chickens, because if you break each joint you will find the most luscious meat which tastes the very best. You have to break the neck all apart and suck each vertebra. Oh, my, it is fine!" Ralph made the gesture of sucking his lips, as though he were tasting the best gumdrops that I could think of. He spent some time in a dissertation which bore the message that the necks of the chickens which he was frying were the most delicious morsels that I could ever ask for. He also said that he was going to be as good to me as grandfather had been to him on that trip to Dakota. I swallowed the story,—hook, line and sinker,—and we proceeded to devour the meal.

As the meal progressed, chicken necks were placed before me, and most thoroughly dissected under Ralph's direction. It beat all how many necks those chickens had, for when I finally cleaned them up, there were no other portions of chicken left on the table. Biscuit filled my vacant crevices at that first meal. Thereafter, I grabbed drumsticks as soon as the platter was on the table. I had learned a lesson.

The first night spent at the ranch was an experience. Our best bed was a roll of blankets on the floor, to which I soon became accustomed. Even the floor was sometimes traded for the ground, because of the mosquitoes. They came in such swarms that sleep was not possible. The air was filled with them, demanding blood in a sullen roar. Large smudges of wood and grass with sufficient sod to keep a smoke for hours were started between the buildings, and we lay down in the choking smoke screen to woo Morpheus. As I lay there looking up through the smoke, I could see a black cloud of humming, roaring insects, hovering just above, awaiting the opportunity for attack. Many reached me, and in desperation I pulled the blankets over my head, until I was almost suffocated with heat and the acrid smoke.

There were other terrors that first night. Strange weird sounds came from the darkness. All were catalogued in after years, but at that time they struck terror into my soul. Shrill screams rent the air, which changed the perspiration on my body to clammy moisture. These were added to by a querulous howl oft repeated, accompanied by a deeper sounding half bark, half growl. There were numberless voices in the night aside from these other sounds. I slept fitfully and was glad for morning. I discovered that all sounds ceased in the hour before dawn.

So terror stricken had I been that Ralph discovered the fact next morning from my questions. Calling me to him, he pointed to a screech owl as the maker of the most blood-curdling sounds. The wolf and coyote he named as the source of the complaining, angry howls. The voices in the night were from various birds.

Timidity would never do on the plains, and so Ralph proceeded in his own way to correct the condition. If I shrank back from a snake in the trail, he made me go ahead and kill it. My terror was not so much of the visible beast and reptile, but of the unseen. Many times he sent me on meaningless errands. I was often sent alone to the bank of the Cimarron crossing, a trip of more than a mile through dense woods, after sundown. Many of the return trips were made in record time, until I caught the first glimpse of light from the ranch houses. His method worked, and gradually I overcame my besetting terrors.

It was a happy day when Ralph finally announced that we would set out for summer camp and my first riding lesson. I had been tending the pony and becoming acquainted with it. We were fast friends and I ached to be on its back. One fine July morning we hitched a team of cow-ponies to the buckboard, took seats therein, and set out leading my pony by a lariat.

We crossed the Cimarron at the Chisholm Ford, reached the southern bank, and headed east parallel to the river through the thickets of waist-high plum bushes. The ripe fruit hung in clusters which were knocked from branches by the team and left a purple trail in our wake. "Swish, swish, swish, swish," came the sound of our progress as we forged ahead on the journey. Many times deer fawn were routed from hiding-places and wabbled away to safety. Young antelope were also in evidence.

Finally we left the river border in a southerly direction, to reach the summer camp on the headwaters of Cottonwood Creek. We reached there about noon, in time for a meal with Perry, the cow-boy in charge. This camp contained a wall tent, placed on a bluff of the creek in a grove of cottonwoods, situated inside a bend of the stream. This bend contained a deep pool in driest weather, being fed by springs. The camp-fire site lay close to the base of a giant cottonwood, the protecting branches of which covered a circle of thirty or more feet in diameter. Cooking was done over an open fire, biscuits were baked in a Dutch oven.

The presiding genius of the camp was a Kansas cow-boy, whose name is all I can recall of his title. Ralph paid him the highest compliment of the country when he said, "Perry has never lost a steer."

Across the creek from the camp, out on the open range, was a well-built rail corral to hold about one hundred head of cattle or horses. A "snubbing post" in the center indicated this to be the real work house of the range, for here we did the branding.

Having arrived at this camp near noon, we partook of our noonday meal at the camp fire. I was anxious to go about my first riding lesson, and Ralph seemed quite willing to give it. Under his instruction I led the pony to one side of the camp, grasped its forelock and forced the bit into its mouth, then drew the bridle over its ears and fastened it. Leaving the reins

The Ring of Experience Grows

with the loose ends on the ground, we placed the saddle blanket over the animal's back, and upon that the new saddle. Then came instruction in the matter of securing the cinches for fastening, in such manner as to avoid bites from one end or kicks from the other. The front cinch came first, and after securing the end-ring in my hand I had to pass the strap through the rings twice before making up. Bracing one foot against the pony's barrel, I made the cinch and secured the strap end with a four-in-hand knot. Then came the same processes with the rear cinch, except that that remained comparatively loose. Next came the adjustment of stirrup length to suit my leg. This was done by taking a stirrup in one hand and holding it under the opposite armpit. The length of strap and stirrup was so adjusted that it just spanned the distance from finger tips to armpit. After this had been accomplished on both sides we were ready to mount.

Before doing so I could not help but admire my new possessions. A pretty cow-pony with the body and limbs of a deer, new bridle, lasso and saddle. Once seated, the rider was secure.

Ralph left me to manage mounting without comment. Having already witnessed such action, I had an idea of the proper procedure. Gathering the reins and passing them on either side of the animal, I grasped them in one hand with the pommel. Then, placing my left foot in the stirrup, I mounted to my seat as the pony commenced to move. To have mounted successfully seemed enough for one moment and I reined the animal to a stop before venturing on my first ride. In fact I was going to stick around for further instruction, and the gentle pony allowed it.

Sitting on the pony with both hands on the pommel, holding the reins, I looked for my brotherly mentor. Almost immediately I saw him and saw that he had not been idle while I had been mounting. Giving the final cut to the trimming of a six-foot switch, he stepped into view back of me. Before I could guess his intention, he raised the switch in both hands and brought it down with full force across the rump of my mount. The pony sprang out and was going at full gallop in one leap. How I managed not to be unseated I do not know, but there I was being carried down the creek bank, through the ford, up the opposite side and away on past the corral to the wide prairie. The pony must have galloped a mile or two before I thought to control him with the reins still in my hands. This I finally did, and in due time I returned to the camp proudly guiding my steed.

Perry joined me and together we rode away to look over the herds about us. Perry complimented my riding, while I swelled with self-importance. Soon he showed me how he rode at a gallop and picked objects from the ground while doing so. I rendered him the compliment of imitation, with the result that I instantly found myself flat on the ground, seeing stars, while the pony galloped away, my saddle turned under his belly. When the escaping steed was brought to me again by the cow-boy, I mounted, content to finish the afternoon with no more circus stunts. On our return to camp at dusk, another feature of newly acquired horsemanship was disclosed. Riding close to the camp fire, I started to leap to the ground and found that I could not leave the saddle. Perry and Ralph lifted me to my bed of blankets where I remained until morning, not even asking for supper.

Ralph called me at sun-up the next day with the unwelcome information that we would ride back to the ranch headquarters on our ponies. It was tough work to move at first, but I managed to eat a good breakfast and saddle my own pony. As the day advanced I found my stiffness wearing away. After fording the Cimarron, Ralph challenged me to a race, and we

The Ring of Experience Grows

finished the last mile of that trip going as fast as good cow-ponies can. Thus I took to the saddle.

It was not long afterward that I was allowed to heat brand-ing-irons in the corrals, and took my first lessons in roping. I tried calves first. A half-grown calf is a real match for a boy of eleven, each on the opposite end of a rope. Many a tussle was wished on me at that time by the older men. Once I got a rope on an animal, it was up to me to get him down with no outside assistance. It sure was fun.

My earlier days at the ranch headquarters were largely spent questioning Ralph as to the history of the locality. My own observations soon brought knowledge of the life of the trails. Altogether I was rapidly developing that ring of ex-perience.

Chapter III

THE weather was pleasant when I arrived at Red Fork Ranch and brother and I frequently sat outside in the shade of the brush porch as we conversed together. Seated on cracker boxes one morning after we had performed our household duties, it came to me that it was almost an incongruity to have found that Cousin Fred had lived many years in the country and that Brother Ralph was there at the time, for one of them had been born in a Quaker cottage and raised in that faith; the other, my brother, was the son of an itinerant minister.

The apparent inconsistency of this seemed to bother my youthful mind and I asked, "Ralph! tell me about Fred."

Then Ralph told me the following story. "You know that Fred, the Quaker boy, was brought into the thick of the turmoil and friction at Darlington Agency before you were born, when he was ten years old. Our Indian friends were just off the warpath, after they had been fighting constantly for twenty years. They were still smarting under the treatment they had received and their spirit was still unbroken. The white people were crowding onto the Indian land so that there was constant irritation. There was much fighting and considerable killing going on all the time.

"You know that Brinton Darlington was a Quaker and most of the agency's employees have been the same. These Quakers seemed to have won the confidence of the wild Indians to the extent that they have been protected at all times by the elders,

The Quaker Boy and the Preacher's Son

even though they were in imminent peril of their lives from malcontents. Fred passed his formative years in this environment. The Indians soon learned that he might be trusted. They knew that the Quakers had control of all the whites about them and would protect them in every way. Fred was soon accepted as a friend and companion by all of our red acquaintances. While his people were teaching them the way of the white man's road, they, in turn, were teaching him their lore and customs. He admired all that was good in them and respected their sterling qualities.

"Another thing which won the Indians over to friendship and fidelity to Fred was the fact that he acquired many of the qualities which they admired. He became a crack shot with the rifle and was often allowed to kill the beef on Beef Issue Day. You know, he became so skillful with the rifle that he rarely took more than one shot to kill his animal. White Shield was his tutor. So thorough was the schooling that he could not only talk the signs, but could tell you the origin and meaning of them all. Another thing which wins the regard of the Indians is to live with them. Fred lived in the camps of the tribes very often, and was taken on the buffalo hunts several years in succession. He would be away a month at a time before his people would hear of him again.

"He frequently sat in the councils with the elders of the tribe, with his mentor White Shield, and other such leaders as The Whirlwind, Stone Calf, White Eagle, Little Robe, Lone Wolf, Little Big Jake. These warrior elders are the best of men in the fundamentals of character, and conduct themselves at all times with the grace and dignity which you may have noticed. Their influence was such that Fred grew up with the same attributes. From them, as well as from his Quaker teachings, he acquired a love of truth and fair dealing, reserve and careful thought before speech. Once his mind was made up there was no turning or faltering in carrying out its decisions. Associating with Indians, Army Officers, Scouts, Frontiersmen and Government employees at the Agency, he grew into manhood before he was twenty years of age.

"His step-mother taught him in his childhood, for you know there was no school for white children at the Agency. When she could teach him no further, they sent him to school at Garnet, Kansas, where he met and chummed with another lad of his age named Arthur Capper.[1] He was always telling me about his friend, Arthur, when he returned here on vacations.

"When Fred was through school, he decided to go into cattle raising, and wrote me to come out and join him. That was when we were living in Indianola, Iowa. I came out here and worked a year in the Agency. Together we completed our plans for buying the ranch, and came here two years ago. We planned operations on a large scale. We felt that we would make a good business here in the trading store and with the cattle corral. We worked together with a few men and put up this larger log house, and that big cattle corral down the trail. That corral is the only one on the Chisholm Trail, of its size, between Texas and Caldwell, Kansas, where you take the stage coach to come here. Then, last fall, Fred got sick and I had to take him down to his father's house in the Agency. He had an attack of typhoid fever which proved fatal. He died at the time we wrote home about it. You will see his grave down at the Agency, beside that of Brinton Darlington. It was hard to see Fred go and I miss him very much, but I do not believe this is any more true in my case than it is with his Indian friends. You would not believe it, Hubert, but White Shield and some of the other Indians cried until

[1] Arthur Capper later became Governor of Kansas and United States Senator.

26

their faces were wet with tears when he was being let down into the grave."

I knew that Ralph had finished school when he left home to join Cousin Fred in the cattle business. He seemed to be, and was, a great friend of the Indians. I think this was so from the very beginning. I know that it was true while I was talking to him, and it was evident that he talked earnestly and labored zealously to teach them the ways and ideals of the white man. I could see that his coming among them with his love of truth and fair dealing was what won their lasting regard. That was why Little Robe and others frequently made the ranch headquarters their home when they were in the vicinity.

Ralph soon mastered the cattle business, I presume, for he seemed to have a thorough knowledge of all its customs and history. With this knowledge he never assumed the picturesque or blatant manner of the present stage representation of cow-boy, and discouraged every inclination of mine in that direction. Like every cow-boy of that day, he abhorred this cartoon of their life, and took every occasion to destroy such ideas. Yet I could see that he appreciated the real picturesqueness that lay about him.

NOTE.—See Appendix, page 289.

Chapter IV

AFTER I had traveled down the Chisholm Trail from Caldwell to Red Fork, I sensed that it was the main highway of the country and instinctively felt the romance of events connected with it. My mind was keyed up to the possibilities for my entertainment and for the satisfaction of the innate curiosity which was my heritage.

Yes, sir, this was a great country, and the realization of that fact became more apparent to me every minute that I traveled in the land. I had come down the trail from Caldwell and knew it from that point to the Cimarron River. On my trips down the trail from the ranch buildings to the bank of the Cimarron, I noted that the "black jack" timber extended for over two miles along the Chisholm Trail at that point. I also noted, on the west bank of Turkey Creek, that this timber extended as far as my eye could reach to the north. I afterwards learned that the width of this belt of timber was from two to four miles. These woods were of oak for the most part, although there were other kinds of trees scattered through the oak. All of this timber grew over the sand hills and extended some seventy miles up and down the Cimarron River to the east and west of us. The growth was heavy, with natural openings or breaks scattered throughout the area. Ralph told me that this made sheltered feeding grounds where the grass was green all winter long, and these spots were in demand by Indians and whites for winter feeding.

Turkey Creek came through this timber from the north and

flowed into the Cimarron. Ralph and I often wandered through the wooded sections bordering the Cimarron River and Turkey Creek on foot. One day we found some strange looking habitations on the west bank of the creek near its mouth. They were still in a fair state of preservation, and seemed to be dwelling places half under ground with walls extending a few feet above ground. They were simply excavations in the earth with walls of sod and dirt which delineated the four sides of the excavation. The roof of sod had been laid upon poles which rested on the side walls. This roof of sod was from eighteen inches to two feet thick, and had been thoroughly knit together by the growing grass roots. Ralph said that these were "dug-outs" placed there by the first white traders who had wandered into the country. He told me to notice that these habitations were placed close to wood and water, and were sheltered alike from storm and observation.

One irregularly shaped, natural opening led through the woods from an opening opposite Kingfisher Creek, where it flowed from the south into the larger stream, and extended to the prairie land on the north border. When the first cattle trailers came north, driving their cattle, they had taken advantage of the natural opening through the obstructing woods. Thus it was that the Chisholm Trail crossed the larger stream just east of Kingfisher Creek, and then led the cattlemen northwest for a mile before they could again go north. I also noticed that it was easy to keep straight west for a short distance to the bank of Turkey Creek if one desired to do so. If one followed this course, after crossing the creek, one entered a dense growth and was lost to observation by any one on the east bank. This made the west bank of the creek a desirable place for any one who wished to hide there. Ralph told me that many cattle thieves hid their herds there from time to time. They left the main trail here to ford Turkey Creek, where they were soon lost in the natural cover. This was their stronghold for years, and they put up cabins which were scattered along the creek for four or five miles. I often ran across these cabins and sometimes found them occupied.

At that time life appeared interminable to me. I had not experienced the first thoughts of old age, which would have been anywhere around twenty years or more, but I did think of things which had happened before. Some of my questions had to do with the history of Red Fork Ranch. Ralph told me that the Cheyennes had been on the warpath only a few years before. As soon as the Cheyenne war was over and after the establishment of Fort Reno, the cattlemen began to lease the range from the Indians. The very first man to locate on the trail was named Reynolds. He erected the old building which we were using for a combination cook- and store-house. He also put up the first horse corral, which was close to the ranch buildings. These improvements were located where I found them, out in the open bottom land, about a half mile from where the trail turns north from the opening in the woods. Reynolds called it Red Fork Ranch. At that time there were no distinct boundaries to it. Following the trend of my investigation, I asked Ralph whether he had always owned Red Fork Ranch? "No," replied Ralph. "Dan Jones bought the place from Reynolds, and held the title for two or three years. Then Jones sold out to a man by the name of Hood. He, in turn, parted with his title rights to Fred and me, and we have called our combination the Williams Company."

(This company continued their ownership from 1881 to 1885 and added to the buildings and equipment. A trading store was first started by Reynolds, continued by the various owners and enlarged by the Williams Company. When they, in turn, sold out, John G. Chapin was allowed to continue the store on the original site until the settlement of Oklahoma in 1889.)

Ralph continued his story to me by describing the construction of the ranch buildings. "You see, the first building which we now use for kitchen and store-house, is a one-story, one-room log cabin built with the logs on end; they call that stockade style. It encloses an area of about ten by twenty feet, with the length lying east and west. The roof is made of layers of sod, to a thickness of about eighteen inches. This roof is laid on a grill work of poles laid flat and level. There is about eight feet head room inside, over the dirt floor.

"The horse corral is of split rails held in wooden stanchions. It is rectangular, with one side toward the buildings and the other toward 'Chisholm Trail.'

"When we took possession, we further improved our holdings. We put up the two-story, two-room log house, a few feet north of the old building. It has about the same outside dimensions on each floor as the older cabin, and you see it is at right angles to the older building and faces west. That has a gabled roof, and we brought shingles down from the 'States,' also the planks for the wood floors." (The ground floor was used for a store and the upper floor, reached by a rickety outer stairway, contained sleeping quarters.)

"We next enclosed the big cattle corral. It is the largest corral between Texas and Kansas, and is also built of logs in stockade fashion. We made it as near a circle as we could, and we ran that division fence through the center from north to south. This corral will hold twenty-five hundred head of cattle. Here the quota is brought in for branding, off the cattle trail for tally."

Ralph was proud of the corral and my own chest expanded at his words, for I felt I was part owner in the enterprise, as though I had taken part in its construction.

During the summer months which followed my arrival at the ranch, I often rested under the sun shelter that was put up alongside of the older building. With boyish inquisitiveness I had investigated it and found the old building to be a combination storage, cook, and eating house. The brush shelter was supported by forked poles to a level with the sod roof of the house, and was outlined on three sides by a "hog-tight" fence of stakes driven in the ground and extending above it about eighteen inches, topped by split rails for a rough balustrade. At the northwest corner of the fence, a well was sunk and a wooden-handled pump installed. A half barrel served as a water trough.

After I had learned to ride, Ralph took pains to ride with me over all our range and I found Red Fork Ranch was an isosceles triangle in shape. One point was some ten miles north of headquarters. The buildings were in one angle, from them the line ran southeast over the Cimarron for twenty miles or more, taking in the head-waters of Cottonwood Creek, where the summer camp was located, and extending on to a cedar grove where the winter camp was held. From here the line ran northwest to the point above headquarters.

It was not long before I had sampled every eatable of the stock in our store. I found such staple foods as flour, bacon, coffee, dried apples, soda crackers, ginger snaps, which were called "smacks" by the cow-boys, and sugar, and there was also a small line of clothing. These were all traded for furs or sold outright for cash. Ralph also said that this establishment was the only trading store between Caldwell and Darlington Agency, a distance of 90 or 100 miles. All supplies were freighted in from the railroad at Caldwell, Kansas.

It interested me to notice that our customers were cattlemen, cow-boys, "mule-skinners," "bull-whackers," Indians,

The Chisholm Trail

United States troopers, outlaws, stage coach passengers, and in the later days, sheepmen.

Soon after my first arrival at Red Fork Ranch, the cattle herds coming from the south increased in number until there was an almost continuous procession. Pursuing my quest for information further, I asked Ralph if the cattle that I saw there were all there were in the world. He said that I could not see all the cattle in the world, but that I was witnessing the passage of all the cattle which came from Texas on the way to Kansas. He further stated that nearly all of the cattle driven up the Chisholm Trail passed by or tarried at Red Fork Ranch. (It is no exaggeration to state that this place was known to all the "Who's Who" of the whole cattle country. The great cattle industry of our West was born while passing Red Fork Ranch from Texas to cattle country north and west of there. A man was truly a "shorthorn" on the great plains in the seventies and eighties who could not say he had ridden the Chisholm Trail and knew Red Fork Ranch.) Again I asked Ralph how old the trail was and who started it. He then told me that Jesse Chisholm knew of the best route to be followed along which cattle could be driven from Texas to Abilene, Kansas, through the Indian country, in comparative safety. Largely under his direction, the first drive was made that marked the path.

He added that in addition to the cattle that were driven by, every traveler passing through the Indian country from or to Texas used this route. The very first drive made a clearly marked path which became more distinct with each succeeding year, as the thousands of hoofs passed over it. Under the influence of cutting hoofs and the action of the winds, this path had become, even on the levels, a sunken road, while at the fords and rises it showed in deep cuts. These cuts were one hundred yards wide, while the roadway on the levels was marked deep over widths varying from one rod to three. Once on this trail there was no difficulty in following it.

By questioning I brought out the following additional information. Each year, the driving season commenced when the grass was a month high, and ended with the next winter's snows. The grass of the old prairies cured where it stood and provided good feed as long as it could be reached. Not until heavy snow did the cattle drive season end. When drives were on, one herd followed another all day, and every day. The cattle driven through in the early season made the largest herds, and were the "stock cows" to supply the new ranges north and west. Those driven in the later summer and fall were composed of four- and five-year-olds for the market. The ranchman at Red Fork kept tally of all passing cattle, which he sent to the stock papers for publication. Some years this ran up into the hundred thousands.

Note,—See Appendix, page 289.

Chapter V

OF THE TRAILS

FROM the very first day of my arrival at Caldwell down to my first view of Red Fork Ranch, I was most intensely interested in everything about me. My questions came in an almost endless flow of words. At the same time that I was acquiring my knowledge of the history of the Chisholm Trail, I was witnessing something every day which gave me information about those who made up its life.

One day I asked Ralph what a cattleman was. Ralph enlightened me by saying, "A cattleman is an owner of a herd on any given range or on a trail. Most of them have grown up in the business from lone cow hands. Generally, they are the older men of any outfit which passes here. The cow-boys call them the bosses.

"It is invariably true of these bosses that they are always ready to take part in any phase of the work connected with the business. While directing others, they will ride in and help rope, brand, ride herd, or perform any service necessary to keep everything moving day or night. While they are on the trail they live with the men and share their hardships on even terms. All of them have a blanket for a cover, a saddle for a pillow, and Mother Earth for a mattress to make their beds at night. At the 'chuck wagon,' the bosses stand in line with the men.

"There are a few cattlemen who are owners while they live away from here. They are called 'absentee' owners. When they come out here to their ranches, you can tell they have not lived the life from the time they were boys, nor are they as practical as the native-born cattlemen.

"All these cow-boys whom you see riding by are mostly Texas born. Most of them have grown up on the range with its life all about them, so that they know the cattle business alone, and do not care much for anything else. They will tell you that it is a man's work, and the *only work* for a man to devote his life to."

I mentally decided that I also would never be anything else but a cow-boy.

I found that many of the cow-boys who came into the store could not read or write. They knew little of the world I had come from in Iowa, and seemed to speak of every portion of the United States east of the Missouri River as "back in the States." They seemed to have a contempt for any knowledge of that foreign country.

I soon learned that a tenderfoot was any one who did not know the cattle business, and was a "curious critter." It never dawned on the cow-boy that any one could think *him* curious.

Cattlemen and cow-boys, tall and short, were all thin, wiry, muscular specimens. Their complexions ranged through every shade and texture of leather. Every time cow-boys came into the store or rode by, I studied them and found their characteristics to be about as follows. There was a certain uniformity in their dress. All of them must have the best Stetson hats that money could buy. These were mostly gray in color, with a leather band. A dark flannel shirt open at the collar was surmounted by the neckerchief. This was knotted hard and had red for the predominating color. Jeans or trousers, buttoned tight about the hips, were tucked into high-heeled boots of the finest leather, with thin soles, and spurs fastened to the heels. Chaps were worn over the trousers and boots for protection from brush while riding. These were fastened loosely at the

Of the Trails

hips. Every man wore a cartridge belt with a holster and "gun" hanging low on the right or left side, according to training. The guns were forty-five Colts, with eight-inch barrels of blued steel mounted on wooden handles. In addition to the six-gun, many carried Winchesters in holsters under the saddle cinches, on the left side, with the stock forward. The best of buckskin gauntlets were worn on the hands. These, with the quirt, completed the usual equipment.

The best stock saddles, full-skirted and double-cinched, were owned by the men. Leather lassos were more popular than "ropes," but one or the other was fastened in coils to the right front skirt of the saddle. Across the back saddle skirt and fastened to it would be the blanket rolled in a slicker. The cow-boy's working materials, bed, and protection from the weather went with him in trim and compact shape.

Many times the cattle outfits would camp near the ranch. On such occasions I was "Johnny on the spot" as soon as the cook brought the wagon to a stop and started his operations. In this way I picked up information and learned still more about them.

Each outfit was in charge of a foreman who might be the boss or a deputy "trail boss." The number of men, including wrangler and cook, was from five to ten. All the cow-boys drove during the day, and took turns on night-herd duty. One and all could ride, rope, brand, scout, and wait on the cook.

To wait on the cook meant that as soon as they made camp at noon or night, some of the men must rustle water and wood for his use. As soon as camp was made, one might see a cloud of dust arise somewhere within a half mile. When this dust cleared enough, a cow-boy would be disclosed riding his pony and dragging a log or bundle of wood at the end of his rope, the other end of which was fastened to his saddle horn. He generally came as fast as the pony, hampered by the drag, could travel. If the camp was not near water, another cow-boy would ride into the nearest stream or pond on his pony, dip up a bucketful of water, and race at full speed back to the cook with it. According to custom, the cook must be supplied with grub, wood, and water; then it was "up to him."

To serve the outfit properly, the cook must have breakfast ready before the sun rose each morning, and rouse the sleepers to eat it. As the herds got under way, he would clean up, pack the wagon, drive until eleven o'clock or so, and then make camp for the noon meal. Here he had to cook and serve, repack and drive on to the camp site for that night. When that was reached, he must again unpack and prepare the meal to be served at sundown. After the clean-up for the evening, he had nothing to do until morning. Three times a day was the same fare served with little variation, and yet there is no record of any man failing to respond to the call, "Come an' git it! Come an' git it! Chuck-a-way!"

As the herds came up the Chisholm Trail to pass the ranch buildings, they hurried through the opening in the "black jack" woods below us and were still speeding along as they passed on the trail back of the horse corral. From there on they were allowed to spread out for feeding and a large herd soon filled the plains to the north of us in its passage. It was there that I often joined the crowd to mingle with the men and converse with them as I rode along for a few miles. As the herds swept along, there was a medley of sound,—lowing and bellowing were interspersed with the bleating of calves. These sounds mingled with the rush of hoofs, clinking of hocks, and clashing of horns. Above these sounds the yells of the men could be distinctly heard as they urged on the cattle and cursed strays into line. Great clouds of dust would hang

Of the Trails

over everything and enter the nostrils with every breath.

I also learned from this contact that all bovines along the trails and on the range were "cows," no matter what the gender. Steers that stood fifteen hands at the withers, bulls, cows, all came under the one designation. They were the "long horns" of story, often having a spread of six feet between tips. All were wild as deer and could rival them in speed. They knew a man on a horse only; a man afoot on the ground was a strange animal demanding investigation.

At the height of the driving season, when the trails were filled with cattle, all other trailers were compelled to work their way along at one side of the main trail. Aside from cowboys, the most numerous body of men were designated freighters. Freighters were divided into two classes—bullwhackers and mule-skinners—of which the first named were the most picturesque of the white freighters, for Indians also come under this heading and were by far the leaders in interest.

Bull-whackers were mostly "old-timers" in the West and in a class by themselves. The days saw them trudging along by the side of their animals and equipment. They were the only men in the cattle country who walked every mile they traversed, following their vocation. For this reason they were looked upon with contempt by the cow-boy, who never walked a foot further than he had to. Nevertheless, the bull-driving freighters were a sturdy class of *doers*.

Impressions of them in bulk is of a crowd of stocky, powerful men. Their dress was nondescript, but in general of a rough, durable type, fitted to their mode of life. Hats of cheap black felt, shirts of heavy wool, loose-fitting trousers, belted at the waist and partially tucked into the tops of broad-toed, cowhide boots. Aside from dress, the principal equipment of each man was the short-stocked, heavy, leather-bodied, long-lashed whip, called "blacksnake." These were often eighteen feet in length and were used with deadly skill. Many of these men could hit any mark within their reach every time. In the hands of such experts, the whip was a terrible weapon, for the lash could take a piece out of the ear or cut the toughest hide. The sound of the lash was that of a loud, clear pistol shot. Every man had a gun in his equipment, but it was only a sheathed Winchester, placed on the load.

The teams which drew the loads were of six or eight bulls each. These were yoked to a chain running back to the "lead wagon" tongue. No feed was carried for the animals. They must subsist on the country, by grazing when they were un-yoked. This restricted the freighting to the grass season.

Loads up to six thousand pounds, placed in two or three heavy wagons, were transported in this way. The lead wagon would have the others in tow as trailers. All the wagon bodies were equipped with bows to support the canvas cover. Many high Conestoga wagons with ends flared up were in use.

These teams and conveyances traveled in "trains" of five and six units, at a rate of from ten to twelve miles per day in good weather. When the trails were heavy with mud, the speed did not exceed three or four. They wended their way across the prairie in fair weather and foul, fording the streams. The men slept on the ground under the wagons or on top of the loads under the canvas. Red Fork Ranch was a haven for them in rainy or cool weather, for there they might come in and make their beds on the floors. It was a hard, lonely life, but the men seemed to accept it with the stolidity of the animals they drove.

I do not know whether it is because most of us naturally smile when we look at a mule, but for some reason the army mules which composed the majority of the animals which were driven along the trails certainly interested me. I presume it was because their ears were so much more prominent than those of the horses, but when a mule cocked one ear forward while he allowed the other one to loll lazily back, it appeared to me not only amusing but indicative of some superior animal intelligence. I also noticed that these mules on the frontier were well worth steering clear of when they were unhitched and feeding themselves. I saw so many proofs of the efficacy of a mule's heels when defending himself from danger, real or fancied, or indulging in pure excess of spirits, that I learned to give them at least ten feet of clearance whenever I passed to the rear of them. This instinctive defense against fighting equine hoofs was so instilled in me in those years that I intuitively follow it to this day by always passing out of reach of any mule's heels. This all shows that I was deeply interested in the mules and their drivers, and I learned a number of interesting things about them.

Mule-skinners might well have been called the "express-freighters" of the trails. They were recruited from the ranks of ex-stage drivers, stove-up cow-punchers, ex-frontiersmen or Kansas farmers. These latter worked on the trails in the off season for farming. Their style of dress was as nondescript as their personnel.

A mule team was composed of six or even eight animals, and the train was made up of any number of such units up to ten. Each team drew one or two canvas-covered wagons. The men drove from the seat of the lead wagon, or from the back of one of the lead mules. A long-handled, light-weight, woven leather whip was the staff of office.

These trains carried from fifteen to twenty-five hundred pounds of freight, and covered twenty-five to thirty miles per day. Provender in the shape of oats or corn was carried, and this was supplemented by grazing at night. Such freight trains worked all the year round, because feed could be carried for the animals.

The mule-skinners slept, as the bull-whackers did, under their wagons, and in stress of weather, they also came to sleep in the buildings at Red Fork Ranch.

The mule teams, swinging along the trails, made an animated picture, while the rattle of harness and the sound of wheel-play under the hub-caps sounded full of life.

When the Indians were first confined to reservations with headquarters at central agencies, freighting was the means of clearing up two difficulties which naturally arose. Confining large bodies of hostile people to given areas from which they must not stray meant that they must be supplied with food and other necessities which had to be brought in on wagons. The job was allotted to the red men themselves, and so there sprang up the most picturesque class of all the freighters. This was a wise move, for it gave them an opportunity for activity which they sorely missed after a life of untrammeled freedom. It also provided a means of support in the wages they earned.

The government issued wagons and harness to the Indians, while they used their own ponies for motive power. The Indian ponies were fully as wild as their owners, and both were new to the work. The first difficulty was to harness the animals, and the initial attempts resulted in much plunging, bucking, and kicking by the frightened, cringing beasts. To get the harnessed pony in line to fasten the traces which pulled the load led to a second fight. After this had been accomplished, the unusual experience of going forward with a pull on the shoulders caused another series of bucks and jumps in frantic endeavors to free themselves of the strange burden. Every step was fought hard by man and beast, but the processes were finally mastered, and a system evolved which was peculiarly the Indian's own.

Teams were made up of four ponies in pairs. The lead pair were hooked up to a double-tree fastened to the front end of the wagon-tongue and the wheelers next the wagon. The team was started and driven by men mounted on other ponies. The Indian method of driving is best described as "herding the team along." The team was kept on the trail by force, exerted by riding ponies close against the leaders, and so holding them in line. Incentive to keep going came from blows with quirts, kicks and prods in the ribs, yells and curses. Squaws rode on the wagon seat and held a pair of reins or the ends of lassos tied about the necks of the wheelers, but this was no part of the driving.

With this combination, loads were drawn weighing from two thousand to twenty-five hundred pounds. As much ground was covered in the average day as by the mule-skinners.

The Indian freight train was made up of from five to twenty teams. At least two drivers, a squaw and some children to each team, not to mention a chief in charge of the band, made quite a crowd. Old tribal systems were in vogue, so that the train was likely to be manned from one tribe, by the members of one chief's band. The work was allotted in rotation among the bands of one tribe, as well as among the tribes also. In this way, Red Fork Ranch was visited at some time by most of the members of the Cheyenne, Arapahoe, Comanche and Kiowa tribes.

The ranchmen at Red Fork themselves were friendly with the Indians and were known personally to the Cheyennes and Arapahoes. The Indians felt at home while at Red Fork and often camped over night at the headquarters on the Chisholm Trail. During the summer season they passed frequently in large bands, adding much to the local color of the trail.

It was an interesting experience to watch an Indian freight train ford a river at high water. Arriving at the river brink, the lead-team stopped. All of the men divested themselves of clothing, even moccasins, until they stood in breech-clout alone. Then, mounting their ponies, they drove their teams, one after the other, down the bank and into the water at top speed. If the water came to the backs of the animals, they would swim until they could touch bottom again, where the drivers still urged them across the quicksands to the bank, never slackening until they were safe on the trail again.

The whole maneuver was accompanied by yells from the men and cries from the women and children that literally scared the teams through. The men wielded quirts, jabbed with sticks, threw stones and mud to emphasize the verbal prodding. They always got through if passage were possible. Should the elements be too strong, they would wait a more propitious time, but water that made the teams swim was no bar to crossing.

The ford of the Cimarron was the scene of hundreds of such battles with the elements.

The stage-coach outfits were the mail trains of the trails. Never did they fail to bring attraction to the scene. The swaying and creaking vehicle was drawn by the speediest of draft animals. As these were relieved at change stations, they kept comparatively fresh. They trotted most of the time with a rattling and jingling of harness, clearing of nostrils with short, sharp snorts, nickering to each other, and a swift patter of feet keeping time with the clatter of the coach. At rare intervals they walked, making a steady, rhythmical squeak-squeak-etysqueak of leather harness. At a gallop all nickering ceased while the other noises increased. The Jehu on the box controlled everything, and was not the least conspicuous part of the picture, both to look at and to hear, with his skill at the reins and his command of picturesque language.

In the early eighties, there appeared the most listless, slow-moving, dejected, un-picturesque object that ever hit the trails. This was the pariah of the cattle country—a sheep-man. The first herd of a few hundred sheep scandalized us at Red Fork as it was seen grazing its way down to the bottom lands toward Turkey Creek, on an early summer's day. Such animals had been heard of as denizens of that world beyond the knowledge of cattlemen, but to associate them with the West was abhorrent. Here they were, nevertheless, and the surprise was that they had ever succeeded in reaching the spot. The resentment of cattlemen to sheep was so great that man and beasts might well have been destroyed before reaching the ranch.

The bleating herd was led by a giant billy-goat whose odor was as far-reaching as was that of the native turkey buzzards. Of the two, we swore the goat smelled the worse. Trailing behind the herd was a lone man driving a burro loaded with his camp gear and bedding. He stumbled along beside the animal, his head bent, and looking furtively to right and left with quickly averted glances. He never raised his eyes above the herd, nor did he speak. He avoided companionship with other human beings, and in looks and actions seemed on a par with his sheep.

They passed by and forded the Cimarron on the Reno Trail. From the ford, the drover directed his flock southwest into the Indian country bound for the Texas Panhandle. The same man came back the following year with sheep for the market and regularly after that for many years, but never did he evince any desire for human companionship. His was a lonely life of ostracism, which he dared not and could not alter.

In addition to the groups already pictured, a sight of the old trail in retrospect reveals horsemen returning from cattle drives, singly and in groups, roving bands of Indians, Scouts, U. S. Cavalrymen, lone travelers on honest business, horse thieves rushing to cover, and pursuing officers.

Ralph told me in conversation that he had seen a crowd of men who came into the store one day whom he decided were members of the famous James gang of desperadoes. They filled the narrow confines of the store. A tall man with a red beard seemed to be the leader and it was evidently Jesse James. With him were several others. Another tall man with a black beard was evidently Frank, the brother of Jesse. Ralph thought that the crowd included Bob and Cole Younger, reputed cousins of the James boys. One of their number was of such demeanor that Ralph's attention was drawn to him. After one look, Ralph turned away in unconscious aversion. This man's beard and eye-brows were coarse and jet-black in color, and the eye-brows stood out like bristles of a brush. The scowl on his face was like that of the popular conception of a stage villain. He lived up to his looks, for this was Bob Ford, who treacherously shot his friend and leader in 1882. Bob in turn met the same fate at the hands of friends of the man whom he slew.

Many men passed Red Fork in this picture, on the way back to "The States" with a "stake," and never were heard of again. The notorious Bender family of murderers could have told where some of them were buried around that lone cabin on the Kansas prairies.

What an opportunity was missed by the "movie" man, in the passing of this picture of life that has gone forever. It

46

was part of the *real* West, and legend long before the first
Vitagraph announced the birth of the present great industry
of the screen. The film has added characters which did not
exist, and does not portray actual realities in detail as they were.

Chapter VI

BEFORE daybreak one morning, I was wakened from a sound slumber by a fusillade of snaps and cracks accompanied by shouts and yells which roused us at the ranch house to the consciousness of another day, as the first light began to reveal the cook house and horse corral next the Chisholm Trail. The awakening disturbance was the day's opening chorus whenever "bull-whackers" were encamped on the adjacent bottom land, just off the Reno Trail, between the ranch buildings and Turkey Creek.

Crack-crack-crackety-crack-crack-crack-crackety-crack-crack came the sounds as one after another of the men got into action with his twenty-foot long "blacksnake" whip, to limber his own muscles and rouse all the sleeping oxen and bring them up standing preparatory to being yoked and harnessed to the wagons. The animals lost no time in getting to their feet and into line, for experience had taught them that those cracking lashes could clip an ear at long distance.

The beasts of burden were no quicker to respond to the resounding snaps than were the numerous half wild hogs that scurried to high grass in all directions, whence they had come to forage on camp leavings, the wild turkeys that flew from night roosts on the edge of the woods to sheltering grass, quail and prairie chickens nesting for the night within a half mile radius, or frightened does with fawns leaping for the shelter of the woods. Once started on their morning work, these freighters of the old trails aroused every living thing into action in

48

A Day at Red Fork

short order. No alarm clock was needed when they were around, even if such contraptions had been heard of at that time and place.

The whackers had prepared and eaten their frugal meal before the dawn, and were ready to rouse the animals at the break of day. It was not long before the beasts were hitched, bedding thrown on the loads, and camp gear placed. Then the six-yoke teams, each drawing three wagons, began falling into line one after another on the trail, moving along at their steady pace. The creaking and groaning of the conveyances, the shouts and general racket were heard long after the bull-train had disappeared in the woods beyond the big cattle corral.

By that time the sun was rising and we would be preparing our morning meal. If there was fresh meat, it would be fried for breakfast, but more often it was the old stand-by of those days, sow-belly. With the meat would go warm "bread" in the shape of saleratus biscuit, with which the warm grease was sopped from the skillet in the place of butter, and the whole washed down with coffee. Coffee was served without sugar, though at times there was molasses for sweetening. It was good old sorghum. Milk and cream were in a class with butter—unknown. Once in a while there was a side dish of stewed dried apples.

The cooking utensils were the frying pan, Dutch oven and coffee pot. Tableware was solid tin. Tools consisted of steel knives, forks and pewter spoons. Table linen? Never heard of. While there were those who used the knife, fork and spoon, others preferred the simpler combination of knife and fingers. In this case, the thigh encased in jeans or leather chaps served as napkin. The furniture, aside from the home-made pine table, consisted of any handy box in the room or brought from the outside for a seat.

All meals were eaten at typical American speed and the

breakfast was soon finished. It did not take much longer to clear away the few dishes and wash them, out under the brush porch near the pump. Haste in the preparation, consumption, and clearing up of the meal was not a necessity as a general thing, for time often passed slowly at that lonely spot. A day so busy as the one recorded here was unusual.

Be that as it may, if the usual system was adhered to, cleaning up the breakfast dishes was immediately followed by tidying up the place. The table underwent a mopping with the dish rag, the box seats were lined up against the wall or thrown aside, and the dirt floor was rendered speckless by the simple expedient of opening the door and sweeping all refuse outside. Next came the sweeping of the yard between the buildings, and the floor of the storeroom, followed by a trip to the sleeping quarters above the store to sweep that out, if necessary. Beds of blankets were never made up; such fussing might spoil the restful indentations made by the body of a heavy sleeper. All was now set for the rush of chance travelers that just *might* come.

Often a freight train of mule-skinners would swing into sight and line up in front of the store on the spot vacated by the bull-whackers, while the drivers came in to trade or simply pass the time of day and exchange news of the trail. More often, there would be only chance lone travelers, or none at all until the down stage came from the north about ten o'clock in the morning.

This was the big event of the day, for it brought the news from civilization, and the way-pocket was handed in with precious letters and newspapers from "The States." The approach of the stage could be noted by the dust it raised coming down the butte, by way of the trail two miles to the north. Always watchful eyes looked for this sign, and on the days that "Dobe" was known to be the driver, there was sure to be an apprecia-

A Day at Red Fork

tive, expectant audience of all sojourners lined up in front of the buildings to witness its arrival at the Red Fork Station.

Under the urge of the lash, the six-horse team, propelling themselves along at an average speed of six miles on the stretches, and whipped into a gallop for the last hundred yards, were swung in a wide circle off the trail to the left toward the buildings, and brought to a stop in two or three strides, halting finally in a cloud of dust before the frontier store, and held in leash by the master hand controlling them,—said hand being aided and abetted by a booted foot on the brake-lever of the Concord coach.

The stage road was some seventy yards to the west of the buildings, and the intervening space was worn bare of grass to a hard-beaten, sun-baked surface over which to maneuver. Dobe loved to show his skill in driving, and at no other place on the whole length of trail were the conditions so favorable for the show as here. As a result, the arrival of the stage from the north with this driver almost always included this grand flourish as a finale, to the accompaniment of a flow of language such as only these old time drivers could command. If perchance he did not find his audience in waiting, the volley that ensued brought us out of the store in short order.

Most often the audience was made up only of Ralph and me, for the other men were scattered on duty over the broad expanse of the range, but it mattered not to Dobe, for there was joy in the performance for its own sake.

We admirers would dutifully wave greeting to him as he came to a halt, while yet the vehicle rocked and teetered from the inertia of arrested motion. After acknowledging the greetings of those on the ground with a nod of his head, the driver would turn to the other side and eject a stream of tobacco juice to the full limit of his range, no mean distance, then turn back again and break out into a broad, self-appreciative smile, as much as to say, "As a driver, I am the bully boy with the glass eye." Then, gathering the reins together, he would hand them down to one of us to hold while he descended to the ground over the front near wheel. Red Fork was not a change station, but the team was watered there out of the half-hogshead at the pump and supplementary buckets.

If there were passengers, they would join the driver in stretching legs while the mail was handed to the ranchman, and news was exchanged of the trail they had come over, as well as the one ahead, especially as to the condition of the river crossing on the Cimarron.

In the interval, opportunity was given any chance stranger to size up this knight of the trail named Dobe. He stood about five-foot-eight in his cow-boy boots. His face was brick red, set off with bushy eye-brows and a heavy drooping mustache of reddish tinge, mixed with gray. His eyes of bluish-gray were set deep in their sockets, and his habit of squinting them at every third or fourth wink gave him a quizzical expression quite in keeping with his character. He wore his boots with the trouser legs tucked in, and a dark blue flannel shirt covered with an old hunting coat of buckskin, elaborately fringed. On his head was a black Stetson, so old and worn that the front brim was pinned to the crown to hold it up.

Like most of the older men in that country, he had been in the West many years. Only a short time previous, he had been one of the white poachers on Indian land destroying buffalo, until the red men in desperation had cornered a band of them in a collection of buildings at Adobe Wells in the Panhandle country about seventy miles west of Red Fork. There had been bloodshed, but the Indians withdrew, and this man had escaped. He drifted about until the stage line was established, when he became a driver. He never chose to give his

DOBE SHOWS HIS SKILL

real name and gradually, because of his part in this escapade, came to be known simply as Dobe.

When ready to start again, Dobe mounted to his seat and took the reins, skillfully backed and turned the team around the corner of the lower building, then, with cracking whip, started out at a gallop which soon settled into a steadier pace that drew the coach quickly out of sight. After watching our visitor pass from view, we busied ourselves with the mail from the outside world, or, if there was no mail, settled down to contemplate our isolation and loneliness. It was this way most of the year, and the memory of the passing of the stage is coupled with the feeling of loneliness that followed, though in the height of the season it would not be long before some other outfit would trail in.

"Nu-mi-nish, nu-mi-nish, n-u-m-i-nish, n-u-m-i-nish po-nee!" would be the next cry that broke the stillness, heralding the approach of some of our Cheyenne friends, freighting for the government or for themselves. That cry was the equivalent of "go" in the white tongue, and literally told the animal to "Go, go on, pony." With the utterance of the words came prods in the ribs and blows with quirts, interspersed with yells and shouts, all together intended to induce the best speed possible. After high speed was attained, the word "Numinish" was long drawn out and signified "All is well, but keep going." When the driver on his pony alongside the harnessed ones withdrew far to one side, the team knew it might come to rest.

In this manner, the first teams of the train would be driven past the buildings a short distance, and we would hear the cry "Numinish" in both long and short meter, mingling with the other calls coming up from the distance until the air would resound with the yells and cries of dozens of buck Indian throats, yelps of dogs, and the treble voices of squaws and children, as the whole band filled the bottom land and came to a halt. If a stop was to be made, the head man would come galloping up to reach the buildings first, where he would hail his friends within, quickly dismount, step inside the door, fill his pipe and step outside again. Seating himself on the ground in plain sight of the arriving hosts, he would light the pipe, and as other Indians grouped about him, each would receive it in turn as he joined the circle. Thus did he signify to all the band that a stop was to be made there until he gave the signal to proceed with the journey.

At such times, the men of the outfit would crowd into the store until they filled it, while the women and children remained outside with the teams. Some trading was done, and talk was voluble and noisy.

As they were to visit a town of white people at the end of the journey, all were excited and came arrayed in their best. Many on these trips were paying their first visit to the "White Man's Village," of which they had heard strange tales. Like any of us going among strangers, they wished to appear at their best both in clothing and deportment, and so, not only did they don their very best, but they observed all the conventions as they understood them. At Red Fork, they were still among friends, and could unbend and be natural. There was no stony mask of seeming indifference while they were there.

Many of the Cheyenne women and girls could still sport the dress they loved so well, of red wool, single piece waist and skirt, trimmed with a black border around the bottom, sleeves and yoke, the skirt coming just below the knee. This dress would often be trimmed front and back with rows of elk teeth. Some wore pretty tanned yellow buckskin dresses trimmed with beadwork, while others had to be content with calico. Their legs below the dress skirt showed, usually, in tanned leather leggings and moccasins combined into a boot, all fringed and made gay with their own beadwork, green predominating in the design. Every woman's and girl's hair was well oiled and braided in two strands, one on each side of the head, with the parting line marked with vermilion. They antedated the flapper of the Twentieth Century, for they, too, often had paint on the face in special designs. Sometimes the cheekbones were outlined in red, sometimes in yellow. Others contented themselves with a single vermilion dot about an eighth of an inch in diameter, placed on the cheek below the eye, or in the center of the forehead.

Styles and modes of dress changed with the years among the wild Indians, and while at this date the women still adhered to their older forms untainted by the white influence, the men were changing their attire in one or two noticeable details.

For instance, many of the men wore the old-fashioned white man's cotton or linen shirts. They were slipped over the head and fastened at the back of the neckband with a thong, as were the wristbands, also. From the shoulders they hung loose, unconstrained by belt or trousers, over the top of the gee-string and leggings. In other words, "the shirt tail was out." To them it was sensible and right; it was the way they wore their leather shirts. The blanket was discarded in hot weather, and the men came into the store arrayed mostly in the white shirt above leggings, gee-string and moccasins. Each man's hair was in two braids, as was the women's, and the parting was delineated with vermilion paint like theirs. No headdress was worn other than the feather of the "brave." Only one distinction was made in the hair-dressing. The women braided theirs from the back of the head, while the men pulled their hair forward over the shoulder to braid it.

(The present day pictures showing every Indian in a group wearing a full head-dress of feathers are all wrong. This was a distinction enjoyed only by those who had won the right to it. The right to wear the single feather in the scalp-lock came only through the Medicine Dance, an initiation of torture which only a real man could endure.)

These Indians, while on the trail, had all the essentials of food with them, so that the trading meant exchange for delicacies to supplement their bill of fare. There was much trade in "smacks," crackers, sugar, and dried apples. There was never a supply of paper bags to wrap purchases in, so frequently the braves were seen returning to their wives and children with "their shirt tails full" of groceries. These visits of our red friends never lasted more than an hour, so the departure was as sudden as the arrival had been, and as noisy.

Along in the afternoon, at about four o'clock, the "up-stage" would arrive. Its approach could not be noted from the store, until the clatter of the wheels was heard, or the driver's voice was raised to urge the team forward. Almost simultaneously the whole equipment would swing into view around the lower building. Often this outfit would not water the team at Red Fork, but would proceed on its way north after a quick exchange of information and the "way pockets."

Then it was time to look for cattle outfits which had planned to spend the night there. The very first sign of arrival would be the "cook wagon." It would be pulled up not far from the buildings, where the cook tenders could easily "rustle" wood from the timber, and water from the near-by pump. To cattlemen this was a luxury.

Following the cook would be the "horse wrangler" with his herd of ponies, which would go by on the run in a cloud of dust. They would be "milled" into a stop close by, and allowed to feed on the bottom lands several hours before bedding down. The wranglers had an easy time here at night, for, although one must be on duty, there were woods on two sides to help hold their charges in case of stampede.

A Day at Red Fork

The big herds were corralled at Red Fork for the night, unless one exceeded the capacity of the enclosure. It was always quite a feat to turn a herd of wild cattle and get them into the first corral they had seen on the trail, but the wing fence helped a good deal. When the cattle were once inside, the men bedded themselves down on the ground around the corral fence. Unless some untoward event occurred during the night, the herd was easily held there, and the night riders had one bit of respite from duty out of the many days on the trail. For that reason, Red Fork was a welcome spot to the old time cattle drivers.

After the cattle had been corralled, the men had their meal, and then would gather in the store for an evening's visit and amusement. Many of the outfits had a fiddler among them, who would bring his instrument into the store and go through his repertoire. Then there would be an evening which every one enjoyed. At first, the men sat or lay about in convenient spots and listened silently to the initial efforts of the performer. Soon the "Arkansas Traveler" or similar tunes would be called for, and as sure as one of these was played, there would be at least one fellow who would arise and keep step in a "jig." This would start every one applauding, and others, becoming imbued with the spirit of the occasion, would join in, until there would be as many as six men on the floor at once going through a "hoe down." There was action, no matter what tune was played. Six men in cow-boy equipment, and all dancing, each to outdo the other, can make some commotion. In the heat of action, stamping feet were abetted by jingling spurs, flapping gun scabbards, and clapping hands to make a noise which was rather augmented than drowned by the yells of approval from the steadfastly admiring audience. Then perhaps some young fellow would become so exuberant that he "would go you one," loosen up with his gun, and pour out the six shots into the air or floor.

After the evening's entertainment, every one would disperse for the night's rest. Cow-boys and cattlemen would then go to the corral, take saddle for head-rest and blankets for cover, and turn in, while the ranchman slept on the floor above the store. Soon the noise of the playing, singing, dancing, and shouts of the evening would give place to quiet and the night sounds of the prairie. At dawn would come the clamor and confusion of the departing hosts of cattle and their attendants.

This is a picture of a typical full day at Red Fork Ranch during the height of the driving season when the cattle business had reached its halcyon days. To have been on this busy corner of "Main Street" (the old Chisholm Trail) was a privilege which few people experienced, and no one will again.

Chapter VII

O N the slope of a sand dune, at the edge of the black-jack woods, in plain sight of the Chisholm Trail, just below the buildings at Red Fork, lay the stockaded graves of two young men.

They had been members of Wild Bill's gang of horse thieves. One had been slain by the other with a forty-five bullet ranging from the apex of the head down to the face. It was a treacherous shot from behind, and the murderer had been promptly sent to the beyond by the rope-route, to join his victim. A dispute over cards. The bodies were buried side by side, making two more permanent residents of Red Fork Ranch. These graves were unmarked and all identity of their occupants lost.

Pat Hennessey, whose grave was beside the trail below Bull Foot Ranch, met his death with four others at the hands of Indians on the warpath. He was more fortunate in being known, and the tale of his death was often told. (Hennessey, Oklahoma, is named after Pat.)

On a convenient knoll, by the trail, they laid him. This would describe the location of many graves of those who "cashed in" while on the old trails. A knoll was a frequent resting place, for knolls were numerous on the north river banks, close to the fords where so many went under the turbulent high water as the cattle were being forded across.

If you had ever seen these raging waters in spring freshets, you would wonder that there were not more graves of those who had fought them. There were swift currents of muddy waters in the channels, and swift eddies with leaping swirls near shore; battering-rams of floating trees, crumbling banks which gave way as one tried to scale them. Then there was the added risk of accompanying a herd of panic-stricken animals into the flood. Often men, animals, and floating logs became a confused, inextricable mass in the middle of the stream. Men and animals were swept back from low banks again and again until they were engulfed. Yes, many graves were the result of these crossings.

Then there were the graves by the trail out on the wide prairie. These may have been filled by the bodies of men trampled out of human semblance in a stampede. Others fell in argument over cards, or were victims of raiding Indians, and were laid to rest by the survivors. Some fell victims to white human hyenas, with the vast areas as the only witness of lone murder. Oh, there were many ways to the grave on the old trails!

Those who filled them were never the victims of wasting malady which brought lingering death. The grave fillers died suddenly, and were buried quickly, without benefit of clergy.

Most of the burials were made deep, and all graves were protected from the wolves and coyotes. This was done by driving stakes deep into the ground in a rectangular arrangement on the sides and ends of the grave mound. These were driven deep enough and set close enough together to discourage digging. A platform of stakes was fastened over the top of the enclosure to keep animals from leaping over and digging straight down, inside the stakes. Somewhere near would be a rude headboard, if such were obtainable, with the name, if it were known. Many graves had no headboard. Marked and unmarked were alike in being "lone graves"—soon for-

FORDING THE FLOOD

gotten and unattended. Many mysteries lay there, for no one knew whence they came, or who was awaiting their return. Some of their occupants were the only permanent residents of Red Fork Ranch.

One day I rode with Ralph headed north. When we had reached a point about a mile and a half from the ranch and had entered the "black-jack" woods bordering Turkey Creek, we entered a clearing at the head of which was one of the lone graves which was staked out in the usual manner described. This was placed near an ash tree which was marked as a headstone. This grave had been filled before Ralph or I came to the ranch. The complete story is as follows:

One pleasant day in summer, when the grass was high on the plains and bottoms, and the wild plums and mulberries were in full fruition, a strange herd of ponies were driven down the trail from the north to the bottom lands of Turkey Creek near Red Fork. Arriving late in the afternoon, and finding feed and water plentiful, the herd was allowed to browse for the remainder of the day. They were in charge of a young man in full cow-boy rig. He seemed furtive in his actions, and at times displayed a violent temper.

He was soon followed by a man of some forty years, mounted on a good saddle horse, accompanied by another man and a woman driving a covered wagon which contained a mess box and camping utensils.

The whole outfit was the nucleus of a horse ranch, yet unlocated, somewhere in Texas. The owner, named Wanamaker, was the one riding the large horse. He had bought his stock and equipment in Emporia, where he had also engaged the young man to herd the stock. The man and wife, new to the West, had agreed to accompany the owner to his new ranch, and act as handy man and cook.

On arrival this afternoon, the owner selected an open spot in the black-jack on the bank of Turkey Creek as a camp site for the night. Supper was prepared by the woman and the meal was finished as the first shades of night were falling.

The young man then proposed to Wanamaker that he go with him into the woods for a wild turkey hunt. It was roosting time, he said, and they could not fail to make a full bag in short order. Aside from the usual weapons of Westerners, there was a shot-gun in camp, and the young man selected this for his hunting, in addition to his "six-gun."

The two men left camp and stepped into the woods to the north with the older leading the way. They were immediately lost from sight in dense brush and the gathering gloom. In fact, it was too dark to see turkeys unless they were silhouetted against the sky on an overhead limb. It is a good method of hunting this game, coming under them at roost, but the couple left in camp were "shorthorns" and told each other that they could not understand why any one should try to hunt in the dark. An indefinable dread of the young man had taken hold of the honest couple. He seemed so vicious, and had such disregard for others' feelings at all times, that they had learned to distrust him. His manner always gave a sinister shade to every word and act.

And so it was that the two left in camp nervously awaited the outcome of affairs. It was not long before the loud report of a gun-shot broke the quiet of the wilderness. To have heard a shot was to be expected, under the circumstances, but it startled and frightened the anxious listeners. There was only one shot, followed by an ominous silence.

A premonition of deadly import held the two spellbound in camp, until there came a crashing sound through the brush, followed by the form of the young man bounding into the firelight. His manner was that of a fiend, and the others shrank back in terror before him. Striding to Wanamaker's horse picketed close by, he hastily saddled it, filled the saddle bags with provisions, and picking up the rifle of the owner, vaulted into the saddle and rode away into the darkness. He left the "shorthorns" alone in what was to them a wild, unknown, Indian-infested country. If they had only known it, the worst that they could fear had left them.

The couple spent a night of terror, not daring to sleep, and tortured by the unfamiliar night sounds of the wild places. At earliest dawn they hitched the horses to the wagon, and not stopping to eat, drove from the woods out on to the trail. There they met a strange man on foot to whom they told their story.

This stranger, it happened, was a bull-whacker camped lower down on Turkey Creek, who was on his way over to Red Fork Ranch when they met him. The couple did not know they were so near buildings until the freighter pointed them out a mile away. To leave the vicinity of their nightmare was their only thought, and they could not be induced to return. The freighter directed them to Darlington Agency, thirty miles away, where they might notify the authorities of what had occurred.

The freighter went on to the ranch and told Dan Jones the story. Dan and his foreman rode over during the day and found the scattered herd and camp site, but look as they would, they found no trace of the missing man. At length they gave up the mystery, rounded up the ponies, and started with them for the ranch. When close to the buildings, they were overtaken by the head man of a band of the Sac and Fox Indians.

This Indian reported that his band was deer hunting, and had encamped in their tepees on the west bank of the creek, not far from where the whites had been the night before.

They had heard the shot and witnessed the hasty departure in the morning. Divining that something was wrong, they had made an investigation. Almost at once they hit the trail followed by the two hunters the night previous, and found the body of the murdered man. It lay on its back in a small clearing, with arms outflung. A hat lay close by and the pockets of the clothes were turned inside out.

As the Indians interpreted the signs, the murderer had followed Wanamaker as the two passed along. When they reached the clearing he had called to his victim who had turned about. As he did so, the shot-gun had been held close to his face and fired. The result was instant death from a wound which carried away much of the face and extended through the skull.

Now the Indians were no fools. They knew that if they were found to have been in the vicinity of a white man's slaying, theirs would be the blame. Every unsolved murder in that country was laid at their door. They had witnessed the search by Jones, however, and knew they were not suspected by him. Now was the time to clinch the matter. So the Indian rode after the searching party, brought Jones back to the woods and showed him the victim's body as it lay.

Another day had reached evening darkness by the time Dan knew the location of the body, and it was then too late to remove it. That night a troop of cavalry with Tom Donnel, the scout from Fort Reno, came to Red Fork and went into camp. They had been sent by Agent Miles upon hearing the story of the man and wife who had arrived during the afternoon.

Cavalrymen, scout and ranchman went to the spot the second morning after the murder and buried the victim. The body was wrapped in a blanket and buried deep, at the base of a towering ash tree. The usual stockade defense was placed about the mound. Dan started to carve the name Wanamaker on the tree for a headboard, but stopped for some reason after having finished the first two letters "Wa."

Thus did they lay away this stranger in a strange land. Now he was a permanent resident of Red Fork Ranch. Who knows where he came from? Perhaps some one waited in vain for a letter, a summons to share a new home in the distant, unknown land never reached. Who knows?

Tom Donnel took up the trail of the murderer at the spot and tracked him down into the Texas Panhandle. He was brought back to Fort Reno and tried by court martial. The evidence of the married couple was sufficient to convict him, and he was sentenced to hang. Given into the custody of a United States Marshal for removal to Fort Smith, he escaped on the way and never was heard of again.

Chapter VIII

OUR uncle, Benjamin F. Williams, was a frequent visitor at Red Fork Ranch during my stay there. He was in the midst of his activities as Deputy United States Marshal, having jurisdiction over all the country embraced in the old Cheyenne and Arapahoe reservations. For the majority of years of his tenure of office this territory was buffalo range and Indian country in which a mixture of white outlaws and Indians roamed. It was his duty to rid the country of outlaws. In the performance of his duty he had already been forced "to kill his man" and he was feared as well as execrated by those who desired to live in the country as a hiding place from the law.

Uncle Ben was one of my heroes and was always followed about the ranch during his visits by my admiring, hero worshiping glances and impertinent inquisitiveness. At that time, he was a five-foot-eleven, one-hundred-and-eighty-pound, black-bearded specimen of authoritative, self-reliant manhood. He handled himself with the agility of a cat. His method of mounting a horse was to place his left hand on the pommel of the saddle and vault into the seat. I often watched him as he proceeded to the horse corral in the rear of the ranch buildings to secure his horse. He never used the bars or took the time to let them down as he entered, but placed his hands on the top rail, which was about chin high, and sprang up and over the fence. He was an uncle to be proud of in that wild country and I often beguiled him into telling some of his history.

One of his most important and nervy transactions had occurred in the cook-house of the ranch only four years prior to my coming there, when the cook-house was the only building on the site. This involved his capture, single-handed, of a certain "Wild Bill" and thirteen of his men. This was not the famous Wild Bill Hickok, but a very cheap imitation of that frontiersman.

Uncle had received a warrant for the arrest of this pseudo-Wild Bill and his men to be delivered "dead or alive." The story as he told it to me at the ranch is as follows:

Uncle's first problem after receiving the warrants was to locate his men. The country in which they might hide was extensive. His work was so in accord with the interests of the Indians themselves, for they wanted every white man off their land, that he always had their hearty support and coöperation. Accordingly, he first went to Little Robe for any possible information. The old war chief had runners out every day, and his young men were on the scout continually. In this case, he was not able to help his friend with direct information, but they both agreed that the most probable place to find them was on Turkey Creek near Red Fork Ranch.

He decided to scout up that way, and set out alone from Little Robe's village. He camped one night in one of the old dug-outs at the mouth of Turkey Creek, for it was in October and the weather chilly. His plan was to ride into the ranch in the early morning light before he could be observed by any chance looker-on. Once there he might secure information from the ranchman.

He accordingly arose at dawn and mounted his pony. Crossing the creek he was soon on the trail and riding toward the ranch from the south. As he approached at a single-foot pace, there was no evidence of life about the spot, except for the smoke issuing from the chimney. This was as it should be, for the ranchman would be preparing his breakfast.

With this thought in mind, he spurred up his mount and

rode briskly around the corner of the building, straight into some fourteen ponies tied close together in front. They were bunched so that no one riding from the south could see them. The droppings about them gave evidence that they had been there all night.

Here was a ticklish situation for the marshal to meet, for, as he instantly divined, here was a full array of the men he was after. From the silence prevailing, he felt certain that he had been seen by those within. His mind had to function at top speed. There was only one thing to do under the circumstances, and that was to face the music right then and there. It would be folly to ride away in the clear morning light, for to do so would draw the fire of those inside.

In addition to his six-shooter, he always carried a Henry rifle, and on this he largely relied. His *modus operandi* was to carry the rifle in the crook of his left arm, and shoot from that position, keeping his body with the left side to the target.

Without hesitating an instant, he alighted from his pony, strode to the door and kicked it open, holding his rifle in position. He had stepped into a room full of men all standing to receive him. There were all the desperadoes he was after, with Wild Bill in the lead.

Uncle Ben knew his men and they knew him. His speed and daring had carried him that far unscathed. The men were both surprised and confused, or they would have fired as he came through the door. Right then was the time to have shot him, before he himself could see where to shoot. As it was, he now had every man covered with his cocked rifle and his swift glance. He could in any event get two or three of them in case any one opened fire. No one seemed desirous of attracting his personal attention, and all stood like images. The marshal stood still also, for he couldn't hope to arrest fourteen men single-handed.

Both sides studied the situation for some minutes, each prepared to join in the shooting as soon as it started, but no one had an inclination to begin.

Finally Wild Bill broke into a grin as he realized that he and his men held the upper hand. He began to taunt Uncle Ben with having blundered in on them there, and disclosed the fact he knew there were warrants for their arrest.

"Whyn't ye arrest us, Williams? Here we be, an' glad to see ye," he boasted.

Uncle had not answered the taunts of the desperado, but to the question he made reply, "I'm not fool enough to try to arrest you, fourteen to one. Now that I know where you are, I'll keep after you and get you, every one, when I have the chance."

This seemed the psychological moment for a retreat, but how was he to get away alive? He considered the matter for a few moments longer, never relaxing his vigilance and seeming to fix every man to his place with his unwavering glance. Something must be done, however, and he decided to leave. He began to sidle out of the door a step at a time. As he retreated toward his pony he kept glancing from side to side as he covered every man every second of the time. His glance seemed to compel belief that he would shoot on the slightest pretext, and every man was so reluctant to draw the first shot, but yet as reluctant to let the enemy escape, that all unconsciously moved forward step by step after him. Thus they drew together so that all could see out of the door, and could be seen by the man outside. By the time he had reached his horse, the gang were all outside.

Then in a flash, he sprang into his saddle and in the same second recovered his drop on the crowd. Once seated, he backed and sidled his pony to a point where by applying the spurs he was carried from sight in one bound around the corner of the cabin, and was so far on his way before the gang recovered that they did not fire a shot at him.

Uncle lost no time in reaching Fort Reno, where a troop of cavalry was placed under his orders. He returned to Red Fork Ranch the same night, and took up the trail in pursuit of the gang who were now in full flight.

The second day of the pursuit he overtook and surrounded them so that they had either to fight or to surrender. They asked for a parley and Williams rode forward to meet Wild Bill. He said to the robber chief, "I told you I would arrest you, and now you will have to surrender, or I will turn these soldiers loose on you." The whole gang surrendered without a fight, and Ben Williams saw them convicted and sentenced to long terms of imprisonment at Fort Leavenworth.

This broke up one of the worst gangs of horse thieves that ever operated in the Indian Nation.[1] The finish of such traffic by this gang started with that one meeting in the cabin at Red Fork, between the nervy Deputy United States Marshal and the unnerved outlaws. He had them "buffaloed," "the Indian sign on them," he was "the jinx of the number thirteen."

They had been all bravado before this man faced them, then Wild Bill's name was changed to Tame Bill.

[1] The old Indian Territory was always spoken of by Westerners as the Indian Nation, or simply as the Nation.

Chapter IX

CHEROKEE BILL

I FIRST rode over the trail from Red Fork Ranch to Darlington Agency via the stage coach. After my return by the same route I knew the trail and thereafter used my pony on most of my trips. I had been absent on one of these trips when on my return Ralph told me of what he believed was a peculiar incident which had occurred while I was away.

One day four or five men were driving by with a herd of about four hundred head of beeves. They seemed to be under the leadership of a handsome, smooth-faced young man, not much more than a boy. He was a tall, slender youth with copper-colored skin, ruddy cheeks, and long, wavy black hair falling to his shoulders. Cow-boy apparel of the best texture clothed him, and he wore a "four-gallon" Stetson. The trappings of the horse were in keeping with the man,—Spanish saddle, lariat of black-and-white horse hair, and silver-mounted bridle.

When the man alighted at the store and came in, he displayed a grace of motion and show of equipment that made him a marked man,—out of the ordinary. After picking up what information he wanted of trail conditions and cow outfits which had passed, he mounted and rode to join his men who had driven on.

Ralph would have thought no more of this man, except possibly as one different from the usual passerby, had he not come in again two days after his first appearance. Again the leader brought his companions and this time they all came into the store together. They were in the best of spirits and quite talkative.

It was gathered from the conversation that their herd had been destined for the market, and that they had sold out to another outfit on the trail. The transaction had been for cash, which the leader carried on him. He had between three and four thousand dollars in gold.

He paid the men about two hundred and fifty dollars each and they prepared to go on at once, saying they were bound for Texas. The ponies they rode had belonged to the leader, and he sold them back to the riders. After all business had been concluded among them, the men purchased some supplies and rode away leaving the one man behind.

He asked if he might stay the rest of the day and the coming night, and whether he and his horse could be fed. Being assured that he would be taken care of, he put his horse in the corral and proceeded to enjoy his day off.

The men had all addressed him as Bill, and he told the ranchman he was known as Cherokee Bill. Later, he amplified this statement by saying that he was the son of a white father and a Cherokee woman. His looks belied the statement, for he had curly hair that belonged to no Indian and to very few whites. Ralph put him down for a half-breed, negro-Indian, and later information gave it that his father was a negro and his mother a Cherokee.

No matter what his parentage, Red Fork Ranch was entertaining a young man who was as full of life and the joy of living as ever passed that way. He let go all holds, unbuckled his reticence, and gave himself over to the full enjoyment of unfettered talk. His life's history (his own version), stories and anecdotes came in a constant flow. He sang ditties, danced jigs and indulged in good-natured banter at the expense of the ranchman, to while away the afternoon and evening. His good spirits were contagious, so Ralph entered into the occasion, and the two young men had a real "bully" time together until they retired to their blankets at about ten o'clock.

They both arose at dawn and while breakfast was being prepared, Bill went to the corral and fed his horse oats. Coming in, he ate a hearty meal and then led the horse to water. After saddling he came back to don heavy clothes for the ride.

As the weather was cool and he was going to strike across for the Panhandle, Bill bought that which would add to his comfort, a heavy ulster, overshoes, and a pair of heavy buckskin gauntlets. Taking off his spurs, he put on overshoes and fastened the spurs over them. He shed his gun belt for an instant to don the ulster and replaced the gun outside that. Picking up his Winchester, he placed it in the saddle holster.

The air was clear and bracing, and man and beast both were in fine fettle. When ready to mount, Bill took reins and saddle pommel in one hand and leaped astride the animal.

For two or three minutes he reined in the beast with one hand and allowed it to buck-jump from pure fullness of spirits. With every jump of the animal, the man let out a whoop of the same joy that animated the broncho. Then giving the horse the rein with a final yell, he tore away, turning in the saddle to doff his hat in graceful adieu, and waving it to and fro till he had passed from sight.

What a perfect picture he was, that bright October morning, of happy, blithe, buoyant life as he galloped away with his hair flying in the breeze and his body gracefully swaying with every motion of his steed.

They were headed down the trail and it was also the start of Cherokee Bill on the downward path.

He never came back that way in peace again. Always it was in mad flight, one way or the other, to escape the avengers of the law. Never again could he enjoy the carefree companionship of another as he had that one afternoon and evening.

Companions in crime were ever open to suspicion, and he killed some of them in fear. Every man's hand was, in the end, against one who was naturally of a genial, pleasant nature. What a contrast the subsequent news of his exploits made to the one pleasant day we knew of him. Does the crime trail lead to happiness? Ask the shade of Cherokee Bill.

Cherokee Bill passed us several times while he was evidently "on the dodge" and I had my first sight of him. We knew he was piling up a reputation for reckless, unpitying murder.

NOTE.—See Appendix, page 293.

Chapter X

KILLERS

WE no doubt entertained many killers at Red Fork Ranch, some of whom impressed themselves upon my mind, making an unforgettable memory.

A herd of some fifteen hundred Texas longhorns came up the trail to Red Fork Ranch one summer's day, late in the afternoon. They were driven into the corral by a full outfit of cow-boys. The drive had been tiresome, and all hands looked forward to this spot as a haven of rest for one night. Here the cattle could be held in a corral and night-herd duty dispensed with.

By early dusk, all stock had been corralled, and the men descended in a body on the cook and his evening offering of food. All was jollity and good feeling, for they were going to have a night off and an evening's entertainment, consisting largely of a performance on the violin by one of the outfit. His skill was attested to by his comrades who proclaimed him a "jim darter."

The men came into the store and announced the coming entertainment to Ralph. Of course he acquiesced, and set about gathering an audience by passing the word to near-by freighters and the men employed on the Ranch. Accordingly an audience of more than twenty assembled in the building in full expectation of an enjoyable evening. These old timers had few opportunities for entertainment, and to listen to a violin was all that any of them could ask.

The store-room where the program took place had a waist-high, pine-board counter along one side and one end, making an ell. Diagonally across the room from the corner of the ell was a door opening from the south, while in front was the door facing toward Turkey Creek.

Two of the visiting cattle outfit acted as an arrangement committee and disposed the audience for the performer. They insisted that every individual in the vicinity be present in the room. After making sure that all were there, every one was seated on boxes and on the counter. A cracker box was placed in the corner of the counter ell for the performer. After all had been seated, the man of the evening suddenly appeared in the south doorway. Quick and lithe as a cat, he sprang into the open door and balanced there. He was above medium height, thin and muscular. Garbed as a typical cow-boy from head to foot, he carried a fiddle and bow in one hand, and a Winchester rifle in the other.

He hesitated a moment in the doorway as he swept the faces of every one in the room with a keen, comprehensive glance. In another moment he was striding like a panther, softly and swiftly, toward the ell in the counter. Arriving there, he wheeled about in the fraction of a second and glanced about again to see if any one had moved. Placing his violin and bow on the counter at his left, and never lowering his eyes, he felt for the box, placed it, and sat down.

Once seated, he placed his rifle against the counter on his right. Then followed some moments of adjusting his rifle at exactly the right angle from which to snatch it in the least fraction of a second and balance it for a hip shot. The same action which snatched up the gun would cock it. Without removing his glance from the room an instant, he tried the gun position several times, snatching it up, and replacing it until satisfied.

With the same quick, cat-like motions he picked up the violin

FIDDLE IN ONE HAND, RIFLE IN THE OTHER

and bow, and commenced to play without tuning up. As he played, he was only partially seated, with both legs drawn up under him ready for a spring. There was never a second that he did not cover every man in the room with his glance, as he turned slightly from side to side. He could, and did, play almost every selection familiar to the audience. Encores were given, and every tune called for, he played. He was there to please, and did so.

It was good music by a master hand and the audience sat spellbound for that reason, and for another also. Every one there had recognized a killer who was on the look-out for the man who would try to get him. A false move by any person there would have caused the violin and bow to drop, while the same move would have put the balanced rifle into deadly action. Every one knew the type, and that was one audience which did not move its hands or shuffle its feet. Present-day performers might try the same tactics.

The finish came when he suddenly placed the fiddle and bow in one hand, and picking up the rifle, left the room as rapidly as he had entered. Turning at the door he surveyed the roomful of men, and in the next instant had leaped into the dark.

This hip-shot violin virtuoso was a deadly killer well within the cattle country code. His killings were of the stand-up-first-on-the-draw variety. Such killings were not looked upon as murders. This man held the respect and loyalty of every one who knew him. The first killing in self-defense had led to others of the same nature until his life was a continuous every-minute-of-the-day expectation of revenge on the part of some one. In the end, he would certainly "cash in" on the action of some one who caught him unawares. Until that event, eternal vigilance on his part was the ticket to existence on this mundane sphere. Yet this man loved to entertain those who desired his art and not his life. His outfit were his "pals" to a man. Besides corralling every one on the premises, they guarded the windows with their own bodies against a possible shot from without.

Many killers were of the foregoing type. The old West saw many of another kind, also. Stripped of all romance, they were mere murderers. They murdered in cold blood without giving the victim a warning or a chance to fight. Again, they murdered in pure viciousness to vent spite or uncontrolled anger, but never unless they had all the advantage. These men had to make a quick get-away after a murder, to escape the vengeance of the fair-minded. Again there were those who aped others, and in building up a pseudo reputation would aspire to kill a man who had more "notches" on his gun. But such braggarts seldom accomplished their purpose except when they had the advantage of numbers, or "the drop" on the victim.

For a week at one time Red Fork Ranch harbored a real killer while he practiced for a particular murder which he had in mind. He was a "broncho buster" by profession, with a disposition to match the worst "outlaw" he ever rode. He aspired to be known as a "bad man from away back." Gun and knife, both, were his instruments of death, and he was ambidextrous in their use.

He paid his way at the ranch by breaking ponies, and put in his odd time shooting and throwing the knife. All his gun practice was intended to develop speed on the draw as well as accuracy. He wore his gun well down on the right thigh, where it was fastened with a thong attached to the lower end of the holster, and passed about the leg above the knee. On the draw, he passed his finger through the trigger guard, and gave the gun a whirl which spun it once around and hip high before his hand caught it. The thumb caught and held the hammer at the end of the whirl, so that the one operation brought the gun to full cock for the first shot. Subsequent shots were made by "fanning" the hammer into full cock as continuous pressure was put on the trigger.

Red Fork Ranch was infested with snakes of a variety locally named "chicken" snakes. They were small, harmless, yellow snakes, with dark markings, and a slender body not over two feet long. The sod roof of the older building sheltered many, and they ranged through every part of the two log houses. It was a common occurrence to see a snake head project itself downward from the ceiling, followed by the body which would hang poised for a moment, held by the tip of the tail, before dropping to the floor and gliding away to some crevice.

The bad man had much practice inside the houses, shooting the heads from these snakes. There would be an interval of one or two seconds from the first unexpected appearance of the reptile, to the drop on the floor. During this scant space of time, the man would draw and fire at the swaying head, it would disappear, and the writhing, headless body fall to the floor. Rarely did he miss such shots.

Another favorite test was to pin a six-inch square of paper to the building, and place six shots in succession within the space while standing at a distance of seventy-five feet. No misses there. Again he would toss a tin can into the air to a distance of twenty or thirty feet, and after the toss, draw his gun and place two, three, and sometimes four shots in it before it struck the ground.

He was almost as quick and accurate with his bowie knife. It was a favorite trick to draw from the left shoulder where the scabbard held it at the back of the neck. It was covered by his coat collar, and ostensibly was to be used indoors. Like a flash, he would snatch the two-edged weapon with the right hand and throw it at a mark. It was released at the end of a back-handed throw, and turning over once during the flight, would pierce the mark point foremost. Many chicken snakes fell victims to this knife as they were gliding away with the head raised six or eight inches from the ground. He would also throw at his six-inch paper mark, and strike it from a distance of fifty feet. This man was a double-actioned instrument of death.

The real nature of the man was revealed in his treatment of others. I was present at Red Fork during the stay of the killer and was often the victim of his spleen. The very sight of me at any time was the signal for a torrent of foul invective. This was unusual in the cattle country, where youth was an object of solicitous regard.

I was naturally fascinated by the performances of this man in breaking horses, as well as by his practice with gun and knife. As a buster, he was in a class by himself. He would rope, throw, and saddle his mount single-handed. Then he would straddle the prostrate animal and work the binding ropes loose from the feet until the animal jumped erect. The rider never "touched leather" as he sat the first buck-jumps through; then he raked the animal's neck with his spurs, in wanton cruelty. Sky-hunting or side-wheeling, all efforts of the animal to unseat him were the same to this rider, futile.

To discover the boy looking on in wonder and admiration started a string of oaths that seemed interminable in length and variety. As the animal commenced pitching, he and I received abuse in impartial portions, until the beast cut matters short by dashing away. It was the same at knife and gun practice,—curses augmented by kicks if I came too close. Old Chape saved me from actual maltreatment, but he had his hands full much of the time.

86

Killers

The enemy against whom this man was preparing lived at Caldwell, and to Caldwell he betook himself as soon as his confidence had been sufficiently established. He found his enemy on the street and stole upon him from behind, but before he could attack, his victim, warned by some premonition, turned, beat him to the draw, and shot him down. All his practice hadn't supplied him with the nerve to face a cool, courageous man suddenly and conquer. The act for which the victor nearly lost his life was merely that of having faced our killer down in an argument in which he was clearly wrong.

All Red Fork Ranch had breathed a sigh of relief when the killer took his departure, all breathed a sigh of gratitude when it was made clear that he could never return. My gratitude was probably the most fervent of all.

That it took nerve as well as skill to hold the reputation of an old-time gun-man and live is certain. Some of these men with reputations as crack shots have confessed that nerve rather than skill pulled them through. They even disclaimed unusual nerve by saying, "When a man is out to git ye, ye jist have to git him fust." How much psychology was there in it?

Chapter XI

ONE hot summer afternoon, while Ralph was doing his best to while away a tedious time, in heat which registered well over one hundred degrees, he glanced occasionally through the doorway, only to note the shimmering waves of heat that danced from ground to higher levels. He was seated behind the counter at the north end of the room, reading and brushing horse-flies from his face.

Not an animal moved anywhere, while litters of half-wild pigs lay and grunted in the shade of the buildings, and the tumble-bugs gave the only signs of animated endeavor in sight. They were having one of their busiest days, and I was out with them, doing the only thing I had energy enough for, pinning down the rolling balls one after another, to witness the resulting acrobatics. Once in a while I would rise and stamp my foot to see the colony dig in. Then I noticed some of the characteristics of the tumble-bugs.

They were handsome specimens, with shiny, dark brown thorax, and encased abdomen. The upper wings were soldered together, and with the quarter-inch mandibles, made up three-quarters of an inch by half that in breadth of as much concentrated strength and energy as exists in bugdom.

Every section of the old prairie was the tumble-bug's habitat in those days, but he was most evident, and seemingly the happiest, when he could gather the droppings of animals, deposit eggs therein, and roll a ball of manure about a half-inch in diameter with the larvæ in the center. With hind legs hoisted against the ball to push, following along with his forelegs on the ground, he rolled the sphere to the place of burial. There he excavated the ground under and around the ball with forelegs until finally bug and burden would pass from sight under ground.

On any hot sunny afternoon of mid-summer, you could see these beetles by the hundreds, and if there were fresh droppings, you soon would see hundreds of these balls being rolled along.

If you were to fix one of these balls to the ground with pin or needle through the center, you would see the liveliest bug-tumbling you ever witnessed. If the pinning down of the ball were quickly accomplished, the pushing bug would go over the top and tumble in a heap on the other side for the first act. Returning to the original position, he would start the ball spinning on its axis and keep it spinning until he would fall over from exhaustion. Over and over again, spinning the ball, falling and recovering, he would tumble about in frantic endeavor to free it from the spot to which it was fastened. That is how he earned his name.

There were other curious habits to be discovered. When tumble-bugs had the eggs encased in these balls and were on the way to a burial place, if at any moment the ground trembled from man or beast, or from the elements, they would not wait to reach the appointed spot, but would stop rolling and dig in as fast as they could work, burying the balls and themselves in short order.

With this habit in mind, one could watch until there were many on their way with the precious rolling burdens, then stamp on the ground and start them all to digging in at the same instant. It does not take them over thirty seconds to burrow from sight. What is more, it takes only a slight tremor to start them working in. Heavy animals advancing toward the bug colony can set up enough agitation while yet a hundred feet away to send every last bug underground.

In time the sport lagged, and I lay in the dust almost asleep, when suddenly every tumble bug about me began to dig in. This brought me to my feet wide awake, for I knew it portended some approaching animal or man, and that was a time and place where one was ever on the alert against the approach of unseen man or beast. Almost instantly the single-foot was heard down the trail, and a mounted man came pacing around the corner of the lower building. He was a stranger there, and at sight of me he reined in to a stop and hailed, "Howdy, boy."

"Hello," I replied.

Then I began to take cognizance of the newcomer and all his belongings. The man was thin and wiry-looking, with a full black beard and mustache. Black hair, slightly curly, showed beneath the hat band. The skin of his face and hands was white and showed no tan.

He wore an old army hat of black felt, a coat that had been black, but was now so old that it had a greenish tinge on the shoulders, and a vest to match. Both were worn unbuttoned in the heat, revealing a white shirt underneath, with paper collar and string tie of black at the throat. Jeans were belted onto thin hips and hung down over the tops of high-heeled, cow-boy boots. On his back, held there by a strap around his chest, was a cloth case covering a violin, while on the front jockey of his double-rigged stock saddle was fastened another case, which held a banjo. Across the back skirt was a roll covered with a slicker, which seemed to hold blankets for bedding. The pony, the man, and all his belongings were dust covered, and yet there was an appearance of neatness, a certain air of fastidiousness about him that was unusual in that western country.

OLD CHAPE

Old Chape

A low, mellow voice and a gentleness of speech won the boy immediately. The words of greeting, combined with the first scrutiny of the man and his belongings brought the intuitive decision that here was a man I could trust. This faith grew to certainty, and never faded in after years.

Ralph heard our voices and came from the building to greet the stranger and extend the usual invitation to "light." This formality over, the stranger "lighted," and leaving his pony "hitched to the ground" by dropping the single reins there, stepped forward and shook hands with both of us. He was then told to bring his belongings and his saddle into the house, and turn his horse loose in the corral, which he did after watering the animal at the well.

Returning to the house from the corral, he found us preparing the evening meal, and asked if he could not make the bread. This job was allotted to him, and he soon turned out some light-weight biscuits, which he had first mixed, then pounded with the big iron spoon. At the first bite I acclaimed these as biscuits "like mother used to make."

During the meal he stated that he was a stranger in those parts, and that his name was John G. Chapin, that he had no home, and he had ridden up from Fort Reno that day. He had an old friend at Reno in the person of Ben Clark, the Cheyenne interpreter at the post, and as Ben was also well-known to us this fact established the stranger in our confidence. He added that he was going "no special place," and if the ranchman did not mind, would "hang around" for a few days and make himself useful. Thus was Old Chape introduced to Red Fork Ranch, in or near which he was to pass the greater portion of his remaining days.

His coming had been heralded by the tumble-bugs. In the light of later history, they might have been forecasting six years ahead when great hordes of strangers overran the land on a prearranged date and made of it a settled country. No such vision came to any of us on the first night of Chapin's sojourn in the land he was to see pass from virgin prairie to plowed ground before he died. No one thought of such a possibility, nor could he have visualized the reality. Of the three, Old Chape was the only one there when the great stampede came.

After the first meal together we three went outside, and the newcomer took his violin and banjo. Placing himself on a box seat, as his audience did, he took the violin, and after tuning up played several airs, ending with "The Arkansas Traveler." As the twilight deepened, the banjo was taken up to accompany old-time songs of the West. This troubadour sang with his voice always in range, and it never broke. Playing or singing, he was always in the spirit of the part, swaying his body to the rhythm, and giving extra emphasis to the songs by vigorous nods of the head, stampings of the foot and violent strumming of the strings. He would sing or play every waking moment when other duties did not interfere. Well might he have been named "the Troubadour of Red Fork Ranch."

It was not long before I had selected him for a companion and friend. Never did I lack entertainment when Chape had time to play or sing, and the friendship built up between us I foster to this day. Implanted in my memory is the record of his words and the tones of his voice as I heard them forty-odd years ago.

Chape's repertoire embraced "The Wearing of the Green," of Irish memory; "Oh, Susannah, Don't You Cry for Me," from the "Days of '49" period; many of the Cow-boy Songs, in which they were left lying "on the lone pe-rair-ee." He often went to town where he warned the girls:

"Look out for the fellow who wears the wide hat
For he is as tall, and strong, and quick as a cat."

Old Chape

While in town, he met the famous "Madam Brandy" of all cow-boy legend, and told of her famous "Pianner Fortay" as follows:

As I was passin' by her door
An' I heard th' music sweet,
It thrilled me heart with joy
An' I could not keep me feet.

Many verses were required to tell the whole adventure, but each was followed by this refrain:

So, if I chance to sing or dance
I hope I won't intrude.
An' if I chance to sing or dance,
I hope you'll not think me rude.
Oh, my! Don't you wish you was me?
For I feel as happy as a big Bumble Bee,
Bum-Bum-Bul-Bee.

This song was an especial favorite of mine, and I applauded with yells of delight and cries of "Sing it again!" Chape soon learned to give extra emphasis as he sang the final Bum-Bum-Bul-Bee, by shakes of the head and heavy strokes across the strings. Oh, he loved to please the boy.

In Laredo, he witnessed a sad sight as outlined in this verse:

As I walked out the streets of Laredo,
As I walked in Laredo one day,
I spied a poor cow-boy wrapped in white linen,
Wrapped up in white linen, as cold as the clay.

The spirit of the defunct one then sang:

Oh, beat the drum slowly, and play the fife lowly,
Play the dead march as you carry me along,

95

Take me to the green valley, and there lay the sod o'er me,
For I'm a poor cow-boy, and I know I've done wrong.

There were many verses, all of this import, with the chorus after each. It was a cow-boy song often rendered on the trail and on night-guard. The skill with which he could wail out the final words of the chorus had much to do with his reputation as a singer.

"Chape—the bulliest singer that ever was," is still my verdict.

Again in his travels, he had come to a wonderful boarding house, whose cake he honored in the following refrain:

> *There were plums, an' pruins, an' cherries,*
> *An' cinnamon, an' sassafras too,*
> *Oh, it was a cake to make you merry,*
> *An' the crust, it was nailed on with glue.*

Another place he had visited evidently did not suit him so well, for in his gruffest tones he sang in many stanzas an elaboration on the following verse:

> *Th' corn dodgers were hot,*
> *An' th' beef I could not chaw,*
> *But they charged me half a dollar,*
> *In th' state of Ar-kan-saw.*

The evening's entertainment often ended with a rendition of the following:

> *Last night as I lay on the prairie,*
> *And looked up to the stars in the sky,*
> *I wondered if ever a cow-boy,*
> *Would drift to that sweet bye-and-bye.*

96

Old Chape

The trail to that bright, mystic region,
Is narrow and dim, so they say,
But the one that leads down to perdition,
Is staked and is blazed all the way.

They say that there'll be a great round-up
Where cow-boys like dogies [1] will stand,
To be cut by those riders from Heaven
Who are posted and know every brand.

I wonder was there ever cow-boy
Prepared for that great Judgment Day,
Who could say to the boss of the riders,
"I am ready to be driven away."

They say He will never forsake you,
That He notes every action and look,
But for safety, you'd better get branded,
Have your name in His great tally-book.

For they tell of another great owner,
Who is nigh overstocked, so they say,
But who always makes room for the sinner,
Who strays from the bright, narrow way.

Chape was a great addition to the social life on the ranch
and had soon sung and played his way into the good graces
of all who met him. Besides entertaining, he made himself
generally useful about the place. He could do all kinds of
work, and he was never lazy. About a week after his arrival,
and his initial triumph with hot biscuit, he was engaged by
Ralph to act as cook at headquarters, and thus became a "regular" at the ranch.

[1] Dogie, longhorn, cow.—Each means the same: any individual of the herd.

97

During the early days together we learned that he was a veteran of the Union Army. Chape was well versed in the history of his country, a staunch Republican, a ready and thoughtful conversationalist.

In spite of his experience in the army and on the frontier, he retained the habit of clean speech, with a cleanliness of person which marked him apart from many frontier characters. He had never married; he had such regard for womanhood that he never told a risque story. When Ralph was not around, I found Chape assuming my protection. Never did he speak foul words in my presence or speak in anger to me, nor would he allow others to do so. We two became pals; I made a confidante of him in things held sacred by a boy.

It was not long before I began addressing him as Chape, for short. As the intimacy grew, affectionate regard lengthened this sobriquet to "Old Chape." No doubt I would even have spoken of him as "Good Old Chape." Those who understand boys will know by this just how well the man stood in the estimation of his worshiper. Let memory's page record this name in its true meaning (with affectionate regard), for thus he should be known.

Chape at times gave way to his desire for firewater. It was his only method of making a break in the monotony of life. These lapses were not frequent, and never while "on the job." It was either a feast or a famine with him in this respect. A spree depended altogether on his being able to leave the ranch in responsible hands while he went to Fort Reno. It was always while Ralph was away, for he could not bring himself to ask leave for such a purpose. Once when Ralph was away and Texas John present, he chose me to be his companion.

We set out from the ranch driving a team hitched to the buckboard. The down trip was uneventful, and we reached the post without incident. Finding Clark there, Chape alighted and instructed me to go back to Darlington and stay with Uncle John over night. I was to be at the Fort the next day at noon to get my pal and return with him to the ranch.

I duly arrived at the meeting place and was met by Ben Clark. Asking me to drive close to the door of his quarters he disappeared within, and soon appeared with Chape. He seemed to be assisting my friend, and I wondered why. But Chape managed to get to the seat and take the reins from my hands. He looked pale and was not disposed to talk in his usual style.

Through the Indian village we drove, across the ford at Darlington, followed the trail by the trading stores, past the white people's cemetery, on up to Caddo Spring without a word. I missed my companion's usual pleasantries and could not fathom the reason for his silence.

When we had reached a point on the trail well above Caddo Spring, I was surprised at Chape's actions. Suddenly the reins dropped from his hands, and he slumped into a heap on the narrow floor of the buckboard. I spoke to him, but received no answer. The team came to a stop of its own accord. I alighted and worked over my friend until I had him wedged between dashboard and seat so he could not fall out. Then, taking the reins, I clambered up on the seat and placing my feet on the dashboard above Chape, proceeded on the journey. By that time I had sensed that I was attending for the first time some one "under the influence." I also knew that Chape would not be proud of himself when sober again, and felt I must screen him from observation as much as possible.

It was a long journey for me, for we advanced at a walk, lest Chape fall out. On over the high plains to Kingfisher station, through the ford, and past my friends at Phil Block's I drove without stopping. The journey from there to the Cimarron crossing finally came to an end and we were soon across. I drove up to the ranch buildings without my charge coming to life.

At the end of our journey, Texas John aided me in removing Chape from the buckboard to his bed of blankets on the top floor. There he lay for the remainder of the day, through the night, and until the morning of the second day. Then he appeared, awake to the realization that he had returned from another "toot." I, also, had learned much.

Chape's condition while in my care did not breed repugnance towards him on my part. On the contrary, I felt myself to be his keeper, and instinctively protected him from observation and the unthinking grins of rough companions. He had comforted me when I was homesick, protected me from the killer, had sung and played for my pleasure, was my councilor and guide next to Ralph. By my action that day I tried to even scores.

Old Chape was responsive to other natures which were kindred in any degree. He readily made a "pard" of the old plainsman, Pike, and enjoyed the companionship of silent Texas John. Pike was of his age and had had much the same experience; Texas John was rugged, honest, clean, and all three were bachelors who respected all womankind.

With the news of the coming settlement of the land by Payne's "boomers," came the first definite ambition to Chape and his "pard." After Ralph had sold his interests in the ranch, Old Chape secured trader's rights to continue the store until the "opening" should come. He shared these equally with Pike.

Three years before the great change, there were many "sooners" in the land. They even congregated at certain spots. In search of amusement one summer's day, Pike found one of these gatherings in the Cherokee Strip. Drinks were served, poker became serious. The sturdy old man, who had been with Zebulon Pike in a much earlier day, disputed the other fellow's hand. But age had slowed his movements; he was beaten to the "draw," and passed out with his "boots on" to the trail of the hereafter.

Chape went to the scene of his friend's passing, and buried him in one of the lone graves of that country. As sole survivor of the firm, he stayed on alone at Red Fork until the settlement came. A town sprang up in the place of the ranch buildings. Probably those now on the very spot never heard of him. The famous epitaph of the Southwest applies to Old Chape:—"Life is not in holdin' a good hand, but in playin' a pore hand well."

Would that those who read could see this man as my memory last pictures him framed in the doorway of the old log ranch building, smiling his kindly encouragement to my broken, shattered self as we parted. He stood with goodness and compassion radiating as from the Great Friend of Mankind.

Good Old Chape.

NOTE.—See Appendix, page 294.

Chapter XII

ONE day Ralph told me, "The government has sent me an order to fence in our range, and I have got to obey. I am not sure where I can get the help, but as it is Fall and the driving season is over, I will try and pick up some men from those returning to Texas over the Trail." That suited me, I would get a chance to meet more men, have more company. Chape was on hand to cook for any number Ralph might hire.

The first to appear was one who said, "They jist calls me Pike." Short, fat, with bushy white mustache and a cheerful countenance, he appealed to me. I liked him at the start, was glad he was hired to stay with us, and always have regarded him as above the average of our Red Fork acquaintances.

Pike had already been hired when a tall spare man rode up, and was sized up by Ralph, who asked his name and if he would like to work there. "Yes," said he, "I'm outen a job, an' Texas John air my handle." Ralph asked him if he would like to go alone and camp in the woods for the winter. To this proposition he immediately assented, "I sure wud, I'd ruther live alone." Ralph lost no time in engaging him.

Here was a man who was born and raised a Texas cow-boy; who had ridden a horse ever since he was knee-high to a grasshopper. He was about thirty-five years of age at the time, which meant he had lived the life of the cattle country from its earliest days. In addition, he proved to be an excellent woodsman. I took note of his equipment, cow-boy rig minus chaps, with trousers, boots and spurs, but no coat. He was typically Texan in this latter deficiency. Having spent so many of his days alone, he was sparing in speech, especially around strangers. This trait endeared him to Old Chape and Ralph.

Ralph accompanied John on the first expedition to find a suitable location for the wood-cutter camp and noted the aptitude of the man for taking care of himself in the open. Openings in the heart of the woods were found and examined. A location was finally selected on the bank of a stream and miles from either edge of the forest, where fire, wood, and water were at hand. The stream was so narrow that no one would be likely to follow it for a trail. A tent was placed there, with brush wind-breakers on four sides. Standing on a slight knoll in the open, the wind-breaks could be seen from the edge of the adjacent woods, and hid the tent from view. Entrance to the tent was through an opening in the brush wall.

The man seemed perfectly content to remain here alone. No one met him but Ralph, who came at stated intervals to bring supplies. His whole attention was given to cutting and piling fence-posts at spots where they could be reached by cutting paths through the woods the following spring.

John and Ralph became well acquainted during the periods when they were working or spending their evenings in camp. It was then disclosed that the cow-boy could neither read nor write, but he knew every detail of the range and its ways. He could name and draw any cattle brand he had ever seen, and tell its home. Star K, Circle 9, Diamond Bar K, Lazy H, Double Triangle—all these and dozens more were known to him. He had ridden far and wide in the whole West and could tell intimate details of trails and streams, mountains and plains, from the Rio Grande to Montana and the Dakotas.

This old world interested him, but not as a terrestrial ball.

No, sir, the world was a flat plain and if one could ride far enough he would come to a jumping off place. This became a favorite topic of discussion between the two men, but John was never convinced.

In the beginning, Ralph had insisted that John add a coat to his wardrobe. John took it along after much urging, but was never seen to wear it. It lay around the tent with other articles not in use. One day the two men came back in the evening to find that the tent and its contents had been destroyed by fire. Only a few provisions were left. This meant an immediate replenishment of supplies, so, after sleeping in the open for the night, Ralph started early for the ranch to get them. Looking back he said, "Do you want another coat, John?" "N-o-o," said John, "I don't want anuther. I never had airy coat but thet *one*. I'm goin' back ter Texas whar they don't wear airy coats." He was around Red Fork for two or more years, as it turned out, and he never did wear "airy coat." In the matter of coats, John was following the custom of the Texas cow-boy, who wore loose wool shirts as the only covering for the upper part of the body summer or winter.

In the spring of the year, John was brought back to headquarters. Ralph was away often that year and at times the only people at the store were Old Chape, Texas John and I.

On the down trip one morning the stage brought a lone passenger, who proved to be the only negro graduate of West Point ever to reach the western territory. He was on his way to Fort Reno under orders.

The Cimarron had been too high to ford two days before, and the driver came in to get news of crossing conditions. Chape told him that it was not certain that they could cross that morning. The conversation aroused the passenger. He joined in with the declaration that he must go on and that the stage company must take him or suffer consequences. There

was no opportunity to argue the point with him. He stormed
about, flourishing first his sword and then his revolver, and
filling the air with threats and curses. Finally he was left
ranting to himself as the men withdrew to one side for consultation. The three whites were furious at the insults they
were receiving. Chape said that the man could not remain
there, for he and John would have to shoot him if he kept
up his tirade. It was decided that John should take me and
accompany the stage to the river, and then determine what to
do further.

When we arrived at the bank, we found the river still high
but going down, for a sand bank was appearing toward the
southern shore. It was decided to swim the horses across with
the stage and to carry the mail and passenger over in a boat
that was kept there for that purpose. Accordingly the animals
were driven into the water and succeeded in reaching the other
shore with the vehicle safe.

It then remained for the mail and passenger to be taken
across in the boat by Texas John. He first pulled the boat by
hand along the bank up stream until he reached a point well
above the sand bar in the center of the river. Then taking
the mail sacks and the negro officer into the boat, he struck out
from shore. There was a swift current running in the channel,
and the boat was borne downstream rapidly, though John
rowed with all his might.

When he had reached a point well over toward the sand bar
and halfway down its length, John suddenly shipped his oars,
and grabbed the gunwales on each side, tipping the boat so that
it filled half full of water. The negro officer, seated in the
stern of the boat, evidently felt that John intended to drown
him, and sprang overboard into water that came to his arm
pits. To be rid of the passenger was what John desired and
he did not care much if he did drown. He righted the boat,

took the oars again, and succeeded in reaching the north shore a quarter of a mile below the ford. From there he dragged the boat back to where I had been watching the whole performance.

In the meantime, the negro officer, now a wet rooster, succeeded in floundering to the sand bar in the center of the river, where he yelled curses at every one in sight. He stormed up and down the bar and commanded that he be brought to shore. John told him the ferry was not running any longer. He also inquired how he found the water and whether it was good swimming. The stage driver on the other bank would not go for him either, and he was finally compelled to plunge in and wade to the stage coach. Then John ferried the mail over.

John and I secured the boat and set out afoot for the ranch, followed out of hearing by all the curses the negro could command. But John was well satisfied, and Chape joined him in a good laugh when he heard the story. In that day and place, and having a born and bred Texan to deal with, the negro was fortunate to have escaped alive. *Muy bueno*, John.

There was a sequel to this affair during the summer. The Red Fork ranchman had business at Fort Reno and went there pony-back. The negro officer heard of it, and although the ranchman was entirely guiltless in this affair, he evidently decided to get even with any one from the scene of his watery experience.

As Ralph left on the trail for Darlington, he noticed this officer and three colored troopers trailing him. He thought no more of it until he had passed Darlington on the trail north. After he had passed Caddo Spring he detected them again, riding from some black-jack to the west, and something about their actions decided him to put spurs to his pony. For some miles he kept them at a distance, but could see them following hard. It then became a race for Kingfisher Stage station.

Ralph's pony was of good wind and kept ahead, but not far
enough to prevent his pursuers from trying a few shots from
their carbines. Turning on them at the station, Ralph fired in
turn, and succeeded in driving them off. They turned back to
Reno without having secured satisfaction.

Chapter XIII

I WAS destined to meet many kinds of men at Red Fork Ranch, the most blatant one of whom compelled my notice by his manner.

Haw-haw-haw—h-a-w! Ho-h-h-h—o! Har-har-har—h-a-r-r! This guffaw came from a big man in the center of a group in front of the store at Red Fork and drew attention to its creator, who was gazing about him with an expression which plainly said, "Laugh, you coyote, laugh, for Boffman has just told a good one." The big man was named Baughman (pronounced Boffman) and he always laughed first and longest at his own jokes. Often he would be the only one who could laugh. He was so foul-mouthed that hardened old-timers could not find it in them even to smile at his jokes. But if no other laugh was heard, his own never failed, and in such volume that one might be pardoned for thinking that a full chorus of jackasses were giving expression to levity.

He was a tall, heavily built, big-boned man, with bushy red hair and eye-brows. A heavy, drooping mustache partly covered a large mouth with thick lips, set in a red coarse face. A constant sneer showed there when he was not laughing.

His idea of a witticism was to give the most obscene turn he could to an expression; or better yet, to take a sacred quotation or hymn and substitute for the good words all the foul ones he could think of. But with one and all of his offerings came the bray of the jackass to accent the point of the joke.

He never was known to hate himself. Always on the best

The Oaf

of terms with Boffman, he felt himself irresistible in any company, broke in at any time, and proceeded to monopolize all the conversation. Should any one wish to be heard in opposition, Boffman would raise his tones and drown out all other sounds. This he considered a convincing argument.

If any one mentioned any part of the West from the Missouri to the Coast Range, from the Canadian line to Mexico, he had been there. Not only had he been in the section, but he knew every river, creek, water hole, peak, and all the trails that lay therein, and would guarantee to take any one there by the most direct and profane route. Yet he always was careful that his profanity did not apply personally to any one he was addressing. But he sure did hand it out to the unknowns.

With his filthy mind went as filthy a person. Tobacco juice dripped from his mustache unheeded and stained his chin and shirt. Eating with a knife, only helped with the digits of the hands, he wiped his fingers on his thigh and wore the same trousers all the time. Never was he known to take a bath.

He was engaged off the trail to help in getting out fence posts from the black-jack, and stuck to the job all one winter. During his sojourn there he took part in all manner of horseplay that matched his wit. He helped haze with the keenest relish. The first cattle drive of the spring was his excuse for leaving, bound for Caldwell. Mounted on a pony loaned by the outfit, he immediately fell to recounting his stale sickening jokes to the nearest cow-man, and went from sight and hearing with a Haw-haw-haw-h-a-w.

But that was not the last of this man at Red Fork, for he came back in the fall with another outfit bound for Texas, bringing great news of himself. Having arrived at Caldwell with his winter's wages in his pocket, he had decided to go on to Chicago to spend it. Stock shippers always wanted men to accompany trains of stock to water and feed them enroute. Boffman took such a job.

In Chicago he frequented the saloons and brothels about the stock-yards and proceeded to get rid of his money. Within a few days he was nearing the end of his *dinero* and thinking of getting back to the cattle country, but a bad railroad strike was tying up the western roads. Cattlemen were at home in the stock-yards district and even wore their guns. Boffman had invested in an extra Colt, holster, and ammunition belt. He wore the two gun outfits as befitting his voice and his size. He was the bold, bad man from the boundless prairies. "Yes, sir-e-e, he wuz a two-gun man, and a bad un."

As he stood at the bar in a saloon on the last afternoon of his stay, he was approached by a man who had noticed his appearance and manner. This was an official of one of the railroads tied up with the strike. He wanted help, and he had an idea.

"Can you run a locomotive?" asked he of Boffman.

"Kin I? Say, I kin run any iron hoss that goes," answered our hero. He had never ridden in an engine cab, let alone knowing how to operate one.

The railroader surmised as much, but proceeded to unfold his plan. It was for Boffman to appear in the yards at the right moment, dressed in full regalia, and run a locomotive out through the picketing lines of strikers. Boffman never ceased to assert that he could do the trick, and accordingly the following morning was set for the trial.

Here was lime-light for this roysterer, and that was just his pie. He was on hand the next morning at the saloon, where several officials of the road met him. Drinks were served all around, and as all present listened to him and laughed with him at his jokes, Boffman was in fine fettle. At the proper time, they set out for the railroad yards, where a locomotive had been prepared for the trial.

Leading the procession was Boffman with the Chief of Transportation by his side, while a dozen others, in couples, brought up the rear. Striding along, spurs rattling, heels resounding on the old board walks, roaring with laughter at his own jokes, Boffman felt himself "Queen of the May." The gathered strikers were so amazed at the spectacle he presented, so dazzled by the sight, that they relaxed their watchfulness and allowed the whole procession to pass through their lines into the yards. First score for our man.

He was escorted to a waiting locomotive on the main line track, and mounted to the cab. Laying his hand on the throttle, he bellowed, "What's this yere fer?" Taking the reverse lever in hand, he roared, "What's this yere doodingus do?"

So he was shown the moves necessary to operate the machine, and finally announced that he was ready to go. Every one else jumped off, leaving him alone to his work.

Before starting out, Boffman stepped to the side next the crowd, and drawing both guns gave an exhibition of twirling them and cocking for action. Two or three minutes he gave over to this show. Then shooting the guns into the holsters, he grabbed throttle and lever and the machine jumped along the tracks, through the picketing lines, and over to the spot where a mail train was made up. There Boffman's job ended, after he had run the first engine from the yards that had gone out in several days. Thus this railroad strike was broken by a big, bluffing cow-puncher, who would not dare hurt a suckling calf.

The railroads rewarded him well with passes over most of the lines in the United States, added to five hundred dollars in cash. Boffman prolonged his stay in Chicago until he had spent all his new-found money, and basked in the light of his performance. The end came, and he rode back to Caldwell on his passes. There he joined a cow outfit returning to Texas and stayed over a night at Red Fork to recount his glories. He told the story with embellishments; that was to be expected. But the facts as related were verified.

Note.—See Appendix, page 294,

Chapter XIV

ON a certain day I rode up the trail until I was within a mile or two of Bull Foot Ranch. I was brought to a stop by seeing a rattlesnake crossing the trail. I had galloped by and realized that I wanted to see this snake very much after I had passed his location some hundred feet or more. For an unexplained reason I dropped the reins to the ground and dismounted, leaving the pony hitched there. I ran back to the snake and tried my marksmanship with my first six-shooter. I must admit that excitement made my hand shaky so that I missed all of my shots until the chambers of the six-shooter were empty. As there was not a stick of wood or a clod in sight, I finally maneuvered the reptile into striking, and while he was stretched at full length I quickly smashed his head with the butt of my six-shooter. While I was engaged in this occupation, a large herd of Texas steers had come upon me from "down the trail." Before I knew it I realized I had been caught in the worst situation possible by being afoot with a herd of wild Texas longhorns swarming toward me. The herd was evidently spread out for feeding. As I stood there a wild steer suddenly took notice of me. I knew he was not sure what kind of an animal I was, for he tossed his head and raised his tail as he trotted rapidly toward me. He was curious as he came forward, but suddenly seemed to grow convinced that this two-legged creature in front of him must be removed from the landscape. His trot changed to a gallop, and with lowered head and bellows of rage he dashed upon me as I stood spellbound. I do not believe that I was actually "frightened stiff"—it was simply a matter of not having time to make up my mind what to do next. I was far away from my pony and it seemed hopeless for me to try to run away from an animal that was as swift as a deer. In less than a second he was within ten feet of me with his lowered head. Before I could receive the impact of a blow which would have meant sudden death to me, a young cow-boy dashed up on his pony at full gallop. In the fraction of a second which remained to me of life, this horseman dashed between me and my fate and turned the beast back into the herd. I do not believe that I then realized the significance of that quickly acted incident. We had so many narrow escapes on the ranges as we pursued our daily lives that we rarely thought anything of an escape, such as the one described, and rescuers thought nothing of their part in them. Neither one would have thought of giving or receiving thanks.

I asked Pike, who rode up the trail soon afterward, who the young fellow was who had saved me. Pike told me it was Charlie Siringo. (Forty-six years later it seems to me that I should have mentioned something,—"Thanks, Charlie.")

I afterwards saw much of Charlie as he passed our way. Sometimes he would alight and walk into the store. Then I would see an old time cow-boy afoot on the ground. He would come forward head down, eyes picking out short steps, body thrown forward, arms swinging him along, toeing in, and waddling like a duck.

As soon as he mounted his pony you would see a man sitting with the body as erect as a growing stalk, legs in a straight line down from the saddle, feet thrust through stirrups and toes pointed to the ground, swaying gracefully with every motion of the steed, never under any circumstance showing sky at the

A CLOSE SHAVE——PRAIRIE STYLE

crotch, steed and man like a centaur—the same man in the saddle.

Riding from childhood often bowed the legs, and years of ranch life, with frequent breaks poorly mended, made the "stove-up cow-puncher." That was what a man was called at twenty-five or thirty years, after having followed the cows since he was of tender age. The life was no cinch and took its toll.

"Stove-up" is what Charlie Siringo called himself before he was thirty years of age. It fitted him in the days of Red Fork Ranch.

While passing down the trail of life, how few of us stop to think of our influence in the minds of youngsters about us. Actions, appearance, method of speaking, words are recorded in memory for life. This fact is responsible for my grudge against "The Killer." It is also the reason I cherish quite other pictures of Old Chape.

I recall two brothers who frequently traveled either up or down the trails past Red Fork Ranch. When I asked Ralph for their names he simply said, "They are the Miller brothers." In the light of the after years I can add, "They were not the Miller brothers of 101 Ranch fame."

The ones I saw were tall angular men of the old cow-man type. The older wore a mustache, the younger had none. The older never talked to me, but sat his horse at one side while the younger conversed. For all the reticence of the elder, my boyish intuition told me he was of the same nature as the younger. They stand equally high in my memory.

Now that I think of it, the only reason I have retained a lifelong regard for them is that one of them always vouchsafed the answer that sated my impertinent curiosity. One answered, the other complacently agreed.

On the occasion of our first meeting, they both reined in beside me one day as I rode along the Chisholm Trail. Both smiled in a friendly way without objectionable condescension. We exchanged "Howdy." They asked me if I was the boy at Red Fork Ranch of whom they had heard, asking in such a manner that I was proud to answer "Yes." With boyish observation I noted that the middle finger of the right hand of the younger was gone. Even the knuckle joint had been removed, leaving a hollow in the back of the hand. Immediately I asked, "What is the matter with your hand?" Seeming to know that boys want full explanations, the maimed one answered in full. He had been out hunting with a shot gun. While at rest he held the gun with muzzle upward, stock resting on the ground. The urge came to try the bore with his finger. The digit fitted so well that it stuck there and seemed impossible to remove. In the resulting struggle, the gun was discharged and removed the finger from its mouth and from the man's hand as well.

On another occasion I overtook the Miller brothers on the same trail. I had been up to Bull Foot and was on the return trip. We fell in together and visited as we rode. Again there was curiosity on my part. It appeared the younger was again a victim. I noted a livid, red scar on his throat at the Adam's apple, and true to my form asked for particulars. I was told of their being in camp a few days previous, when, at the evening meal, the younger had broken off and swallowed a tooth. It had stuck and refused to be dislodged. A hasty trip had been made to Caldwell, where the obstruction had been removed by cutting down to it from the outside. They were just returning from town after the operation when I overtook them.

In simple encounters such as these the Millers engraved

their personalities on me, so that I say now as then, "You both were the real stuff." May they be alive to read this.

One day I noted a negro cook for a cattle outfit which was passing. He had come into the store and called Ralph outside, where he unburdened his mind in the following words: "Say, boss, I has a gal back dere, and we is promised to git mah'ied when I gits back fum dis drive. I-I-I wants you to write me a letter to her. You jes write fer me an fix it up, jes like fer you'se'f. Dat will be all right, boss, jes like fer you'se'f."

Like most of the cow-men he could neither read nor write. He had been on the trail many weeks with the memory of his sweetheart as his only solace. No word could reach him from her, none come from him unless some one would help by writing. No doubt she would keep her part of the compact, yet he feared others might press their claims in his absence. A letter telling of continued fealty to his lady love with assurance that her Romeo still lived and expected to claim his reward at the appointed time, would help ever so much. Such ideas were often confided to the importuned scribe, and of course he never failed to oblige.

Paper, pen and ink were procured, and the writer went to work with the swain at his elbow to prompt, and hear the thoughts as they were written down. The more that appeared on paper, the greater the lover's satisfaction. Ralph searched his mind for every synonym for love and told it to the man, who immediately sanctioned its use, framing an additional sentence. At last when there seemed no more to add, the lonely swain watched until the precious missive was placed in the way pocket, to go out by stage to Kansas, thence to Texas by train.

Many a marriage contract was clinched by the ranchman at

Red Fork. It was good training in the art of writing to the opposite sex—both dark and fair. "No thanks, boy, the pleasure is all mine," quoth Ralph.

Experiences were coming to me in varied form, all tending to develop that first ring. One morning while the driving season was still young, two cattlemen rode up to the store, dismounted, and came inside to complete a conversation which evidently engrossed their thoughts.

After greeting Ralph and me they continued their talk as they leaned against the pine counter. It was disclosed that they had been partners in the cattle business for years. One of them had decided to go back to "The States." Evidently parting came hard to these two pals; they had prolonged it by riding together from Texas.

The man who was going back east evidently owed money to his friend, for he paid over some four thousand dollars in gold. The recipient removed from about his body a money belt. In our presence, he filled this belt with the gold and fastened it about him where it would not be seen. As soon as this was done, the two hastily shook hands in parting. One rode up the trail, the other slumped down on a box seat and covered his face with his hands.

Finally he asked if there was some place where he could lie down, as he did not feel well. We then noted that his face was broken out in livid blotches. His illness made him weak, and Ralph assisted him to the upper floor and placed him on a bed of blankets.

During the day he became delirious. Then we disrobed him and made him as comfortable as our equipment allowed. For two or three days he tossed in delirium as we brothers attended his wants. Ralph told me the man was suffering from a disease contracted in the red-light district of some cow town.

His constitution pulled him through, and he finally arose from the bed, dressed again and rode away out of our further knowledge. He had been helpless in our hands with a fortune in reach, yet rode away with it intact. It was the western way to give service freely where required without reward other than the consciousness of having done the right thing. That was the pay we received.

One blustery, cold day in the late fall, Dobe came into the ranch cook-house where we were preparing the evening meal. With him was a lone passenger carrying a cow saddle. Dobe did not usually stop on the up-trip and he immediately explained his reason. He had seen a horseman back of him on the trail that afternoon who rode so hard that Dobe decided he was trying to overtake him. The passenger had seemed anxious about the pursuing horseman. Dobe decided to stop there and learn the reason, if possible.

It was dusk in the room but I recall the appearance and actions of the passenger. Retreating to the rear, he placed a table between himself and the door. There he cringed and trembled. We had not long to wait. The door was kicked open, and there stood young Hubbel, the trader, covering us all with his gun. Discovering the man in the rear, he strode toward him, and soon the situation was made plain.

It appeared that the man was a thief who had been stranded in Darlington Agency for a day. While Hubbel was absent and only the Indian clerks were in sight, he had pilfered the cash drawer, picked up a saddle from the floor, and as the stage swung to a stop, had boarded it as its only passenger. He rode on top with Dobe and had watched the pursuit.

Covered as he was now, the thief fairly groveled on the dirt floor and cried out in abject terror. Finding that he was unarmed, Hubbel simply kept him covered while his fate was settled. Ralph did not want him around, Hubbel did not want the bother of taking him back to the Agency, so it was decided to give him in charge of Dobe to turn loose in Caldwell. After requiring him to disgorge all the money on his person, Hubbel took his saddle and left for Darlington after warning him never to show his face there again. I suspect he never did. In that day and place he was fortunate to escape as he did. Our cow-boys would gladly have tendered him a necktie party then and there.

I have told you of the first sheep-man passing by Red Fork Ranch. Another man of different stripe gave us another idea of the business.

During my first summer there he came by with a herd of two thousand sheep, driving to Texas. He had a cook wagon and much equipment with a full quota of herders. As the herd filed by the ranch, filling the air with the varied sounds of hundreds of sheep, the owner came into the store for a brief visit. He proudly drew attention to the size of his herd and the completeness of his equipment, stating that he was on his way to Texas to enter the sheep business.

To our surprise, this same man came into the store in the fall. He was alone on a return trip to Kansas. Naturally Ralph asked him how he liked the sheep business. With a disgusted expression on his face he said, "There is only one thing in this world with less sense than a sheep, and that is a damned sheep-man." He had sold out.

One hot evening in late summer while Ralph and I were alone at headquarters, I retired to the upper room for my night's rest, leaving Ralph downstairs.

My bed was on the floor, I had a cracker-box for chiffonier, light from a tallow dip. The method of retiring was simple.

Eye Has Seen, Ear Heard

Place candle on box, slip off shirt and trousers, slip between blankets, pull them about the shoulders, blow out the light from that position, and go to sleep.

On this night the system had progressed as far as blowing the light out. On turning to it I noticed the candle behaving in an unaccountable manner. The light was waving about in slow measure just as though it were beating time as cheer leader for three rousing hurrahs. One more wave followed for the tiger as it fell over on its side and extinguished itself. I thought no more of it and was soon in the land of Nod.

Next morning a cow-boy rode in to report a stampede among the cattle, which had been caused by an earthquake. Subsequently news came of the great disaster which claimed thousands of lives in Java and Sumatra. I claim to be the only one in the old Indian Territory who recorded that catastrophe with a tallow candle for a seismograph.

The majority of our Indian friends and acquaintances of that day still were of athletic build, a hold-over from their former free life of activity. How supple their motions, how proud and graceful their carriage as they rode or walked! The sight of one never failed to fascinate me.

Then there was the human side. Intensely curious about all new objects, they plied their friends for information. With changing conditions, they realized there must be a change in their mode of life. Many of the warriors attempted (without urging) to follow the new trail when they saw in it a means of taking care of themselves and their families.

I had no sooner become well established at the Ranch than my Cheyenne warrior friend, Red Lodge, descended upon us, accompanied by what seemed to be all of his relatives. The six or eight men with their women and children made a considerable band. They had apparently come for a stay, for two tepees were set up on the bottom lands in front of the store.

Red Lodge came in and as soon as he saw me he said, "How, Vehucus," using the name he had given me on the train. I was glad to renew the acquaintance and accepted his invitation to visit the Indian camp. There I took up my Indian education where we had left off. From him I had my first lesson in the use of the Indian bow and arrows. During the first evening also he bestowed upon me my real Cheyenne name, Nevaw, meaning Left Hand. I was born to use my left hand, and he, in typical Indian fashion, fastened the name of my peculiarity upon me. Such recognition gave me the keenest satisfaction.

The crowd of Indians had brought a plow with them in a new farm wagon, all issued to them at Darlington. No doubt Red Lodge had told Tosimeea (the Agent) of a desire to "follow the white man's trail." That afternoon and evening at the ranch passed without his saying a word to us of his new intentions. Respecting his reticence, we never asked the first question.

During the next day, from dawn to setting sun, the Indian camp was deserted by men, women, children and dogs. They had gone somewhere into the woods on the west bank of Turkey Creek.

Asserting my privilege of adoption, I went to the camp as soon as I discovered the Indians were back and preparing an evening meal. Soon I learned of the day's doings. They had taken the plow with their ponies to a spot in the black-jack and there plowed virgin soil for the first time in their lives. Watermelon seed had been sprinkled on Mother Earth after scratching her bosom. It had been a great experience for every one, including the ponies. Neither man nor animal in that crowd had ever before taken part in such a task. It had been a lark.

Just how they harnessed the ponies to the plow that first time is left to conjecture, but it had to be according to the wild Indian's imitation of what they had seen at the Agency. The fatherly government had not appointed instructors in farming at that time. They had a harness for the wagon and this was used. The ponies had bucked and struggled to escape the load put upon their shoulders for the first time. Once in the traces, they had been herded along, as on the trails, by men mounted on other ponies. The plowman had no knowledge of thrusting the plow-share into the soil and holding it there. It required agility and unusual strength to do this with a wild team of horses dragging the plow at breakneck speed. Sometimes the plowman went sailing through the air as the ponies raced ahead. Straight furrows were not thought of; the results, no doubt, had the appearance of scratches here and there on the surface of the ground. But they had persevered for the day and reported a crop planted.

Around the camp fire that night there was much rubbing of sore muscles and attention to bruises and abrasions. But how they did laugh at the spectacle each had made in the battle! How they did josh one another! It was fun and they took it in that spirit. The work finished, tepees were struck and the crowd returned to their village the next day.

Some three months afterwards, while Texas John was at the headquarters before his winter's isolation, he took me with him on a scout for strays to the west of Turkey Creek and north of the black-jack. After a day in the open, we were returning to camp as the sun neared the western horizon. Reaching the creek, we rode down its western rim searching for a good ford. The way led into the woods, and in pushing through one dense growth of underbrush I rode into an opening of more than two acres' extent and could not believe my eyes as they beheld what seemed to me wagon loads of ripe watermelons. Here was Red Lodge's farm.

The prolific soil had aided the amateur efforts of Indian farmers to a bumper crop. Even at that time I could note the indifferent plowing the ground had received. There was more virgin soil than plowed, and the seed had not been planted. Yet so much had taken root that vines reached over almost every square yard. I called John to me and we each appropriated a large melon and took it with us. To my knowledge, this was the only watermelon crop grown on Red Fork.

Red Lodge and all his band returned to Red Fork the very day after my discovery of his melons. Again the tepees were pitched, again the crowd disappeared over Turkey Creek. There was feasting for two or three days. Yes, I was an invited guest. The orgy over, they went away with a wagon load of the last of the melons. They were no doubt finished at the tom-tom's invitation the first evening they were back home.

Looking up the trail one morning at about ten o'clock, I called Ralph's attention to a little cloud of dust moving along the Chisholm Trail toward us, as yet two miles away. It was hard to detect, it seemed almost not to be, but the cloud persisted. It was not large enough to be made by animal or vehicle. It seemed odd to me, but Ralph immediately knew the portent. Crying, "Cheyenne Charley," Ralph hurried to the cook stove and placed a pot of coffee over the fire. I remained outside watching the approaching dust cloud. Quite rapidly it advanced until I made out a human form to which it acted as a tail.

It turned out to be a long, lean Indian brave. He was six

feet tall, torso bare, belt about his thin hips supporting his leggings, moccasins on his feet, hair braided forward over the shoulders, leather packet fastened about his neck, no weapon but the knife in his belt, bare headed. As he drew near with the short, springy steps of a long-distance runner, I could see every muscle rippling under his bronze skin. Arms folded to his sides, he came forward easily and stopped at the door with a smile which was infectious. Knowing Ralph of old he greeted him first, then stepped inside to the table where Ralph had set the steaming pot of coffee and a tin cup. He did not show the least strain even in his breathing. No perspiration was apparent. With a satisfied grin he seized the coffee pot and poured the cup three-quarters full, then took the bottle of pepper sauce we always had on the table and filled the cup the rest of the way. He drank this rapidly, then followed with another of the same mixture, and another until he had imbibed four.

As he talked to Ralph I sat and took in every feature of the incident. Having finished this repast, for the hot drink was all he wanted, he rose from the table, stepped quickly to the cabin door and sprang into a trot which soon carried him from view down the trail.

The man was known as Cheyenne Charley. Acting as runner for one of the Chiefs, he carried news to and from the Indian villages on the North Canadian. These athletes performed their duties following the old customs of the wild Indians. No doubt there were runners in every Indian tribe on the American continent. The plains tribes had them in every village to carry news to distant points. Charley was among the last. I believe he had news from Amick Covington at Caldwell to carry to his village that day. He had camped out on the trail the night before, and had traveled some thirty miles before reaching us,—would cover twenty-six more before reaching Darlington. While on these trips, he ate no food during the day, but Ralph had instituted the custom of giving him hot coffee as he passed us. This man often ran sixty miles in one period of daylight. Soon I was emulating his calling. I often practiced then and in succeeding years, and at one time accomplished the feat of running forty miles in one day. All honor to Cheyenne Charley, athlete.

Hearing a voice on the outside one morning as we were cleaning up our breakfast dishes, Ralph and I stepped to the door of the cook-house and beheld an elderly Indian and a white man in front, close to the pump.

The white was a mule-skinner who had evidently been on his way to the store when he had met the Indian. The Indian sat his pony erect, his blanket dropped about his waist. There were the usual braids of hair drawn over his shoulders to the front, but in addition I noticed that each was wrapped in otter skin. To his scalp lock was fastened one gray eagle feather. Under the blanket was a black shirt. His legs were clothed in beaded buckskin leggings, and moccasins covered his feet. The moccasins showed the wearer to be a Cheyenne by the design of the beadwork and the predominance of green. Ornamented tobacco pouch and knife case showed at the belt. As this rider sat his pony he appeared to be acting as audience of one to the white man. He kept an impassive face, but drummed with his heels incessantly on the pony's ribs. I learned later that this (beating a tattoo with the heels as they sat a passive pony) was typical of the horse Indians.

The white man talked in a loud voice and gesticulated. "You heap big chief?" he inquired in a roar.

"Me heap friend," he assured the Indian, with hands clasped before him.

Eye Has Seen, Ear Heard

The man then proceeded: "Me come long way—three sleeps," illustrating the rests enroute by placing hands together shoulder high, resting his head on them and closing his eyes. There ensued a torrent of information about his business, his ownership of the near-by outfit, details of the size of his family and questions as to the number of squaws the red man had. Speaking at the top of his lungs, between pidgin English and a sign language of his own, he poured out a story which the red man did not comment on or show that he understood. The freighter evidently forgot his errand at the store, for he ended his speech by hastily walking away toward his camp. As the man left, the Indian allowed his gaze to follow the white out of sight, then turned to Ralph with a grin parting his thin lips and made his first utterance. "Heap damn fool!" said he, as he flipped a thumb over his shoulder at the retreating form.

This was the fawning type of white man who disgusted him,—the one who would cheat an Indian every time he could, one who would take his land away without a qualm. The man was a coward also, and showed it. The Indian read him and had only amusement from the encounter.

Ralph greeted the Indian as one he knew well, and expected him to stay for a visit. He was Little Robe, the Cheyenne War Chief. In him I beheld the friend of our family of whom I had heard so much. He also took me into his consideration at once. On the first day of our meeting, he adopted my Cheyenne name of Nevaw to address me by. To me this seemed on a parity with his naming my cousin Issenon after his own dead daughter. I was now one of the family.

On this first morning, Little Robe's mind dwelt on his experiences with whites. The freighter had evidently recalled unpleasant memories. His remarks showed his resentment, which, however, never applied to us personally. At first he had received traders in his own village; he had smoked the pipe with them and they had all taken a puff as it reached them in the council circle. Little Robe had then allowed the traders to go about his village and had even asked his people to trade with them. But one of the first transactions had been the exchange of a finely tanned buffalo robe for a little piece of round silver which he now knew to be *Oko-muckite* (one half dollar). One of his young men had been persuaded to part with a fringed hunting shirt for the consideration of one box of fire sticks (the old sulphur matches). He resented this utter disregard for his people's rights by the white men, and this trading on their innocence.

He spent several days at the Ranch, riding about with us, telling of his life, thoughts, and feelings. Red Fork Ranch had been the scene of many events with which he had been connected. He had wanted to locate there when the Indians had first accompanied Darlington to an Agency site. Most of the tribe had spent several weeks in the vicinity before Darlington Agency site was chosen. At the crossing of the Cimarron he paused one day and pointed to the spot where he had found his son on a certain eventful day. This same son came to join his father on that visit at Red Fork, and between the two we have the story in the next chapter.

NOTE.—See Appendix, page 295.

130

Chapter XV

A GREAT and fast moving cloud of dust out of which came the thunder of a thousand equine hoofs was passing down the rise from the north to the bottom lands of Turkey Creek, on the Chisholm Trail, headed for the most direct opening in the black-jack to a ford of the Ho-to-oa-oa.

Close inspection would have revealed a fan-shaped herd of ponies running at break-neck speed. Muzzles stretched out in front, tails straight out behind, ears laid back, legs doubling under like jack-knives to reach the longest strides, bodies almost touching the ground, the whole herd came on in full stampede.

It was a controlled stampede, however, for they headed in a straight line for the opening nearest Turkey Creek. Through the dust cloud the forms of fifteen Indian youths could be seen driving and directing the herd. Each rode a pony stripped for war, guiding him with knee pressure. Every man of them was wielding his quirt unmercifully, both on his ridden mount and on the driven ponies as well. Bent forward, hair flying, arms and bodies rising and falling in regular rhythm, men and animals made a composite picture of deadly earnest action. The roar of the herd's hoofs drowned all other sounds. The ground trembled.

On one side at the head of the herd rode Oakerhater, the Cheyenne sub-chief, while Taawaytie, the Comanche, rode opposite him. These two were "on point" and directed the course. Following along on the edges of the herd, equally divided on each side, rode others, among whom were Okstei and Zotom. Altogether, there were fifteen young bucks including the Son of Little Robe, who brought up the rear, all working together to carry out a preconceived plan, which was to get the herd across the river in time to escape the interference of cattlemen and cavalry, to the number of forty or more, who were in close pursuit. Once across, they would be comparatively safe on their own land.

Sometime previously white traders had visited the village of Little Robe, the ranking War Chief of the Cheyenne, and, under the guise of friendship, had succeeded in making away with a herd of two thousand Indian ponies. It was a hard blow to the Indian's trust as well as to his material wealth. A party of volunteers, young men under Oakerhater, had set out in pursuit of the thieves and had followed them almost to the Kansas line unsuccessfully. Turning back, they had picked up all herds that came their way, to replace the stolen stock, and had accumulated about a thousand head.

Cattlemen had pursued them and hung in their rear awaiting an opportunity to attack. A few miles north of the Hoto-oa-oa, a troop of cavalrymen, out on a scout from Fort Dodge, had joined the cattlemen. Hence the wild flight for the ford.

As the galloping herd neared the opening in the black-jack, Oakerhater and Taawaytie rode forward in front of the leaders and slowed them to a trot, while the other men worked along the sides of the herd to the same end, until finally, as they neared the ford, the whole herd was subdued. The water was not deep that day, and the animals trotted through to the south bank. As they emerged from the stream, they were headed south-west until all were across.

On the Banks of the Ho-to-oa-oa

As the Indians reached the opposite bank and were starting across country to their home, the Son of (Skiomah) Little Robe made a brave resolve. His father and his people had been sinned against. They had been deceived, and they had been robbed in a way that hurt. Their wealth lay in the pony herds; without them they were crippled as well as impoverished. Moreover, to steal the ponies was an affront to all the tribe. The boys had attempted to recover their own, and failing that had taken back from the white tribe what, according to their reasoning, was only a fair recompense. "If the pursuers could be held back at the ford," thought this son of the War Chief, "the other Indians might reach home with the herd in safety." Why not perform this act, and save his people and their property?

Those who had gone out to rectify their wrongs were expected to do just that. To hold back pursuit at this point would clinch the result. Then again, here was an opportunity to win a place on the honor roll of the tribe, a place beside his father in the Ho-tam-i-tan-i-u (Dog Soldier) Band. Surely, He-am-a-wihio (Great One Above) would look down with favor and help his son.

Speaking to Oakerhater of his purpose, Skiomah took his stand and saw his friends pass from sight as the sun went down on this fateful day. Let the brave Indian youth tell the story in part in his own words.

"When we had left home two suns past, my father had told me not to fight the white man, and I had done my best to follow his orders, but here we were with ponies which rightly belonged to us, and the white men were coming to take them back if they could. All were safe on our land now; yet these white men never admitted that we had any land which they could not take away. Always, they wanted all and gave little.

If they caught up with us now, they would fight us and some of my friends would be killed and we would lose our ponies, for the whites numbered more than two to our one.

"One of us could hold the white men for a time at least, and that was what I decided to do. I felt that I might be killed, but to die in battle had always been an honor among my people, and here alone I would earn the honor. Oakerhater said the plan was good. As I watched my friends ride away on the trail to my father's village, I trembled a little and gripped my pony hard, for I saw our enemies appear on the other bank.

"At first, I sat up erect and yelled at the top of my voice to attract attention. Then I raised my hands over my head and made the sign, 'I will fight.' Then I made the death sign. The white men all rode back to the woods and began to dismount and to hide. I was happy, for now I knew they were afraid to cross while I stayed there.

"Soon I saw the sand in front of me spurt into a cloud and heard a shot; many more bullets followed; I then clung to the side of my pony opposite the river and raced up and down the smooth sand next the water, across the ford of the trail. At the end of the run I would turn about, and throwing myself on the opposite side, race back. I kept this up for some time. Without ceasing, I gave my war cries and sang the songs that the Medicine Man had taught me. I did not tremble now, but had faith in The Wise One Above, that he would bring me safely back to my father and to the girl who was promised to be my wife.

"The sand flew into my eyes many times and there seemed a cloud of it in the air. No white man left the other shore. At last, I felt a pain in my right arm and my rifle fell to the ground. A shot had caught me as I changed sides. I could not shoot any more. I rode up on to the bank to find shelter, and as I came to a buffalo wallow another shot went through my left thigh and into the pony, so that we both fell into the depression. That was all I knew for some time.

"Then I remember feeling pain and found both my arm and leg were broken, and I was bleeding so that I thought I must surely die. Close to me was my pony lying so still that I knew he was dead. No white man came, and soon it was dark.

"Again I slept and woke in darkness to find that much rain was falling. I was not bleeding now, but I felt cold and could not move. I thought my death was near, and tried to sing my song to He-am-a-wihio, asking him to take me to him. I was too weak to make him hear and fell asleep once more.

"I dreamed that the sun was shining and that I saw my father and that he looked upon me and said 'Son.' Then I opened my eyes and saw that the dream was true, for the sun was shining and there sat my father on a pony's back looking down into my eyes. Then I knew all was well with me. There was no enemy in sight. I felt happy, strange and weak. I fell asleep again, and did not wake up until I found myself in my father's lodge, with my family and the maiden who was to be mine caring for me."

Oakerhater and his band had reached the Indian Village with the ponies the night before, and had reported to the chief, Little Robe. They told of leaving his son alone on the river bank, and of the shots they had heard as they galloped away. They had little hope that he still lived. The stricken father prepared at once to go to the scene of the fight, in case the boy had not returned at day-break. A "travois" was attached to a lead pony, and shortly after dawn, Little Robe, mounted on his best pony and leading the other, set out to bring the body of his son home for burial.

He told his people that he wished to be alone with his dead. He knew also, that if troops were to be met, he could deal with them best alone. The village had lost many warriors in the past few years, and he did not want more trouble to come to them. The young men were aroused, and if they met the soldiers, he feared that nothing could keep them from fighting. He admonished all to remain calm and to do no rash thing before he returned. Here let us take up the story of the father's return to the Ho-to-oa-oa, in his own words.

"I felt that Ahk-tun-o-wihio (The One Below) was visiting some punishment upon me, and I searched my mind for the cause, as I rode over the prairie. I had promised Tosimeea (Brinton Darlington) at the Medicine Lodge that I would not fight either my white or red brothers from that time. I made the promise after the medicine pipe had come to me from my right side, and I had not touched the bowl. This promise I have kept and have made my followers do the same.

"We have sat down on the place the White Father told us to, and for three winters we have remained there. The country from the Hon-ne-o to the Mitsun, and from the trail of the Woha (Chisholm Trail) west to the country-where-the-buffalo-come-up-out-of-the-ground (Texas Panhandle) was to be ours. But my young men report many herds of woha on our land north of us. Why is this? We have kept our word, and these white men should keep theirs. They should not come to our land. They are driving the buffalo away from us.

"I can not blame my young men for taking the ponies. They belong to us in place of those which the white men stole. I gave my heart to these very white men, we smoked the pipe together. No one of my people has ever stolen that which belonged to those with whom he had smoked the pipe. I will keep the ponies,

On the Banks of the Ho-to-oa-oa

"But worst of all, my brave boy is dead, the one I taught and for whom I gave away many ponies when he became a man, he who has loved me and always obeyed my word. All these thoughts and more came to my mind.

"Because of all these thoughts, my heart was very sick as I came near the place where my boy had been seen last. I looked for white men, but saw none. All was quiet as I drew near the river, and rode down on the sand next the water. There I found many tracks of one animal pointing both in the direction of the rising sun and in the direction of the setting sun. The sand was thrown up and I knew the pony had been driven hard. Then I found the rifle which I had given my boy lying in the sand. Running up the bank from this was a single track. This I followed and from the top saw the bodies of a man and pony. It was my son and his pony. 'Both dead'—I thought. Oh! it was hard to come on my boy lying there lifeless. With a sick heart I rode close and cried out with sorrow, 'Son!'

"The Great Wise One Above came then and opened my boy's eyes and he looked up at me and smiled—then he slept again. My heart felt good and I hurried to the boy's side and found that he lived, for his heart was beating. He lay in much blood, and one arm and one leg were broken. I brought the pony with the bed to the side of my boy and carefully laid him on the platform. I was much heartened when I knew he was not dead. I was sure we could cure him of his hurts if he could live till he had reached our lodges.

"I bound up his wounds, and laying his rifle beside him, started back. The sun had been down a long time that night before we reached my village. It was a long journey for me. The boy did not complain, but slept from weakness most of the time. As we came into the village circle, the crier told all that we had returned, and the first to meet us were my wife and the girl my son was to marry. Together, we lifted the boy to his bed and there re-dressed the wounds and bound up the broken parts. In time he came back to health, as you see him now."

The simple stories of the father and son give the bare facts of an heroic episode. This young Cheyenne had made as brave a stand for his people and their rights as did Horatius of ancient Rome. For what he believed to be his right, he had brought forty well-armed Indian fighters to bay. They had dismounted, and taken to cover two hundred yards away before they dared to fire. Each of these troopers was armed with the latest Henry rifle, six shots to a loading. The rifle fire at the Indian was almost continuous after it started. His return fire, he had realized, would not be effective. Only the body of his pony and its speed which made him a difficult moving target, protected him.

Even when he could no longer either fight or run, he still held the vantage, for the troops thought that he had ambushed himself in a buffalo wallow and would surely pick off any one who attempted the ford. Darkness came before any maneuvers could be made to cross above or below him and get in his rear. All knew he was a fighting Cheyenne, who would resist as long as he was alive. All the whites withdrew in the darkness, the troopers returning to Fort Dodge, and leaving this one boy victor against forty-to-one odds.

The whole affair had been so against fair play, and such a violation of agreements with the Indians, that Little Robe was unable to prevent his warriors from taking up the fight the next spring. Most of the tribe went on the warpath to protect their rights. The old war chief did not break his word, however, but remained at home while the rest fought. This was the real cause of the Cheyenne War of 1874.

On the bank of the Ho-to-oa-oa, within the boundary of the future Red Fork Ranch, this saga was enacted.

NOTE.—See Appendix, page 295.

Chapter XVI

EARLY one morning, I stood in the doorway looking on to the trail when a very sheepish looking cow-boy drove up and came to a stop. He was in charge of a two-seated farm wagon. A stranger sat with him while two others occupied the second seat placed midway of the length of the wagon bed. The rest of the wagon was filled with bedding and hunting gear.

The three strangers were ruddy-cheeked, clean-looking young Englishmen. Strange to say, they spoke the language without an "I say," "fawncy," "bah jove," or "well, rawther," as we had understood they did. In fact, they talked as real Englishmen of the educated class. The one sitting with the driver seemed spokesman, and asked if they might stay a couple of weeks to hunt and to watch the operation of a cattle ranch. Ralph replied that they were welcome to stay if they could stand every-day fare. On the assurance that they would be glad to live as the natives did, the word was given and the three men alighted. Then it could be seen why the cow-boy driver was looking so apologetic. Each man dressed very much as the golfer of to-day—knickerbockers, golf stockings, low boots, wool shirts, and caps. The like of this had never been seen in the cattle country before and we were as astonished as the cow-boy said he had been. The latter did not have a clear conscience until he had taken Ralph aside and excused himself for being seen in such company. He ended by saying disgustedly, "Hell, they wears pants, won't ride a hoss, and talks langwidge." With this indictment he strode back to his wagon and, refusing all invitations to stay over night, drove away. He would have driven all night or camped out rather than remain in such scandalous company. Some of the boys might "ketch" him there.

Ralph returned to his guests and assisted them to settle in the upper room of the larger cabin. During this process, the leader of the three introduced himself as an Englishman named Wilson, and the other two as friends of his. Later the others told Ralph that this man was Lord Wilson of the English Peerage. The other two were not titled, but had been his classmates at Cambridge. After graduation the three had set out on a tour of the world at the expense of the Peer. They had visited India, Malaysia, Australia, and Japan. Then they had spent some time on our Pacific coast. Now they wanted to see the cattle country at the heart of it.

We had only read of men of this type. That our reading had led to erroneous ideas of the English was soon proven. The books had told us that Englishmen dined every day on choice viands. Ralph was much worried in spite of their assurances to the contrary. He was afraid they would not like his fare of sow-belly, hot biscuit, and coffee served straight. For the first meal, he stewed some dried apples to "give sauce to good digestion." They ignored the sauce and centered all their attention on the amount of pork Ralph could fry. They kept him at it until he saw they could equal him in their capacity. He never had to worry after that except as to quantity.

The four young men were soon on terms of mutual regard, and the companionship was enlightening to both sides. Frank, honest exchange of ideas brought them all together. While the Englishmen were absorbing the strange ways of cow-boy land, we learned that poise lay in good-breeding. But the average cow-boy could not change his preconceptions.

In a country where everybody rode, even if he had only a tenth of a mile to go, these men insisted upon walking. They often walked eight and ten miles before breakfast, then put in the remainder of the day walking unheard-of distances. The cow-boys attributed their refusal to ride to no other reason than cowardice.

When among strangers they were as sparing of speech as the cow-boys themselves. They never vaunted their station in life, or their prowess. Strangely enough this reticence was misunderstood. If they were not sissies, reasoned the cow-men, why didn't they talk United States, not "langwidge" that couldn't be half understood.

Then they had habits which were simply scandalous. We were surprised one morning to find our guests lined up in front of the pump, soaping themselves all over and taking turns at being rinsed off by buckets of water wielded by the others. Ralph later joined this water line and the adoption of the Englishmen's "daily tub." Whoever took a bath except when the river was handy? Silly.

In cow-boy land one was thought to be a fool to be taken in by any cock-and-bull story one might tell you. These were often tried on new-comers. They were tried on the Englishmen, who accepted any man as telling the truth. For this the cow-boys set them down as plain fools. Ralph frequently straightened them out on these yarns, by stating facts.

Lord Wilson displayed his true democratic spirit in his treatment of the friends who were traveling at his expense. They brought one cot bed with them. Our accommodations allowed of sleeping on the floor only. Did Lord Wilson take the cot for his own exclusive use? He did not. Each used it in turn, and there was much good-natured kidding as to whose turn came next.

The evenings of their stay were spent in visiting with cowboys and hearing the lore of the country with embellishments. The days were filled with long tramps, hunting, and witnessing the cattle business at the summer camp.

The time for their departure arrived all too soon. There was mutual regret on this point. If they had been protected from insult at Red Fork, they were not to miss a hazing after they had reached the border cow-town at the end of the trail. We did not go with them there. The same cow-boy who had first brought them to us was prevailed upon to return for them with his wagon.

No doubt it was the desire to redeem his social standing that moved him to publish the hour of the arrival of these "cowardly, queer critters" in Caldwell. A delegation of mounted cow-boys met the arrivals down the trail and escorted them into town. Surrounding the wagon was a group of twenty or thirty cow-boys, cavorting about, shouting and firing their sixes. Every resident of the town seemed on hand ready to enjoy the game.

Down the one main street they rode in their wagon to the one pine-board hotel and engaged rooms for the day and night, for they were desirous of seeing the cow-boy in town. A self-appointed reception committee escorted them from the hotel to a round of the saloons and dance halls. In each of these the drinks were on the strangers and they entered into the spirit of the occasion to the extent that they paid the score in every place, to the shame of the usual cow-boy prodigality. Every cow-man in town joined the procession and it sure was a day from which to reckon time.

Each hanger-on took turns as raconteur of the badness of certain others in the crowd for the delectation of the paying visitors. Cut-throat Jack was pointed out as the one who always took this means of helping his victims to leave this vale of tears. Eats-their-heart Mike was one who copied the Indian stunt of taking courage from his victims. Various other sanguine men were pointed out as having their own private grave yards.

Hunting yarns followed, and many tales of strange beasts. The Woolly Woofs and such did not gain credence, but the old, time-worn story of the "snipe hunt" was swallowed entirely. It was agreed to engage in one that very night. The Englishmen had noted the great abundance of bird life on the prairies and could anticipate very full bags of game.

At dusk, a cavalcade of some score of cow-boys set out with the visitors for the hunting grounds. They went down the Chisholm Trail, passed over Bluff Creek, and then stationed the men with the bags on the level plains fully a mile apart. Each of the guests was told to wait for the drive; the crowd would spread out and make a record round-up of the snipe and point them to the runs where they were waiting. Then the cow-boys drove back to town as fast as they could, congregated in saloons and regaled themselves with liquid refreshments and with the tale of how they had taken in these innocents.

The three men came to a realization of the joke sometime during the night. They succeeded in finding each other in the dark and set out to tramp back to town. They arrived in the middle of the morning and went to their hotel at once.

On the long tramp back they had talked over all their experiences in the country and finally approximated the reason for the hidden slurs they had received during the past weeks. Lord Wilson determined they should not leave until this idea was refuted in a way the cow-boy could understand.

Lord Wilson

He went to his room and selected the best rifle he had, and filling the magazine with cartridges, he strode with it to the center of the cow-town and stood in the middle of the street with the cocked weapon in the hollow of his arm. Then he raised his voice and called on all to hear what he had to say. He told in decisive tones just what he thought of them. They were cowards and damned liars, not worthy of notice by decent people. If any one differed with him, he might come and shoot it out. No individual appeared to dispute him. Then he made the invitation all inclusive, and said they might come in a bunch. Still no response. Then laying down his rifle he asked any or all to come forward and be trimmed with his fists.

After an hour spent in an endeavor to get satisfaction, he stated that he would be in town until the next train time, and was ready to meet any one with gun or fists during the interim.

The law of the range protected him from assassination, and anyway he had won the respect of the men there. They were ashamed of themselves, and a committee waited on him during the day to apologize. The same crowd acted as a bodyguard for the departing gentlemen when they went to the depot to entrain.

The whole experience with these Englishmen had been an enlightening one for the cattle country. It would not have been that without the sequel on that last day. If the cowboys had been scandalized by the unheard-of doings of the trio, they were equally amazed that these men had courage of the kind they admired.

"Why, those English sons-of-guns sure called the turn there," said one when recounting the scene on the main street that day. "Say, I reckon they kin walk ef they want to," said another. "Their langwidge is sure *muy bueno*," chimed in a third. "An' say, you kin bet I don't want them fellers to beleeve anything I say," was the final capitulation to the lesson they had learned. It was long remembered in cow-boy land.

(In "Burke's Peerage" appears this title to a record: *Sir Raymond Robert Tyrwhitt-Wilson of Stanley Hall, 4th Bart., Bridgenorth, England.* This was the title of the "Lord Wilson" of this story. He has since died.)

Chapter XVII

WHILE life was thoroughly interesting and instructive at headquarters on the Chisholm Trail, there was still more of interest at the summer camp on the Cottonwood. I spent many days there where we were in the center of our cattle range. Perry and I would often be alone and it was he who instructed me in much of my knowledge of cattle country life, though I often scouted about on my own. With him I rode over all of our range, and learned of the winter cow-camp in a log house located in a cedar grove away to the east corner of Red Fork property.

Many were the sights strange to me then, not the least of which were the wild cattle scattered over the plains. I soon learned to keep to my pony, if I wished to avoid investigation by curious cattle who did not recognize a man on foot. After being among the cattle for a while, one observes many human traits. I firmly believed that cattle could talk to one another.

This idea first took hold of me while Perry and I were riding over to the cedar grove one day. We had reached a spot several miles from the Cimarron River, while the Arkansas was further to the east of us. Water was miles away in any direction.

While riding along to the rear of Perry I thought I saw a form of some kind on the ground partly under a bush. Wheeling about I rode back and saw a young calf flattened out there. It could not have been over a week old. The body lay with its fore legs stretched out in front with the head lying partly on them and turned to one side. Eyes were half-closed and staring. The hind legs were doubled up, one under the body, the other beside it. I called Perry back and we dismounted.

The calf had not moved or winked an eye-lid as I watched. Perry approached and lifted it from the ground as high as he could. The whole posture of the baby never changed. He dropped it to the ground with a thud, but there was not a movement of a single muscle. As the body thumped against the earth, I thought it a dead animal, but Perry explained, "It's mother has left it there to go for water."

We mounted to ride away, and then I saw ever so slight a movement of the front legs as the animal reached out and drew itself slowly into the same spot it first had been moved from. I was to witness a finale to the scene.

After riding a short distance I met a bawling cow trotting along with head in the air. Perry told me to watch her.

She passed along in the general direction of the recumbent calf. She finally stopped and let out an impatient "Baw." It seemed to say, "Child, where are you?" In answer to the query the apparently dead calf sprang to its feet and gave a querulous, glad cry as much as to say, "Oh, I thought you would never come." Soon the calf was being satisfied at its fountain of youth. Then Perry explained.

The calf had been born far away from water and was yet too weak to travel far. The mother had gone miles away to the nearest river for a drink. Before she had left, she had nosed the baby down by the bush where I had seen her. Prowling wolves were all about scouting for food, of which a baby calf was the choicest. Now I claimed that mother must have explained the situation to the baby in language which meant this: "I am going away now, and as you cannot go along, I must leave you here, for I cannot stand it another hour without a drink. Mr. Wolf will be looking for you to eat you up. If you do what I tell you, all will be well. Now you lie just the way I put you and don't you move a muscle or an eyelash." That was just what baby did. I leave it to the reader, did or did not mother talk to baby?

I have spoken of the mother cow talking to her baby before going down to the river for a drink and of the baby's understanding and fidelity in following instructions. All the cattle talked.

Watch that eighteen-hundred-pound bull there. See him stalk majestically to the center of a group of cattle and let out a roar which says as plain as day, "Give me room according to my strength; I'm about to turn myself loose." Every steer and cow in the vicinity understands and removes itself to a safe distance without delay.

Bull looks about and then lowers his head to "make medicine." Muzzle held close to the ground he blows a mighty blast from his nostrils which fills the air with a cloud of dust. Slowly he draws one fore hoof over the soil, gathering all the dust and gravel he can, and throws it up and over his body. At the same time you hear him say in his lowest bass voice, "Ur-r-r-r-r-r-r-r-Ugh," "Here I am that can lick any other feller on the range!"

After the first blast he does not raise his head, but you can see his eyes glaring defiance about him. All the cows about had first stood watching; now some of them resume feeding with a toss of the head which says, "I've heard you before, it is old stuff. If you want a rumpus, it is none of my affair. I told you the last time."

Not having an opponent to dispute him after the first challenge, Mr. Bull proceeds to throw dirt on his back with the other hoof, showing impatient determination, and raising his voice, roars, "Ur-r-r-r-r-r-r-r-r-Ugh," "Hear me, I want to fight. Oh! you cowards!"

As time elapses without an opponent, the bull rakes dust onto his back, faster and faster, as his voice rises in a continuous roar which can be heard a mile away. In the meantime some have looked him over. Younger bulls trot up and retire to an inconspicuous position after one look, and resume feeding with a toss of the head which says, "Not for me, wait awhile longer."

In the bedlam of sound now coming from the one bull, you will finally be conscious of another sound approaching, and turn to note another gentleman of the herd approaching with voice raised. Majestically he moves forward as all others make way for him. He approaches until he has reached the ring about the challenger. There he gives a final roar and rushes at top speed at the one who has insulted him. The challenger has noted his approach, but has never ceased his roar. The two voices mingle for a moment and cease with the crash of two skulls coming together. With the issue joined, the two beasts cease roaring and give all their attention to the battle. But they did talk when there was breath for it.

When driving a herd to the trail for market, it was a usual sight to see some steer who had been left behind come trotting to join his mates. Wild cattle love company and if their folks are driven away, leaving one to solitude, that one will do all he can to join the crowd, and he will talk about it. Before he has discovered the missing ones, he trots along, never pausing except to voice his inquiry of "Where are you?" Once he discovers the missing ones he proceeds at his fastest trot, scolding the while that he should have been left behind. When he has found his friends and relatives again, he falls into line, giving a final satisfied bawl.

Take baby in the herd. Life is full of fun, let's run about a bit. Dashing here and there in playful jumps, one finds mother out of sight. Never intended that should happen. I must find her quick, "Ma-a-w!" No answer, "M-A-A-W!"

In the meantime mother has heard and answers without looking up from her feeding, "M-o-o-o; yes, child, what is it?" Baby does not see mother and becoming frightened, gives an agonizing "M-a-a-w-a-aw-a-aw. I am lost, come to me." Then mother starts to the rescue, giving a warning to all other elders, which says, "Clear out of my way, for I am *going* to my child." Then she plunges straight toward the child's voice and they all make way for her. I have heard them as plainly as if they talked English. I learned to interpret it for my own edification and protection. One needed to understand when a mother voiced her intention of running one down as baby was being held for branding. It was well to mount your pony in time.

Cattle were always real companions to me on the range, especially when I was doing herd duty through long hours and there was no other companionship to be had. It was a pleasure to me to go on herd in the early morning hours when the cattle had not yet risen from their beds on the sections of ground made warm by their own bodies. In this they were human, for on a cool frosty morning they seemed as reluctant to leave their own warm beds on the ground as I had been to leave my blankets. The night herder would come in to eat his morning meal which Perry had prepared, and I would get the word "All quiet." This would be my cue and I would ride forth to the great prairies in the early morning light and hunt up my wild charges. When in sight of the recumbent figures on the plain I would start my rendition of some one of the cow-boy songs I had learned, continuing until I was riding through the herd as it lay.

Then I would cease singing and start greeting my friends. "Hello, Tom," I would say as I passed a long-horned steer.

At the greeting from me he would scramble to his feet, rear end first, stretch out his legs to the greatest span, bow his back until his belly came near the ground in a curve, twist his tail into a curled appendage, and open his mouth in a wide yawn accompanied with a most audible "Ow-o-o-o-ou." It was a most human touch. "Life is such a bore, wish there was something to get scared about other than that human horse that I see every day." "Well, I better get some breakfast now I am up," he seemed to say as he dismissed me with a look and fell to feeding. Those morning greetings were human to me, I understood what he said and he had the same knowledge of me. Thus I would ride through the herd noting all the old friends in sight, strangers, new babies, Old Red, the lord of the herd for the nonce, and his younger rivals. It was "Hello, Tom, Dick, Harry, Jack, Bill, Red," as I greeted my way among them and as one after another went through the same motions as Tom had. Not to neglect the opposite sex, the greetings included Ivy, Sal, Mariar, Polly, Susy, Lizzie, and the rest. They may not have been ladies in the perfectly human yawn they executed in company, but they did the same as the gents, and even scratched their bellies in the same open manner.

After reaching the far side of the herd I would circle the whole in a leisurely manner and note that my charges were all feeding by that time. Some baby would finish soon and with the vigor he had imbibed would start his antics to work off the energy. He would see how high he could jump, skyhunt, sunfish from end to end, kick at the morning sun, and buck until he was tired, all the while letting out blats and squeals. While in the ruckus mood, baby would strike strange mothers as he heeded not where he went and said mothers would give him a boost with their horns which sent him on his way until finally he would bring up against his real mother, get his breath, and fall to feeding at his own fount of life. The second potation would start calfy looking for trouble with other kids on the block. Walking up to Skinny he would give his friend a smash in the side, then with playful jumps swing around in front of his chum, lower his head, and butt head on. "Yes, sir, I feel like I can do you up in ten pound packages and eat you whole," says one to the other. "My pa kin lick yours," is the retort. "I am going to lick Red some day," comes back the first. "There, I licked you!" says the other as he pushes his opponent to the ground with a well-placed blow in the side.

During the long days on herd I would sit my pony with leg thrown over saddle horn, asleep some of the time, and rouse at any unusual disturbance, including the bull fights which occurred several times daily. With the life of the herd about me I came to believe in animal language, and now class every species of their tongue as among the others spoken on the face of the globe.

There was entertainment and instruction in it. It beats all how inflection, tone, manner of delivery, give different meaning to the same general sound. But it is there, and along with my knowledge of English, Spanish, Portuguese, Cheyenne, I rank high the attainment of cow and horse talk, gleaned during the otherwise lonesome days on the old unfenced ranges of the West.

One day, when there was a man to leave with the cattle, Perry and I rode over to Phil Block's camp for a pleasure trip. Perry being from Kansas did not have the animosity toward Indians which most Texans seemed to have. Phil was a white man who, when a child, had been stolen by the Cheyennes. He had grown up among them and had married into the tribe. Indian usage decreed that all the relatives of the women were now his relatives. I do not think Phil ever objected to this arrangement. At least, his camp always harbored many Indians, and in Indian style he kept open house.

In a bend of Kingfisher Creek, where it swung in a large arc from west to north, he had a log house for winter use. This was to the east of the Reno Trail as it led down to the ford of the creek. Across the trail, opposite the log house, was the summer camp, consisting always of three tepees,—more when there were callers from the main villages. To this spot Perry guided me.

Phil greeted us and made us welcome. I was soon exploring the tepees for strange sights as Perry gossiped with the older men. Indian style, there was a large iron kettle simmering over the fire in the center of the largest tepee, which I knew contained food of some kind. This would be meat, for they did not have vegetables. It smelled good to me, and soon I was hanging about in the vicinity of the savory odor.

After a few minutes, a buck went to the kettle, lifted the cover, and speared down into the contents with a pointed wooden stick. He drew out a luscious-looking piece of meat on the end of the stick and seating himself on a back rest, proceeded to devour it with noisy gusto. His eye was upon me all this while and he finally signaled to me to help myself with another stick. Needing no second invitation, I followed suit and took a generous helping. Picking out a vacant back rest in the tepee, made of rawhide and bones (like the arms, seat and back of a chair, minus the legs), I also sat down and proceeded to devour my share. I liked the taste enough to accept a second portion. I ate my fill and cherished the last taste in my mouth until it was time for Perry and me to set out for our return. As I shook hands with Phil I gave a final lick to my lips and asked him what it was I had been eating. He grinned and said, "Hota" (Dog).

On the Range

The assembled Indians interpreted the look of dismay on my face and broke into a laugh. They had led me on purposely. I fooled them on one point, however,—I thought enough of my food to retain it.

As I rode back that afternoon with Perry the day seemed perfect though hot, and I little thought I was soon to be plunged into an unusual scene, the memory of which has remained vivid to this day.

On the open prairie a man on herd sat his pony with one leg thrown around the saddle horn and the other extending to the stirrup. His body was hunched forward with arms crossed on the bent knee, and he was almost asleep. The pony stood on three legs. Man and beast were both resting in the hot sunshine of a July afternoon on the range of Red Fork.

The herd was scattered over a wide area peacefully feeding, or lying down and chewing the cud. Here was a scene of peace and content.

A sudden gust of wind out of the still air brought the man erect in the saddle, and the pony to all fours, both wide awake in an instant.

That rush of air had come like a slap of the hand, raising the hat brim, twisting the neckerchief about, and tossing the pony's forelock back between the ears onto the ruffled mane.

Following the first slap by a few seconds came a very, very faint breath of air, touching the man's cheek as gently as a girl's breath. The cattle were now all on their feet moving about in the sunshine to discover what had disturbed them. All eyes were finally focused on a low-lying bank of clouds on the horizon to the northwest. That was all there was to look at, for the sky overhead was clear and serene.

Then came breaths of hot air at intervals of a second or so as though a giant hand were slapping the air, first from one direction, then another, to clear away the unwelcome, heat-laden humidity. The cloud bank now looked larger.

The sun was suddenly obscured, and with this blotting out there came a steady push of hot air from the northwest, as though an unseen giant had made a pop-gun of the universe and was pushing the plunger through the barrel with this air ahead of it.

As far as the eye could reach over the scattered herd, individuals were now seen to be trotting toward a common point where the herder sat his pony. Animal instinct told them to come to the voice now raised in a cow-boy song of soothing.

As the animals came toward the focal point, each would stop a moment in his flight to wheel about with head erect and gaze in the direction of the clouded sky, then resume again the path toward solace and comfort. Here and there would be heard cries of anxious inquiry. There were no cries of defiance now from the lords of the herd. Unthinking calves first thought it a lark and gamboled around their mothers, but were soon told that this was a serious affair, after which they cried in querulous doubt of the ways of this old world. Man and beasts now realized that they were to have a storm of wind and rain. Perry, as he joined the other man, told me to keep clear of the herd.

The two riders could not expect to stem the drift of hundreds of hoofs in a storm, but they could quiet the nerves to some extent and stay with the herd to bring them back. Already the cattle were starting to walk away from the oncoming storm. Louder rose the human voice in song as the men rode along the sides and rear of the herd.

Then came the hush before the storm. Not a breath of air stirred and the clouds enveloped the whole sky. The heat seemed to bear down as if to crush everything to earth. Nature's scenic painter had colored the heavens from dark gray to slate black, and suddenly commenced to work here and there with shades of green and copper placed on cloud borders, as the air changed.

Then came a cool gust of air with the smell of rain and clarified ozone. Then the atmosphere became charged with electricity. It crackled in the hair, and from spurs to belly of my pony, while sparks sprang across from the animal's ear tips when he threw them forward. Darkness fell and sparks of static could be seen on horn tips throughout the herd. Then one great dart flashed from the clouds, and striking the ground, gathered itself into a ball of fire as large as a house. It rolled away over the prairie to disappear with an explosion that shook the breath from the body.

That flash seemed to take the plug from the bottom of a great reservoir of water above and it came down in cataracts. Flash followed flash until balls of fire could be seen rolling in every direction, and the reverberating concussions fairly stalled the motion of all living things. At times men and animals were tossed like corks in a cross sea, from side to side, and with the sound of celestial artillery came the all-embracing shriek and roar of the wind. With each succeeding bolt of lightning came more rain until the surface of the ground was buried in water.

At the height of the storm, the almost continuous flashes of light revealed a mass of milling animals which moved about in circles not knowing where to go. Water coming down in torrents added to the blinding flashes of lightning, and the roar of the wind joined with the bellowing of the frightened animals, to make a perfect picture of bedlam and confusion. The crooning song of the cow-boys had ceased when it could no longer be heard, but the men were still there.

As the electrical display first slackened, and the flashes with exploding balls of fire became less frequent and further away, the herd broke into the first stampede of unreasoning terror. With tails out and extending themselves at fullest speed they ran in a great mass. They ran with the storm as occasional balls of fire still lighted their path. The cow-boys kept with them, while I followed in the rear.

As the fury of the storm abated, the roar of the herd became the dominant sound. For some time they ran until they tired and slowed down. Then the cow-men rode close to the leaders and, by shouting in front of them, turned the direct line of travel into a curve. Soon the herd was running in a large circle, then a close mass of milling animals, and the stampede was over.

With a final lightning flash away on the horizon in the southeast, the sun broke through the cloud banks in the west. Just above the horizon its slanting rays flooded the land. It lighted up all the retreating cloud banks, and while accentuating the blackness, it also painted every color of the rainbow there. The air was clear and bracing, and earthy smells rose from the ground. Danger and terror were gone, all was peace again, and the cattle, hearing again the songs of the men, fell to feeding about them.

These storms of the old prairies were unlike any in the settled communities of to-day. With no outstanding eminences to strike, the lightning hit the ground without entering, and gathered into great balls of fire that raced over the level country for miles, and always burst with a final terrific explosion. One of these explosions was awe inspiring, but when the height of the storm was reached the display was fearsome. The flashes of light ripping their way from the clouds, with the balls of fire shooting over the ground in all directions, kept men and animals helpless in one spot to be buffeted about by the tornado of wind. The sound of the air closing in on the

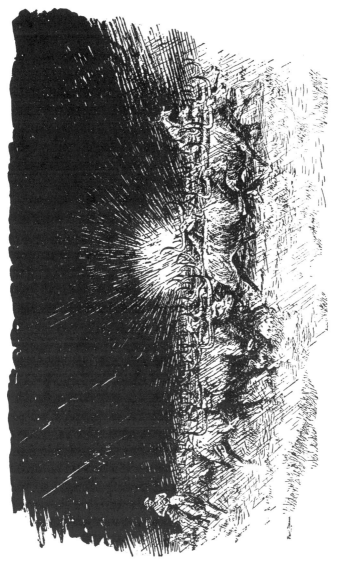

STORM AND STAMPEDE

vacuum created by the electric current transcended all others, and was approximated only by the shriek of the wind.

The electrical display often continued for over an hour in the worst of these storms, and took as long to die away. The start came with the suddenness of the rush of the wind, but descended gradually from the peak of pandemonium and confusion to a peace and quiet enhanced by the purest of air.

Chapter XVIII

RETURNING to the headquarters from the summer camp, I was soon to meet a different demonstration of nature.

One afternoon the cook of a cow outfit chose to pitch his camp in front of the store where he had water handy. I watched his skillful preparations of the evening meal.

He started his fire on the bare soil of the trail, and had bread baking, two gallons of coffee boiling, and bacon frying by the time a herd of cattle began to be worked by to the bottom for night feeding.

Much fried sow-belly lay heaped on tins near the fire, and the coffee pot was opened for a final stirring when I brought proceedings to a stop with an exclamation of alarm.

I had glanced up the trail just in time to note a terrifying black cloud swooping down upon us with the speed of the wind. This cloud was black as night, reaching from the ground to the heavens and spreading from Turkey Creek on the west, across the trail and out of sight to the east. The cook looked up at my cry of warning and without an instant's hesitation broke for the shelter of the houses. I followed as a close second.

Then came fifteen minutes of darkness as we huddled in the store, choking from clouds of dust which penetrated to every recess of the room, the while we were bombarded on the outside by a hail of gravel and dust.

The dust storm departed as quickly as it had arrived, the sun came out, and we returned to the abandoned camp fire.

Natural History

There we found the fire smothered under a blanket of dirt. The open coffee pot, and skillets with bacon, were filled level with sand and gravel. The log house was marked with bruises and some window panes were broken.

The cook emptied everything out onto the ground, cleansed his utensils and started all over again on his evening meal, while I meditated over the experience of a sand storm on the plains. We had been more fortunate than I was to be in other years when caught out in the open by one of these.

They were simply wind storms which caught up all the loose sand, soil, and gravel, and hoisted tons of it into the air thousands of feet. The atmosphere would be so charged with dirt as to shut out the sun to the darkness of midnight. In the open, one had to dismount and lie on the ground until the fury had passed. Cattle and horses drifted before such storms until they had passed them by. In this instance, the cattle which had been driven by in the afternoon, drifted back past us and were rounded up afterwards.

In this manner, trails were scooped into the semblance of sunken roads on the levels, railroad cuts on the rises. Thus were sand hills picked from dry river beds and placed along the borders of the streams.

Our cattle corral at headquarters was built in a manner that would lead one to believe it impregnable to any attack cattle could direct against it. Six and eight inch logs placed closely together deep in the ground and rising to six feet above seemed strong enough to hold any herd. This was true in ninety-nine cases out of a hundred. The one exception was when blind terror took hold of the herd. I was witness of this, and here is the story.

Toward the end of the season, a good-sized herd of cattle reached us one afternoon. It was driven into the corral and the cow-boys came into the store for relaxation during the evening. A warm, comfortable, moonlight night came on, everything was serene. The cattlemen made their beds on the ground about the cattle corral with trouble far from their minds. Among them was a shorthorn cow-boy who was on his first trip up the trail. He became the key to subsequent happenings.

After others had gone to sleep, this shorthorn lay awake with his head pillowed against the fence. Inside the corral a steer was also moving about, unable to go to sleep.

Arriving at a point where he could look out between two logs of the fence, Mr. Steer discovered the strange dome of thought belonging to Shorthorn. Treading noiselessly, he came forward, put his muzzle through the aperture, thrust out his tongue, and licked the strange thing there. He smelled salt and tasted it.

Shorthorn did not know steers yet. Realizing what was happening, and in a playful mood, he reached over his head and took a firm grip on that bovine snout with both hands. It was a new and terrifying experience to Mr. Steer. Immediately he sent up a bellowed cry of agony and fear. He tore loose and wheeled into the herd to escape the fearsome thing which had attacked him. With his first bellow, every other steer in the corral was on its feet, gazing about in fright with tail erect for the extreme emergency. It did not take long for those milling animals to rush blindly against the fence. Sheer weight finally forced an opening through some of the corral posts. Before the awakened cow-boys could reach and saddle ponies, the herd was pouring through an ever widening gap in the fence with the speed of an express train. They headed north toward open prairie and as they passed the ranch buildings we were awakened there by the roar of a herd in full flight.

Natural History

We could not understand the cause of a stampede, on that perfect night, nor could the cow-boys in charge. It was revealed only on the confession of Shorthorn the next afternoon, after the scattered herd had been brought back. We at the ranch could hardly believe the herd had escaped from our strong corral, but were forced to admit it after an inspection of the ruined fence. This was repaired for reception of the same herd as it was rounded up. That Shorthorn developed his first ring from the experience.

My first prairie fire was witnessed in safety from the ranch house, as it passed on the other side of Turkey Creek. Clouds of smoke appeared north of us and to the west during the late afternoon. By night the smoke was carried in dense clouds on a northerly breeze past us to the south. For an hour or two we were lighted up by the blaze as it passed through the black-jack. One could read by the light. The flames leaped high in the air; they caused a roaring rush of air; a crackling sound reached our ears. At one time in the evening, we could see this conflagration reaching for miles from the Cimarron to the north. The picture remains vivid to this day. I was soon to experience another prairie fire, equally vivid, with myself and a companion escaping from its devouring menace.

Pike and I set out one day to go from our headquarters to Phil Block's camp. After we had crossed the Cimarron ford, a short distance south, three antelope leaped across the trail in front of us. Bounding a short distance, they stopped in their tracks, wheeled about and gazed back, wheeled again and bounded away. We looked and could see no cause for their fright. These first animals were quickly followed by jack rabbits and more antelope in full flight from some unseen terror—unseen by us but evident to them. It was not long before we two saw the smoke of an approaching prairie fire in the west. Then we knew and spurred our ponies into a gallop along our course. As we hurried forward great flocks of quail and prairie chickens whirred and whistled past us in the course followed by the animals. Even rattlesnakes crossed the trail in evident uneasiness. Both birds and beasts seemed to have lost the fear of man in the presence of a common danger. At times the trail would be filled with exhausted birds who walked as they gathered strength for another flight onward.

The first light gray smoke now reached us and the ponies did not need urging to proceed at their fastest pace. The fire was approaching rapidly, and knowing there was a fire guard at Phil's, we determined to try for it.

We could see tongues of flame burst out through dense smoke as the terror bore down upon us from the west. There was a roaring sound and heat was borne to us with the choking smoke. Pike and I both doubled over the ponies' necks as we rode the last half mile to safety. From there we saw the flames cover our trail and pass on to the bank of the Kingfisher, where it died out.

Riding back on our trail in the afternoon we beheld a country swept bare of every growing thing. Here and there smoldering heaps of grass broke into flame as gusts of wind fanned them. We had escaped death by fire that morning, yet Pike did not even remark on the fact. He had seen death too many times. The reality is pictured in my mind with galloping sounds finally drowned in a roar, sensations of heat and choking that almost overcame me.

I contracted malaria at Red Fork Ranch, which made itself manifest by fall of the year 1883. It was the good old "fever and ague" of which I had heard father tell in connection with his early days in Iowa. In view of later knowledge I could call it "intermittent fever." There was a glow of satisfaction in discovering I was heir to something that father had told us about, but no pleasure in the agonizing reality.

About eleven o'clock of a morning, when I was entertaining visions of our noon-day meal, a feeling of nausea would come over me which was relieved only by most energetic vomiting. This would last for some time as I vainly hoped for surcease from the visitation, for the vomiting would be succeeded by headaches and raging fever. I would go to the upper floor and wrap blankets about me as violent chills took the place of the fever. No amount of cover could keep out the chill which seemed to come from my bones. When I finally broke into violent perspiration the attack was over for the day, and I answered the call for supper. There would be one day of respite before the next attack. On my off days, the world resumed its roseate hue, my optimism told me there would be no more sick days. But I was wrong in that belief. Relief came only with cold weather.

It seems I was inclined to keep a diary, along with memoranda of observations, during my early days at Red Fork. The diary did not last long; in fact, I can find only two days' entries in a paper-back note book.

Looking at this book cover ornamented with a pink star inside a pink circle brings to memory the picture of the whole stock of them as they lay on the lower shelf of our trading store. A full dozen reclined there in the remaining half of a paper carton, which had been torn from about them. Flanking the note books on one side was a 6 x 12 inch box of raisins, while a similar box of prunes guarded the opposite side. On a higher shelf were pasteboard boxes containing "boiled" shirts, and paper collars. This end must have been the home of the luxuries, for I do not recall a single sale from either shelf on the north side. Not only was there no call for them from customers,—we did not use them ourselves. I say we did not use them. It is true that we did not cook prunes for ourselves, that would have been extravagant. Dried apples were our limit. The raisins were not served in puddings or otherwise. Yet both raisins and prunes disappeared from their shelf without being sold. It always happened when I was present.

I find the following entries:

AUGUST 12TH, 1883—MORNING

One freight wagon and one Indian.

NOON

One freight wagon I have bin fixing the store while Ralph is sweeping.

EVENING

One cow-boy and four freight drivers.

AUGUST 13TH, 1883—MORNING

Two men came here and stayed all night and ate breakfast this morning and are now off. One man came here alone and bought a few things and went on. Ralph is washing and I have cleaned up the yard.

NOON

Nothing atal has come this noon nor stage has not come one man just—

Not much excitement in this account of our life, even with visitors "on" and "off." I note I was at one time "fixing things," "cleaned up the yard." I did not mention cleaning up prunes and raisins.

Natural History

My sudden break in the important annals of Red Fork Ranch at noon of August 13, 1883, leads me to believe that day was one when the "fever and ager" visited me.

As to the observations set down by myself in this same book when I was eleven years of age, they cover Indians, beasts, birds, reptiles, and wild grasses. While not material which will be accepted by the Heye Foundation or Smithsonian Institute as accurate, it is a class of information of interest to a boy and in his language. Here we have it:

INDIAN TRIBES

Cheyenne	
Arapahoe	
Ciawa	(Kiowa)
Sock	(Sak)
Cherokee	
Pawne	(Pawnee)
Comanche	(Commanche)

Then come studies in natural history with my own comments:

PRARIE DOGS

Prarie dogs are littel things not much bigger than a musk rats. Their holes are littel mounds which they make themselves. They scratch their holes with their feet. They dig one long hole just like a hall and then make one room for themselves and for an owl that lives with them and one other for the yung ones. Their tails are like an squirls only they are strate. When you pass them a ways off they stand on their hind feet and bark at you. If you start at them they get all off their body in the hole but they leave the head out and watch you til you get up to them then quick as a flash they disapear from site.

LIZARDS

Lizards are littel things about 4½ inches long. They are littel thin things and have a long tail. Its hole is strait down and then turns off to one side. They feed on worms and bugs. There is a lizard called the cow killer which is black in the middil and red on both ends which stings. Its stinger is an inch long and stings very hard. And there is a horn lizard which horns. And there is a poisen lizard which when it bites it poisens very badly.

RATTEL SNAKES

The rattel snake grows from 1 foot to 10 feet long. Their hole is 14 feet in the ground just big enough to go in. When the littel are raised and are out with the old ones and there is danger the old one opens its mouth and the littel ones run down the old ones mouth. When the danger is over the old ones opens its mouth and they run out again as happy as ever.

WILD CAT

The wild cat lives in the woods and make their nests in the trees and live in the tops of them. Their cry is very queer and it is like a childs cry when hurt. They run in the tops of the trees and keep crying all the time.

LEOPARD

The leopard stands 4 feet high and are very feirce. They will attack a man in the night while they are sleeping and tear them all to pieces. When they have yung ones they are very feirce and attack you any time.

SPREADING ADDER

The spreading adder is a fearful snake it is worse than the rattel snake. You go along and you see one the first time and you think it is dead. You will go to kick it over and it will whirl around and bite you. When you hit them their head spreads out 4 times as big as its head.

THE DEER

Deer inhabit the forest. They are very wild but if you catch a fawn you can tame it so you can do anything with it. The buck deer have horns every year in the spring. When they get old the bucks rub the horns on trees and they come off and you can find them in the woods.

PAMPAS GRASS

This grass grows all over the prarie very thick and very high. It grows so high so a man on horse back can not hardly see another in front of him. In the spring it is green and in the fall it gets dry and old so a man building a fire will start a prarie fire.

BUFFALOW GRASS

This grass grows all over the prarie in bunches.

CHICKEN HAWK

The chicken hawk that lives down here is fearful large they are large enough to carry away 6 chickens at a time.

CHICKEN SNAKE

The chicken snake are very thick around where there is any chickens. They follow a hen with a brood of chickens and springs on the littel ones and swallow them up. They are very poisen when they bite a person they will kill them. When they see a person they keep darting their fangs out and bite you. They are 1 foot long when they are born and they do not grow atal but grow big and fat.

The prarie chicken live on the prarie in the grass. When you are riding along they will run out in front of you.

I suspect I had set out to jot down items with which to regale my playmates back home when I should again reach there. My observations seemed inclusive of all about me, conclusions often wrong. I saw most of which I wrote, Ralph told me some, imagination filled the other items.

The reader will recall my first day's efforts to dig out a prairie dog. I did not get far in my excavation. I imagined the rest of what I recorded. The boy's description of the animal and its ways are not so far from the truth. I was fantastic in my theories of the lizards, also in reference to rattlesnakes holding the young in their bellies. Years of subsequent experience never revealed this capacity.

I am sure I never saw a leopard. I must have been referring to the mountain lion, of which there were, however, none in that country.

As to the spreading adder, there is some proof of my observation. I recall walking about the cattle corral one day with Texas John riding by my side. I came across an adder curled in the sunshine asleep. Unthinkingly I kicked it awake before John could warn me. Then it was that the reptile's head swelled in anger as it struck once before gliding away.

Deer were ever present with us there. Hardly a day passed without our seeing some of them. The winters found them congregated in droves. Many times we came across fawns and sometimes we chased these on pony back. Antelope were numerous.

Buffalo had left the country a few years before my coming,

and their bones were strewn about on almost every acre. Uncle Ben Williams, while visiting us one time, was reminded of an experience with a buffalo bull on a spot he pointed out just south of the Cimarron River near the trail. He had purchased his first shot-gun while in Caldwell. The salesman had told him he could kill buffalo with it when using buckshot. Uncle Ben believed this and on the down trip was watching for an opportunity to prove the assertion. He was riding in a buckboard and as he passed up the rise from the ford, he noted a group of buffalo feeding a short distance away. Driving his team back out of sight, Uncle Ben left them and stalked the buffalo on hands and knees. He was able to approach within fifty yards of the bison and selected a bull for victim. He fired at the spot back of the shoulder as the forefoot was brought forward. The animal threw up its head and let out a bellow of rage. Instead of dying according to schedule, he rushed his man, chased him back to his team and then galloped away.

We had one species of wild life at Red Fork which was the progeny of former inhabitants of pig sties. In my time there, these had become a considerable herd of wild hogs. They had reverted to such an extent that no one could lay a hand upon them. When a hog was wanted for meat, he was hunted as other denizens of the wilds.

These wild hogs had plenty of nature's food, in the shape of acorns in the black-jack woods, roots, and the offal of the ranch house, and never rejected a feed of corn. In order that they should not wander too far afield, Ralph fed them shelled corn at certain times. Taking a bag on his arm he would advance to the center of the bottoms in the open and start calling to the beasts. Soon they would come running from the cover of grass and woods, from every direction, and one heard others answering from the further places as they also heard the call to feast. I was able to tally over one hundred.

I see by my notes that I had the pampas grass growing over the prairies. It was found only on bottom lands bordering streams. The buffalo grass grew all over the prairies to the Rocky Mountains.

My days were filled with investigation of the new and strange and then we had the ladies with us.

Chapter XIX

LADIES

LONG NINE stood in the doorway of the log house at Pond Creek Ranch and eyed us as we rode up. With arms akimbo and level gaze she met our advance, then turned her head and spat tobacco.

Long Nine was a tall, angular female character of the Chisholm Trail. Six feet of muscular femininity won her the sobriquet she was known by from Caldwell to Texas. She was the only female who would go unattended into any camp that wanted her services, and protect herself at all times. Earning her living as cook for whoever would employ her, she accompanied cow outfits if desired, and also worked at ranches along the line. Miner had her at work when I first met her, and I saw her often as she passed us.

No bi-furcated skirt cow-girl was she. Just a plain calico gowned one. Her hip was not adorned with a flapping holster and six shooter. Boots did not adorn her feet, just plain shoes. But a look at her stern, determined face, a glance at the evident muscularity of her body, caused one and all to respect her.

Pete, the attendant at Skeleton Ranch, once told us of persuading her to leave Miner and come to him. She did not stay long, there was a sudden termination of her stay with the man at Skeleton.

Pete must have become careless or reckless, both perhaps. He told us the trouble started one morning when he objected to the quality of her cooking. No sooner had he voiced his objection than he was seized by shirt band and trousers, and thrown bodily through the door of his cabin. By the time he had scrambled to his feet, the door had been slammed and latched so that the owner had to cool his feet outside until the stage came in from the south. Then the indignant lady strode forth with carpet bag in her hand, demanded and received her wages, stepped aboard the stage and was borne away.

She was then a frontier woman over forty years of age. Her life had been spent in single blessedness at army posts and in frontier towns. No one knew her full history or name. To one and all she was known simply as Long Nine.

Red Fork Ranch was never graced with the female sex but once in the time of our history. It was practically an Eveless Eden.

The exception came when a party of ladies arrived under escort from Darlington Agency to spend a few days. Our cousin, Anna Williams, with Sue Miles, the daughter of John D. Miles, the Agent, were the ladies, and their escort was Lafe Merritt, a young newspaperman. The party arrived in a buckboard.

The advent of ladies among men who seldom had enjoyed such companionship caused much excitement that was kept well concealed. Anna Williams had just come from her graduation at Garnett and was the life of the party. A more vivacious young lady never lived than she. She kept all the men on the jump, and as for me, I was her devoted slave.

They arrived just before supper time, and the two ladies turned to and produced a meal which for variety and tastiness was the best ever eaten there.

Chape made an immediate hit with the damsels and spent the evening in playing on his violin and banjo for their pleas-

Ladies

ure. A jolly crowd they were, and the evening breezes caught the sound of female voices blended with Chape's mellow tones, singing "Oh, Susannah, Don't You Cry for Me," "Old Uncle Ned," "Old Black Joe," "Swanee River," and other favorites to the accompaniment of the banjo.

The night was warm and we sat outside between the log houses with Texas John, Pike, and some strangers for an audience.

During the evening it was interesting to note the innate gentlemanliness of these rough men of the frontiers brought out by contact with pure womanhood.

Pike, who was the oldest and possibly the roughest in personal appearance, showed the most courtly of graces combined with genuine consideration for the desires of the ladies. He placed boxes for them to sit on and equaled Sir Walter Raleigh in placing his bandanna on the ground for the feet of one of the girls as she sat down. His battered sombrero was in his hands most of the time.

Old Chape was always courtly so that he did not make such a contrast to his usual self. He was simply a shade more assertive in his natural consideration for the feelings of others.

Texas John was not to be outdone in signs of Southern courtesy, the result of his boyhood contacts in Texas. His demonstrations were a trifle stiff and showed lack of practice. He did not realize that his best move would be just to act his natural self.

Ralph, presuming on the relationship of one of the young ladies, was entirely at ease in their company, and being young and single, he and Merritt both twitted the ladies and made good-natured fun.

The upper floor of the large cabin had been allotted to the use of the visiting ladies, and when it came time to retire, they started single file up the rickety ladder stairs. Anna held back and said that she was too tired to climb the ascent to bed. Ralph promptly proposed to Merritt that he carry the young lady up. Taking the suggestion literally, Merritt grabbed Anna up in his arms before she knew what was coming. He started for the stairs, but his burden was so lively, kicked so hard, and scratched his face so heartily that he was forced to drop her.

The following morning two buckboards were brought with pony mounts to carry the party to the summer camp. The ladies, Ralph, Merritt, and I made up part of a gay party. There was much skylarking on the trip and I demonstrated expert horsemanship for the delectation of the ladies, but I was considered as all younger brothers seem to be,—properly to be seen in a moderate degree and not to be heard at all. My exhibitions met with a cold reception.

When we arrived at the summer camp, Perry was abashed into a silence that was broken only when he was spoken to. He and I became the two silent admirers, ready to do or dare. With the camp for a base, picnic parties were carried out on trips to the cedar grove, and every one had a delightful time for two or three days. Here the ladies were allotted the tent for their sleeping quarters, while the men took their blankets and slept on the ground near by.

One day there came a rain storm of such violence that Cottonwood Creek was bank full in a short space of time. The ladies had taken refuge in the tent. At first all was serene, but when the waters rose from the raging stream and covered the land thereabouts, the tent and the cottonwood tree that sheltered the camp fire were on the only dry bit of ground. Suddenly, as the men stood under the trees watching the water rise, piercing screams began to issue from the tent. The screams denoted terror and agony of mind.

I was the first to rush through the water to the tent. Lifting the fly, I beheld the two women standing on two cots holding their skirts tightly about them. Crawling about the floor were two large rattlesnakes, some garter snakes, and a half dozen land tortoises, all driven there by the flood. Then did I perform deeds of valor as I killed, one after the other, all the crawling vermin there. Was I acclaimed a hero? I was not. No sooner had I removed the danger than I was ordered peremptorily from the sacred precincts, and retired a most crestfallen champion of the fair sex.

When the time came for the departure of the ladies, Ralph and Merritt accompanied them on the trip across the country to Darlington, leaving Perry and me behind. We were twitted and joked by the party, and thus received the only direct attention that had been our lot during the visit.

When the fair ones had gone from sight, I turned with tears in my eyes and looked at Perry. I did not need to be ashamed of my show of feeling, for there stood the grown cow-boy with his cheeks also wet with tears.

Chapter XX

THIS famous center of the Cheyenne and Arapahoe life of those days has already been mentioned as the scene of some of my experiences. During the late summer and fall of 1883 my presence there was more frequent as I left Red Fork Ranch to find new experiences. Beef Issue days were the gala occasions which I most enjoyed with the Indians. Beef Issue Day was Christmas to the Indians, as they then received from Uncle Sam the dole intended to keep them quiet under their changed conditions of life. To me it was Circus Day, for I saw the Indians with their families from all sections of the reservation assemble in all their finery. On these days I met or saw most of the famous red men of the two tribes.

The government beef for the Indians was driven into the corrals near Fort Reno, to be issued thence "on the hoof." This system enabled the Indians to reënact the buffalo hunt of earlier years, and there was excitement for them as well as for me. I do not say that Uncle Sam counted me in the deal, but I never failed to see to that myself. Uncle John Williams, Tun-hun (pounding man), was at that time government issue clerk in addition to his duties as government blacksmith. He it was who held the precious pieces of paper with the names of those who were entitled to a beef on the hoof, and who called out the name at the proper time and place. Uncle John was Santa Claus on Issue Day and I basked in the reflected light of that glory—Assistant Santa Claus, by my own appointment.

No doubt there have been Beef Issue days which were cloudy and drear, but my memory makes them all sunshiny days with everybody dressed in their best raiment and with holiday manners.

These days began with subdued excitement evident all about the camp. Criers could be heard giving out news from one village to another; boys, girls, and dogs were on the move early; the older people were looking to their hunting gear. The women were cleaning their camps and harnessing the travois to the ponies chosen to bring home the spoils. Young ladies who were "promised" were braiding and oiling their hair, marking the part with vermilion, a final dab of which showed in dots on cheek or forehead. I saw all this as I scampered about the camps, always keeping track of Uncle John to note when he would start for the government corrals. Although the crowds were on the way early, his appearance, driving his buckboard through the waters of the ford as he crossed to the south bank of the North Canadian, was the signal for the rush of the crowd of "curtain raisers." I either sat with him on the buckboard, or rode a pony beside him. I preferred the latter, for then I could get to more places. As we advanced over the prairie, thousands of Indian men, women and children were to be seen coming from all directions, to join the main crowd about the "man of the hour."

As Uncle John and I rode along the trail toward the government corrals, many of the older men of the tribes would fall in line on either side of us. They had no duties to perform other than to grace the occasion with their presence. They came clothed in all their ceremonial dress and riding in "party style."

As I have never seen a picture of Indians riding in party

style, and as it is not likely that the movie of to-day would be so realistic, it may be well to explain this feature of the day. Every plains Indian was a horse Indian, and as such rode horseback from early babyhood. For all other purposes, they rode bare-back or with a blanket which only covered the pony's withers. They had saddles of their own manufacture, made of two saw-buck arrangements fastened together for pommel and cantle. Two stirrups were attached to the seat. These stirrups were short, possible adjusted for some child of the family to use at other times. But grandfather must use the saddle for certain occasions, such as riding to Beef Issue. So he did. Taking a tame pony of the family string, he placed the saddle on it and fastened it. Seating himself in place, the rider would then show he knew what stirrups were for by drawing up his legs until each foot was in its proper place. As the Cheyenne are six feet in stature on the average, one can imagine the spectacle they made with their feet secure in these shortened stirrups. The grown man was borne along, his knees rising close to his shoulder level. Many rode this way to the party.

I well remember one strapping buck riding close to me on one of these occasions. The pony was guided by a nose rope, while his master sat atop with knees drawn shoulder high. Though he had never felt the need of any head covering in all his life, he had a black plug hat fastened with a thong under his chin. His braids of black hair hung well below it. There was an added note of elegance in the shape of a lady's sunshade, pink, with ruffled border, which he held stiffly erect with one arm resting between the elevated knees. Several of the chiefs carried silver-headed canes in the crook of one arm as they would a baby. Former attendants at some treaty wore army coats with epaulettes on each shoulder; others had enormous silver crosses fastened by a thong about the neck, lying on their chests. There was only one use common to all the various articles named—ornament. After they had affixed their mark to some treaty, they were made the owners of these ornaments. As Beef Issue Day was of official significance to all of them, it was the time to show the officially bestowed presents. Thus did they indicate to fellow tribesmen and doubting whites that they were among the elect. A crowd of the leaders would arrive with us at the corrals and there dismount and form a circle on the prairie, seat themselves, and start the ceremonial pipe among them as they talked. In this manner they gave their sanction to the occasion.

Other bucks rode up stripped as for war or for the chase. These would be individuals who were to receive an animal for food. Women came riding ponies dragging travois on which they later would carry back to camp the coveted meat. With the women would be children, either seated with the mother on pony back, or on the platform of the drag. All were dressed in the best they afforded and happy in anticipation of the day's developments.

Arriving at the corrals we found the herd of cattle therein and a crowd of Indians ready to assist. A steer would be singled out and driven into a chute, where he would be held as the government brand was seared on flank or belly before he was turned loose. Uncle John would then cry out the name of the man to take the animal, and as it raced from the branding chute into the open the prospective owner would ride forward on a pony bare of saddle, as was the rider of all but breech cloth. The animal was smarting from the pain of branding and usually came forth from the chute at full gallop, bellowing rage.

The men chose a variety of weapons for killing. Some rode forward sucking the muzzles of forty-five Colts, others held Winchesters. Little Big Jake and some other older men still favored their old hunting bows and arrows. With the first steer turned loose, the real fun started.

A vast stretch of level prairie lay before the animal, and soon he would be lined out in the direction of his old home, going as fast as he could travel. As he gained headway, the Indian rider raced up alongside. Silent as death he would reach the proper position and fire. They always tried for a shot in the lungs as the forefoot on one side was brought forward exposing these vitals, or they tried to reach the heart by the same maneuver. The bowman played for the same spots in the same manner. Often the arrows were buried up to the feathers in the animal's side. Pistol, rifle, or arrow, each soon took its toll of bovine life.

The workers in the corral were rapid, and Uncle John soon was calling names in quick succession. One after another of the animals was released and pursued by riders until the whole plain was covered with racing animals and mounted men. Soon the air resounded with shots, and the cries of women and children, as they saw their father or brother bring down the coveted meat.

As the individual took after an animal, that man's women and children took after him with the travois. As soon as the animal was killed, the women came and proceeded to skin and cut it up for transportation. The children took part by snatching tid-bits for immediate consumption, for all Indians liked meat rare, if not absolutely raw. Some parts were devoured raw from the still warm carcass. These Indians were skillful butchers and it was not long before the racing animal was converted into separate hide and quarters.

These beef hunts often took up the greater part of the middle of the day, and at the height of action there was excitement for me. I never could keep up with all the individual incidents, and that worried me. At one time I followed Little

BEEF ISSUE DAY

Darlington Agency

Big Jake and watched him make his kill as I rode within fifty feet. He started his pursuit with three arrows in his mouth and a buffalo bow in his hand. His pony was an old buffalo hunter, with only a rope about its lower jaw for control. The man rode bareback stripped to leggings and moccasins. He let the animal go until it had an eighth of a mile start, then took after it at top speed. I was put to it to keep near him. The animal had slowed to a trot until it heard the pursuing gallop of the pony, when it again broke into a mad pace. Silently the rider rode up alongside, and instantly loosed an arrow into the lungs from the right side. This arrow showed only the feathers as the rider's pony leaped to one side. The animal was crippled, hampered, in movement by the wood shaft. The rider raced his pony in a small semi-circle back of the wounded animal and at full gallop came up on the left side and placed another arrow in the heart which dropped the animal in its tracks.

As the hunt progressed, there was much talk in the circle of older men near the corral. The scene brought up memories of the old buffalo grounds. The majority of them were of the opinion that buffalo still "came up out of the ground" over in the Staked Plains country. There were those who claimed in all honesty that they had witnessed this phenomenon. They felt they could still find the wild game if allowed to go off the reservation.

By the time the last shots had sounded on the plain, many families were to be seen wending their way homeward with the addition to the family larder. Soon all of us scattered.

During the remainder of the afternoon, all the camps were scenes of animation. Here and there tepee flaps were raised shoulder high and joined with neighboring ones to connect two, three, sometimes four homes into one banquet hall. Everywhere could be seen the fresh meat hung in strips where the sun could dry it, pots of meat were simmering over fires, the family tom-tom began to beat out its invitation—come, come, come. All were welcome as long as the feast lasted, and the succeeding nights after Beef Issue were given over to feasting.

On these nights there were dances, story telling, and pow-wows, young lovers stood encased in common blankets in the shadows, younger brothers passed remarks about older sisters or brothers in such an embrace.

The outstanding memory of those Beef Issue Days is the holiday air which pervaded the camps and homes of these people. Struggling to meet the demands of unprecedented conditions, puzzled as they took the strange trail of life, daily losing faith in their white captors, this day offered relaxation and a temporary supply of food secured as they used to secure it under free conditions. Opportunity was given them to parade before each other in gala dress and exploit their skill. The tom-toms beat all the old calls, sociability reigned and the young folks made love as in happier times.

A daughter of Ben Clark, we called her Jennie, was taken into Uncle John's home after her mother had been killed in one of the fights in the seventies. Aunt Sally Williams became her white mother. Jennie was larger than I and older, and often initiated me into the mysteries of Indian life and customs. It happened on a Beef Issue Day, after the kill, when we were at the house for the evening meal, she told me in confidence of a well-hole full of black snakes over by the Arapahoe school building next the white burying ground in the Agency. This information made me the spectator of an Arapahoe family tragedy which had all the essentials of pathos.

I had proceeded after supper to the well next the school

building and, having investigated with a long stick, had found her information correct, for I speedily stirred up a hissing that made me back away in terror. As I dropped my stick, another sound struck my ear which made me forget snakes. It was the wail of an Indian woman mourning her dead. Close by where I stood was an entrance to the school building, and from this ran a slight young Indian woman clothed in elegant Indian dress. A fringed smock covered with porcupine work and beads came halfway to her ankles revealing combined leggings and moccasins of the same texture of smoked orange-yellow buckskin. Her hair was sleek with bear oil and in two braids. Her copper-colored cheeks were set off with red coloring in the centers, but her face was set in lines of the greatest anguish as she wailed her sorrow. She seemed to say some one was dead.

Divining that the cause of her sorrow was in the building, I walked in as the woman rushed away toward the Indian camps with her cry. In the first room a tableau revealed itself which is vivid to this hour.

The scene was lighted by an oil lamp placed on a table in the center of the room. On one side stood the Arapahoe School Superintendent. By him stood an Indian boy eight years of age. In front stood a tall young Indian buck, evidently the father of the boy. The white man was holding the father back by the force of his gaze. None of the actors seemed to notice my intrusion.

The Indian father stood erect as an arrow and I could not help but notice the elegance of his dress. I never have seen finer. A fringed buckskin shirt, of the same coloring as the woman wore, had the appearance of velvet. Leggings, moccasins and gee-string of the same quality, all were exquisitely worked with beads and porcupine quills. The moccasins each had a four-inch tassel of the same material as the rest of the dress, attached to each heel in place of buffalo tails. A leather belt held a tobacco pouch of the same quality as the clothes, and a knife sheath with the weapon in it. The boy was a small replica of his father in every item of dress but the tobacco pouch and knife.

The child stood erect with his gaze seeking the face of his father and the white man alternately. The Indian father had his hair done up with an eagle feather standing in the scalp lock. He was a "brave" of the tribe. As I came in the door, this father's gaze never left the face of the white man, and his eyes blazed murder. As I reached the center of the room at one side, the white man laid his hand on the boy's shoulder. Instantly the father snatched the knife from his belt and sprang with it to give a thrust in the side.

He was an Indian athlete in prime condition, quick as a cat, but the white man was quicker and stronger. He met the thrusting arm and twisted it so that the weapon fell to the floor, and, as if the two had rehearsed the action, both fell back to their original positions and again stood looking into each other's eyes.

There they stood as the white man talked in quiet, even tones to the father. "I must do to your boy as I have done to the others," said the white man. "We must cut his hair and take his Indian clothes from him."

After gazing a few moments more the Indian brave seemed to accept the inevitable. He bowed his head, picked up his knife from the floor, and strode out into the dusk. Then I learned the story.

This young Indian couple had promised to put their only child in the school to learn to read and write,—to follow the "white man's road." They had been told the requirements but had fondly hoped the boy might be allowed to keep his Indian dress and his long hair. Like all wives and mothers this one wanted her man and boy to appear their best on such an occasion. She had spent weeks making the apparel they all wore that night. She must have been one of the most expert guildwomen of the tribe. The dresses were beautiful, and each made a splendid appearance.

Waiting until the evening of the last day to fulfill their promise, the parents had come to the school with the boy, arriving just as I did on my quest for snakes. The mother had fondly hoped as she worked that the fineness of her work in contrast with the miserably fitting government clothes and brogan shoes would appeal to any eye, and win for her. She had seen the children of her neighbors so changed in looks by the change of clothes that one hardly knew them. Give the Indians credit for knowing how ridiculous they looked in the clothes given them by a bountiful government. They had pride and resented the change. To the mothers it was akin to losing their boys by death to see them thus humiliated in spirit and forced to act the part of scarecrows.

With these feelings, mother and father had stepped into the room with their bright boy looking his best. They had asked at once if the boy might not study the new ways clothed in his lovely native dress. They were told there was no hope of their desires being fulfilled. Realizing the futility of further entreaty on the point, feeling she would now lose her boy, the mother took one last look at him and fled from the room, wailing as for his death.

Thus, with everybody else happy on Beef Issue Day, feasting and dancing all about them, this family faced what was to them a real tragedy. The red people had many such tragedies in those days.

Little Robe and Red Lodge were the first in my thoughts among the older warriors, because of my early associations with them. Many others gained a place in my memory by reason of their thoughtfulness and willingness to help me on one way or another. Every one of these red men was a gentleman. This assertion I maintain in the face of the record which made old timers brand them as savage.

A more desperate man never lived than Powder Face of the Arapahoe tribe. A stocky, broad-shouldered, dark-complexioned man, he grew up in the tribe and took part in all the battles during the sixties and seventies. He was versed in the use of all the Indian weapons of those days—war clubs, lance, knife, bow and arrow, revolver and rifle.

In one of his fights during the seventies he became separated from his fellow tribesmen and was surrounded by six or seven troopers armed with rifle and cutlass. His pony was shot under him, and as it fell the warrior landed on his feet with lance and knife in his hands. Silently he met the attack of odds, warding off blows with the lance and hoping to come to grips with his knife. Round and round him the troopers circled, raining blows with their cutlasses on his head. He withstood the attack for several minutes before he finally sank to the ground helpless.

Left Hand was the War Chief of the Arapahoe when they first came to the reservation of which Darlington Agency was the center. Later on Powder Face succeeded to the position, due to his desperate, determined fighting qualities.

I met him first in one of the trading stores during my first summer there. As I came in the door I found the eyes of an Indian fixed on me. He was sitting on the pine counter, with moccasined feet dangling. His blanket had dropped about his loins, one arm was held akimbo with that hand resting on his knee, the other rested on his thigh with open fingers close to an ornamented knife handle in his belt. This posture was characteristic of the man while among strangers.

Darlington Agency

He gazed severely at me and then broke into a grin as he seemed to recognize me. I soon learned that he had previously observed me about the Agency. He held out that knife hand to me and said, "How, Nevaw! Me Powder Face."

I noted that many of the other Indians kept clear of him and did not speak in his company. Many times his face was fixed in a scowl. I presume he had won his way at the expense of some family feuds. But I never feared him from the time of our first meeting. Soon I was to know him better.

On first meeting I was struck by his scarred face. Great cuts had been made which criss-crossed scalp, forehead and cheeks,—souvenirs of his meeting with the cavalrymen. His voice was a deep bass, welling up from his throat.

Scampering about the camps one day, I was brought to a halt by a spectacle before me. A tepee was opened in the front with the door flap propped on sticks to form a sunshade. To the right was a totem stick with some scalps showing in hoops of willow. In the shade I first noted a slender Indian woman with a pleasant face, seated between the knees of an Indian buck, who was combing her hair. From the latter came the voice of Powder Face in the hail, "How, Nevaw." Thus I found my new friend at home.

He did not rise, but continued his ministrations to his wife as he bade me be seated. No introduction was made, but I knew the woman to be his wife, of whom I had heard. Aunt Sally had said she was a nice Indian and that Powder Face was good to her.

The two had been married many years, and had no children. Powder Face had never taken another wife, and this one was his willing slave to the day of his death. He helped her with many duties commonly falling to the lot of the women and was a lover always.

On this first meeting with the couple, he did not seem to

mind me and continued to stroke her hair into place as he spoke words of endearment. He oiled her hair and braided it for her. Then they arose and ushered me into their tepee. This tepee was the first fully equipped one I had investigated, and some of its arrangements are fixed in my mind yet.

All tepees I ever recall of these two tribes were set with the entrance facing the east. Powder Face first stooped and entered his home and waved me to the north side, as he took the south. Then his wife entered and passed back of him and took a position west of her husband. We all sat down on buffalo robes which covered the floor, except in the center, where some flat stones covered an area eighteen inches square. In the center of this square sat an iron pot on a flat stone raising it above the fire bed. A fire of small faggots burned there, each faggot pointing toward a common center marked by the pot. To the west of the fire was another group of flat stones with a few ashes strewn over them. Next to this on the west was a rough truss of four upright sticks held by cross pieces, all bound together with rawhide thongs, supporting some objects wrapped in skins. These were the Medicine bag and trophies of the owner. The decorated scalps I had first noticed outside were later brought in and placed on this pile of keepsakes. Altogether, this pile made an altar in the savage home. About the sides of the tepee, which was about eighteen feet in diameter, were placed several devices which I took for rawhide seat backs without legs. These were back rests on top of the floor covering of hides. Here I was in the home of a leading chief of the Arapahoe tribe and soon I was to be entertained further.

Indians never had any regular mealtime, eating whenever they felt like it. When there were provisions in the tepee, something was always simmering over the fire in the pot. So it was in Powder Face's tepee that day. After we had seated ourselves, the wife took a turkey-wing fan and whipped the fire into life as she pushed the unburned ends into the center. Soon there was a steaming which betokened preparation for eating. Powder Face first took some fire and raked it onto the other flat stones. On this he placed a piece of meat taken from the pot in the center. This was a burnt offering. Then each of us took pointed sticks and fished out some of the meat on plates of wooden board. Before eating, the man of the house held a piece of the meat on a stick above the burnt offering and spoke to the Great Being above, then lowered it toward the earth and asked Mother Earth to give him strength. The meat was beef, and in the same mess was what looked like potatoes to me. I afterwards found that these were the roots of cat-tails from the near-by river banks. After I had eaten my fill of meat and cat-tail roots, the squaw gave me a large hunk of dried wild cherries. These had been dried and mashed into a mass which was kept in parfleche trunks about the tepee. We washed this down with water from the river. This couple had traveled to Washington the year before, and had brought back fine ideas. They allowed me a towel to wipe my face and fingers on, though they performed a like office for themselves with the hair on their heads. After eating, Powder Face and his wife smoked alternately from the same pipe.

This couple had no family album to entertain the visitor with, but proceeded instead to show him the trophies on their altar. All was open to the visitor except the Medicine Bag. This was sacred to Powder Face alone. I was entertained as courteously by this savage couple as I have ever been since. Savage and desperate as he was, Powder Face was a gracious host.

Over toward Caddo Spring, near the Cheyenne School, was pitched the tepee of Bear Robe during the summer of 1883.

The nominal head of this Indian family was not boss by any means. Bear Robe was a six foot man and had put on weight until he was all of two hundred and ten in poundage. Mrs. Bear Robe was just as large as her husband, and they did not carry on quite as Powder Face and his wife did. No, there was a sister of Mrs. Bear Robe who was wife number two. The second wife was almost as large as her sister. The situation reminds me of a story Colonel Dodge tells of Stone Calf asking him for the gift of his sword. Curious to know the reason, the Colonel quizzed the Indian Chief. "Me lick one squaw, me lick her heap. Me lick two squaws, they lick me dam site," explained Stone Calf.

For all that, the lodge of Bear Robe had much attraction for me. The man was an arrow-maker and wife number one made me moccasins, while their son Clyde entertained me in several ways.

I do not know the exact reason for the Bear Robe family's living apart from their neighbors, unless it was to be near their son while he went to school. Clyde was the name bestowed upon him by his teachers. It was the custom at the schools to provide the boy with a name which was then used with his father's name. Clyde had gone to school for the prescribed four years and had graduated before I knew him. Leaving school he had largely reverted to the customs of his people, among which was that of the primitive Cheyenne method of courtship. His inamorata was in the school at the time, and, being an orphan, was not allowed to leave the grounds. If the family lived close by for Clyde's sake while he was at his lessons, they must have remained for his sake in order that he might pay court to his girl. More of this later.

Bear Robe had always been an arrow-maker. He made thousands of all kinds, of which I at one time possessed over one hundred and fifty. The great majority of arrow shafts were made of willow withes gathered along the streams, peeled and brought to the tepee for drying. Sticks of proper size were selected by the arrow-maker and cut into lengths varying from twelve to eighteen inches. The nock was cut for the bow string, and a split made at the opposite end for the heads of hunting and war arrows. Then with a knife he scarified a wavering streak down each side from within three inches of the nock down to the end. His skill was shown in this scarifying more than in any other way. In finishing, he left a groove along the length of the arrow on each side which was one sixteenth of an inch wide and scarcely one thirty-second of an inch deep. It curved its way in a succession of parabolas and arcs, as clean cut as though laid out on a drawing board by a skillful draughtsman. Then the shaft was scraped smooth with the knife or rubbed in a bed of river sand.

Wild turkey feathers were prepared by splitting them and scraping the inside surface. They were then cut and trimmed into the desired size and shape, leaving plenty of the quill bare for fastening to the shaft. Bear Robe at all times had his mouth full of deer sinews and strips of deer intestines, soaking until they were thoroughly softened. With these he fastened, one after the other, three feather guides for the arrow. The ends were placed within one half inch of the nock, equally spaced about the wooden shaft, and firmly held by a wrapping of the soft sinew, which dried and hardened. The end of the fastening was pressed down where it would glue in place as it dried. The far end of the feathers was then secured in the same manner.

Next came the fastening of the head of the arrow, and for this purpose the serrated haft was placed in the slot cut at the far end of the shaft. It was held there while a strip of intestine was wrapped firmly about the shaft over the haft of the steel head. I did not see any flint heads used and was told they were too hard to get. I learned the significance of the different manner of fastening the heads. The hunting arrows had the heads placed flat with the bow string; war arrows had the head lying at one hundred and eighty degrees opposite. Hunting arrow heads were long and slender with a shoulder set back to hold in the wound; war arrow heads were short and broad, with no shoulder.

This arrow-maker also made many arrows for hunting birds and small game. These would be finished with a triangular-shaped blunt head of wood. In fact, the head was the original size of the wood shaft which was trimmed down to the size of all arrows. They were all excellent pieces of workmanship. All of Bear Robe's arrow shafts were decorated with yellow ribands painted between the feathers. The blunt heads of the small game arrows were painted this same yellow. Bear Robe seldom spoke as he worked and offered no stories of his past, but answered all questions fully. Once it occurred to me to ask why he decorated all his handiwork with the yellow color. His answer was that that was his "medicine." He added, "Me take scalp, got heap pony." That was what the color signified for him.

Indian wives were never known as Mrs. So-and-So, having their own individual names, as did husband, brother, and son. I never did know this lady's name and so have referred to her as Mrs. Bear Robe. She was one of the moccasin workers among the Cheyenne women and made splendid specimens. Soon after our first acquaintance I was measured for moccasins, and in a few days had them on my feet. Through life I have been able to identify Cheyenne moccasins wherever I have seen them, through familiarity with the work of this woman. One pair of her moccasins lasted me many years.

Clyde was a lad of about twenty when I first knew him.

Darlington Agency

As stated, he had been to the white man's school and then returned to the customs of his people. As with most male
youths, his superior years would not tolerate his paying much
attention to me, though he allowed me to watch him at my
pleasure.

The first summer of our acquaintance he was engrossed in
perfecting himself in horsemanship, and to watch him was
always interesting. Though he had a string of ponies of his
own, there was one which was his favorite, a light gray mare.
He would spend hours with this pony, drilling himself and her
in the technique of horsemanship. Riding her on to the plain
he would race in a circle, leaping from the pony's back to the
ground, first on one side, then the other. Again he would
race along the ground afoot and leap upon the pony's back
while it was at full gallop, never touching it for assistance.
He used to place a rawhide rope about the animal's barrel, and
practice hanging from the side as the animal ran at full speed.
As they raced he would hang low on one side, then change to
the other. At times Clyde recruited other Indian companions
of his age, and put them through regular drills. They made
quite a spectacle as the eight or ten rode together in formation
and wheeled into line, guiding their mounts in a circle as they
all swung on the side in executing the maneuvers of the "sur-
round." Galloping about, leaping on and off the ponies,
swinging on the side, all in regular unison at the command of
Clyde, they were a stirring sight. As they rode their hair
flew about, and they broke into frequent weird cries.

Clyde evidently had thoughts of war much of the time,
but it is certain there were many thoughts of love also. I am
not sure of his having exchanged rings, as was the custom, but
the dusky maiden at the Cheyenne school had his attention.
He had made himself an Indian flute with which he spent
hours in telling her, and all the world thereabouts, of his in-

fatuation. It is not likely that the girl showed by word or look that she knew this stalwart Indian loved her. That was not the way. Evidently he was satisfied, however, for he would spend hours during the day lying on his back in the grass near the school, and blowing the plaintive notes from his flute. There I would go and look at him as he lay with legs drawn up and crossed, holding the flute in both hands and blowing the same refrain of two or three notes over and over again.

He used to take his position in the grass during school hours, where he was technically out of bounds and could not be stopped without a troop of cavalry from Fort Reno. His wail could be heard in every part of the building. My interpretation of it was the words of "I love you-u-u," repeated over and over again. The performer's basic idea was to get that message across, and the longer he could sustain the final note, the better he felt his purpose to be fulfilled. Each attempt seemed not a real success, so he tried it again. After school hours the sound of this wailing was heard inside the big barn-like building and investigation revealed my love-sick Indian lying on a bench in the basement, keeping up the song with unabated energy.

I never heard the sequel to this story.

After breakfast one morning I strolled from the portal of Uncle John's house on to the trail in front and down it to the ford of the North Canadian where I stepped to the side of the water and came to a halt. As I stood there gazing across to the south bank, down the river, up the river, back of me, again in front, Phil Block stepped from the loading platform of the Commissary building and into the road. His appearance there, noticed from the corner of my eye, caused me to turn toward my friend and greet him as he approached. Walking slowly, he came forward until he also stood on the bank of the river at my side. Even the man seemed bent on the same errand which had brought me there. Interest was lying concealed in a clump of plum bushes on the south bank right in front of us. We did not know it at first, but it appeared in a few seconds.

Phil and I stood side by side turning our heads first in one direction, then in another, every fraction of a second, as was the training of that day. Suddenly Phil dropped to the ground like a log, and a puff of smoke appeared from the clump of bushes as the sound of a rifle shot rang out loud and clear. Phil had turned on his back as he lay by my side, and without moving more than my head I looked at him. Blood was starting from a bullet hole in the center of his forehead, a black mark appeared under his skin from the bullet hole under the scalp back as far as I could see. I had already stood close by men shot to death, and I thought Phil had passed on. Of a sympathetic nature, I was instantly on the point of tears over the demise of a friend, as I stooped to aid him if possible. As I bent over the prostrate figure, I noted an Indian as he arose from concealment in the plum bushes from which the shot had been fired. I even knew the buck as a relative of Gray Beard. He seemed fully as interested as I in Phil's condition and stood erect with his eagle feather waving in his scalp lock, rifle held in one hand by his side, one moccasined foot advanced and his gaze fixed intently on us.

I took Phil's head by one hand and turned it over to one side, lifted it from the sand, and noted that the bullet had struck him in the forehead and followed around the side and top of the skull to the back, just below his scalp lock, where I saw and felt it laying. I laid his head down and had started to turn with the intention of running for help, when I saw Phil's eyes open. One eye socket was filled with blood where it had run from the wound, and Phil raised a hand and dashed the gore from his vision. Two or three passes and he pulled himself to a sitting posture, then arose erect on his feet and stood weaving unsteadily. I took his arm to steady him as he continued to shake his head and clear the blood from his eyes as it ran down in a steady stream.

We started to walk toward the Commissary and, as we did so, I saw the Indian raise his Winchester far above his head and cast it from him into the turgid water, as he yelled an imprecation which meant "Bad Medicine." He had made a center shot, but Phil's hard head had turned death aside. Of course the rifle was no good; he should have shot him with a "good old arrow."

Thus did the Gray Beard clan try to even some score with Phil.

Bent's Fort, situated near the present city of Pueblo, Colorado, was a famous spot in our western plains history. The original Bent there was a French-Canadian who married into the Cheyenne tribe in an early day. Three sons came of this union, of which two were famous in all the tribal history from the forties to the eighties. Robert and George Bent married into the tribe of their mother, and each took his part in the wanderings and fights during these years of almost constant warfare. Each was a chief in the councils of the tribe. George Bent was a close friend of my Uncle Ben Williams, as they two were often associated in early affairs on the reservation. George Bent kept his family in the Indian camps at all times. During one of the fights in the early seventies, his wife stood in their tepee with a baby son in her arms, while the fight raged around her. A bullet struck her dead, leaving the boy without a mother. Other women of the tribe cared for him until the Cheyenne school was opened at Caddo Springs, when he was placed there for education. The child was named after his father, George Bent. At school he came under the special care of a teacher named Amelia Kable, and he soon looked upon Amelia as his white mother. I became acquainted with him there and soon we were pals. He was my most constant playmate as we investigated the Indian camps out of school hours, and took part in the games of the other boys.

We heard of the old warrior, bent with his years of hardship, who would soon sing his death song and wished to be buried the same as his friend, Brinton Darlington, and beside him. He had learned to love the Quaker and wept as they buried Tosimeea. Anticipating his end, he had a coffin brought to him in his tepee and had it for a constant companion in the years preceding his demise.

Boylike, George and I would run to this tepee and be allowed to gaze upon this unique adornment of the home. Set on end with the cover removed, the coffin stood back of the altar in the western end. Many times we gazed with awe upon the coffin, as the old fellow would proudly display it.

Together we called on Little Big Jake, to ask him how he had lost his eye. Many times he told us in word and with signs how he had emerged from his tepee one morning to go to the river for his daily plunge. As was the custom, this occurred at the first streak of dawn. He had stooped low to come from his tepee. The sharp end of a trimmed twig of brush had transfixed the optic so that it was drawn out on his cheek before he could arrest his motion. The eye-ball slipped back into place, but the sight was gone.

Indian funerals attracted us at other times; we joined the family and friends as the women wailed their grief and mutilated themselves, as was their fashion. One of these occasions I recall watching a mother stoop over and saw off the first joint of her little toe with a butcher knife. She augmented this wound by slashing her forearms.

Then I witnessed a preliminary funeral procession while with George.

"Ie-ie-ie-ie-ie-ie-ie-ie, oe-oe-oe-oe-oe-oe-oe, o-o-o-o-o-o-o-o-o-o-o-o-o, e-ne-e-ne-e-ne-e-ne-e-ne-e-ne, a-a-a-ayah-ayah." The sound was wafted to us as we stood on the trail leading down the North Canadian one afternoon,—a weird, eerie sound which grew stronger as we listened. Soon we saw four Indian women advancing with solemn tread, bowed under the weight of enormous bundles of wood. Each bundle was at least four feet in diameter and made of sticks broken into four and five foot lengths. They had gathered these on the river bottoms miles away and carried them the whole distance. On they came, keeping step, one behind the other. As they walked, each held her burden in place with one hand on the binding thong over the shoulder, while with the free hand she beat her breast in unison with the others. Their lips were open, their eyes staring, their cheeks wet with tears, and their lips driveled as they emitted the series of terrible sounds. Starting in a low cry held as long as the breath could carry it, they moaned despair for a like interval, then had a period of calling for pity, ending in a choking sound as though the grief were suffocating them. The last sound was fairly beaten from their throats with their fists. As they passed us, the combined sound rose in unison with every shade of despair in the tones. I had never heard it before, and my limbs were stiff and the goose flesh played tag all over my body. The wail of the Indian woman mourning her dead may have been assumed, but it impressed on my mind an unforgettable memory.

These were the wives of some departed brave, and they were carrying the fuel with which to burn his tepee and all his personal belongings which were not buried with his body.

Darlington Agency

Another tragedy of life among these wild people came to my notice while at the Agency, although it had its inception at Red Fork Ranch.

One summer day of 1883 a large delegation of Indian freighters passed us, going south on their way to Darlington Agency. Among them was an Indian youth dressed in the Army uniform, indicating that he came from some government school. He was of my age and we soon struck up an acquaintance as the party tarried for a time about our store. He told me of having just completed five years of school at Carlisle, Pennsylvania, under Captain Pratt. He had met his people at Caldwell and was returning to the villages for the first time after leaving school.

We two boys began to compare notes. Securing a piece of paper from the store, I started to write words to show my writing ability and knowledge of spelling. For every word I wrote, the Indian put down another in his own handwriting. His penmanship was like copper plate and better than mine, and his spelling was without fault. I was so interested in my new friend that I accompanied the party to the ford of the Cimarron River. As the river was high, the party was delayed for an hour or more in crossing, so we were able to continue our mutual examinations. These were typical boyish attempts to "stump" each other. I led off with examples on paper. The trail of learning led all through addition, multiplication, subtraction, and division. Mensuration and fractions were touched on. In every branch this Indian youth was ahead of me. He was proud of the fact, and used every word of his English vocabulary, I think, to show a thorough working knowledge of it. We parted with the best of good fellowship, and I promised to see him in Darlington.

I did not run across him in the camps while I was at Darlington that summer, fall or winter.

I am quite sure it was in the month of May, 1884, that I heard an Indian crier intoning the news of a Hoch-e-a-yum, or Sun Dance. He stood at the eastern end of the Agency street in front of the white burying ground, on a slight eminence. Soon his voice reached me at Uncle John's house, and true to my character, I was immediately on my way to see what was doing. As I walked by the Commissary and Trader's Stores, I saw many Indian youths standing against the buildings in a posture which seemed typical. Each stood on one leg with the other drawn up, foot resting above one knee, leg akimbo fashion, blanket drawn about the body up to the eyes. Silently they were watching and listening. The crier told of who was giving the invitation and where the dance was to be held.

As I started down the street I could see some boys who had signified their intention to enter the tests. They had thrown off their blankets and were dancing in a circle, calling out their intentions, and uttering cries of exaltation just as I have seen old time Methodists do at a camp meeting, when they were filled with "the spirit."

Passing along I naturally glanced at others standing crane fashion to learn whether any of them felt "the spirit" moving them. As I peered into eyes above the blanket shrouds, one pair was suddenly hidden by the blanket as I drew near. Feeling thoroughly at home by that time, I reached up and pulled the blanket away. There was the face of the boy who had stumped me in learning on the bank of the Cimarron.

He cast his eyes down as he saw I recognized him, and would not speak to me. I saw that he was now in full Indian dress and that his hair was long once more, done in the conventional two braids. To all my queries he shook his head, and said, "No sabe." I was compelled to revert to the Cheyenne tongue and sign language. I thought I could divine the cause of his reversion to type.

Darlington Agency

Returning to his people he had not been able to endure the jibes of his fellow tribesmen, and the insistent cry of boys as he passed by, "Ayah, paleface. Ayah, hair cut like buffalo soldiers." As soon as he could he had his mother and sisters clothe him in Indian dress, and he let his hair grow. By the time I saw him he was Indian again, and would not even acknowledge knowing the tongue of the white man.

I did not blame him as I admired the symmetry and elegance of his clothes, the fitness of his apparel, in contrast with that which he had worn home. The brogans of the government with two buckles in lieu of buttons, clumsy and hard on the feet, had always seemed to me the worst of all. His mother had fitted him with smoked buckskin apparel and he certainly looked striking.

The meeting with me brought the struggle to a climax and as if to put an end to all argument, this boy closed our interview by casting aside his blanket and running into the growing circle. He raised his voice above the rest and proclaimed his intention to enter the coming ordeal and prove himself worthy to join the "braves" of the tribe.

Back in the misty past of the tribe, the custom had been inaugurated of taking some test which constituted an initiation for candidates for the coveted place among men of the tribe, one with all the rights of a man among men. Until this test was passed no boy or man could wear the eagle feather of a brave in his tribe. This custom held among all the so-called plains tribes of our Western Indians. These were variations and refinements of detail, but all tribes individually volunteered the tortures. The event came once a year. Among the Cheyenne it was set at a time decided by the Keeper of the Sacred Arrows. Among all the tribes it was a time of consecration of one's life to a man's work. Those having the desire or ambition meditated long hours in solitude while gazing into the sun on bright days, imploring The Wise One Above to send them a sign of some kind which would clinch the decision. Others acted as my friends were doing on the day I speak of, on the spur of the moment, seized with the spirit of the occasion, showing intense desire as the urge of the voice of the Great Spirit ordered them ahead. The momentary urges were called good medicine. The whole process of looking for guidance into the ordeal and taking the ordeal itself were considered a search for and fulfillment of the behest of the Great Spirit. The tortures were accompanied with ceremonies called Medicine Dances. The tribes who also worshipped the Sun as a symbol of The Wise One Above gazed into the sun unblinkingly while in lonely meditation and while they endured the supreme tortures. The ceremony became quite well established as the yearly Sun Dance and was more generally designated thus. The native Cheyenne name was Hoch-e-a-yum.

The occasion was graced by a gathering of the whole tribe at some prearranged place where every one came and was supplied with food for days as each took part in some manner. The affair was also under the patronage of some one individual who undertook the arrangement of details of the program and the feeding of the people. This patron was some prominent man in the tribe, White Shield in this event. How like their white brothers, who must pull off a Charity Ball with the names of many prominent citizens to back the game. Patrons in each of these events served the same purposes. The Indian patron also took care of the fees for the presiding Medicine Men.

I joined a crowd that was pulling down tepees and moving on toward the chosen spot in the West. Long lines of Indian families spread out on the north side of the North Canadian valley until I saw them as far as the eye could reach, ahead and to the rear, for I was not slow in getting into the hegira on my pony. On we journeyed, with White Shield and the other head men far in advance. We traveled some twenty miles and turned off into a draw through the woods to the north of the river, then proceeded through the woods onto higher ground, where the creek ran through a bottom land with hills on each side, the stream bisecting the meadow. There we saw the wild flowers of the country covering the whole ground, so that one had a vista of white, yellow, blue, and even red coloring wherever the eye could reach. The head of the moving horde had come out into the open before I got there, and close by, seated at the top of a bluff, I saw White Shield, Little Robe, Little Big Jake, The Whirlwind, and Stone Calf seated in a circle, smoking the ceremonial pipe. Rapidly the people filed on to the bottom land, and by midafternoon the whole valley was filled with tepees set in circles, with entrances facing east. This was to be the camp for days.

Circles within circles of tepees surrounded an immense structure in the center of the great Indian village. This had been erected the day previous by the men of the tribe, for no woman's hand must touch anything to do with the sacred ceremony, although they could look on and cheer their men to great deeds. (I read a story last summer which purported to describe a Sun Dance, written in authoritative vein. The writer gave women as principals among the candidates. This is erroneous. Either the author is misinformed or is working up a present day version influenced by the "movie" men.) The Medicine Lodge was of canvas covering a space perhaps fifteen feet wide and making a circle of fifty feet diameter. The canvas was held erect by cottonwood poles firmly lashed in place with rawhide ropes, with stout cross pieces secured to them eight feet or more from the ground between the uprights. This covering with its supports rimmed a space where other poles and uprights were placed in the open, like so many crossbars in a gymnasium. The canvas was for the purpose of covering the audience.

It was a solemn time, no one laughed, every one spoke in a low voice or sat in deep meditation. The audience gathered silently and speedily disposed themselves in rows around the large circle. Prominent men took the front places, others ranged back of them. Many of my boy friends were there and Red Lodge motioned me to a place back of him.

At the west side of the circle gathered the group of candidates, each stripped to the waist. They were in low-voiced consultation with older men and the Medicine Men. The Medicine Men sat cross-legged, with a buffalo skull on the ground in front of each, and a long-bladed, double-edged knife lying near at hand.

Each boy there had selected some old warrior as his mentor and guide; these were the older men sitting near by or standing. There was much close consultation. Darkness had fallen; the scene became weird in the dancing light of numerous fires.

Suddenly there came a deep, resonant "bome" from a kettledrum where a warrior struck it, then at long intervals we heard a regular bome—bome—bome—bome in slow measure and the great ceremony was on. The first drum was soon joined by one after another as each caught step and joined in, until there were five or six all sounding in unison. After the first, single, loud sound, that drum and the others gave their sounds in lowest tones. As soon as all were sounding together, one young fellow stepped from the group of candidates and began to rock from toe to heel and intone words. He told of his name, his intention to take the test which would make a man of him, and asserted that he would not fail, for his medicine was now strong. He then looked at his mentor and received a sign to proceed. With that he strode over to a Medicine Man and stuck out his chest, and things happened quickly as the drums kept up a ceaseless drone.

Darlington Agency

The Medicine Man grasped the skin of one breast into a bunch, jabbed the long knife through from side to side and turned the knife over to make a good hole, then passed a wooden skewer through the flesh. The skewer was left in the cut and sinews attached to each end were brought together and tied into a knot. The same process was used on the other breast. The two bunches of binding sinew were made fast to separate rawhide ropes and the candidate then walked to one of the cross bars in the open and was quickly hauled from his feet as he tensed his arms to his sides, all the while looking up to where the sun would be at mid-day. With vigorous tugs, the attendants pulled their man up until his extended toes were a foot from the earth, and there they made him fast. Then the candidate began to shout his story over and over again, the drums now beating in loud unison and with a fast, regular beat, to the time of which the candidate worked his arms so that his body bounded up and down in little jerks. He must hang there until he broke through the skin of his breasts and released himself. Quickly the other five men were treated the same way, and the drums beat louder and louder as one after another was started on his way to torture.

No one retired that night, the morning sun arose on every one there in place, the candidates still at their efforts to tear themselves loose. Drummers spelled one another so that there was continuous drumming. Some of the warriors started to dance early in the evening and passed the night without respite, for they were also entering into the occasion as a religious sanctification, a step higher in the world. These men danced and recounted an endless story of past doings, filling out lines with a "hah-hah-e-yah—hah-yah," all in unison with the beating drums. What a scene! Jerking, yelling candidates, hanging by single lines of rawhide fast to their chests, two score of dancers working around in a circle, leaping and posturing, telling in pantomime of past glorious deeds, rows of solemn warriors seated and passing the pipe from hand to hand and talking signs all the night through. In the dim light of fires outside the sacred circles sat other rows of women and children, cheering the candidates on with words of encouragement which blended in with the pandemonium of sound.

The sun rose on this scene, no one moved, and, as soon as he could each candidate fixed his gaze upon the emblem of his faith as it rose in the sky. Their binding ropes slowly spun them around at times, but they all tried to gaze fixedly into the blazing orb as they continued their intoning in voices that grew weaker or ceased at times. Near noon, one of them fell heavily to the ground, the first to pass the ordeal. He was quickly picked up and rushed off to a tepee where a Medicine Man bound up his wounds, and he was given his first nourishment for days. During the afternoon I noted that my friend of Carlisle School experience had ceased to jerk his body up and down. His whole body hung limp, and as it turned from side to side one could see the binding sinews holding his flesh high from his chest. He had fainted. Quickly he was let down and borne off to another tepee where he finally came back to the consciousness that he had failed. His years at school had weakened him and thus paid him for his study.

That same afternoon saw the end of the torture for each of the others. One after another they slumped to the ground and were taken care of. The second night in the camp was given over to sleep and rest. I took mine with Red Lodge and his family.

The morning after, each successful candidate came back to the Medicine Lodge, his breast bound together with sinews, and came again to the Medicine Man, who was now seated in front of his buffalo skull with a tomahawk in his hand.

There I saw the reason for Cheyennes being called Cut

INITIATION INTO MANHOOD

Darlington Agency

Fingers in the sign language. Each boy stepped up, stooped over, and laid the index finger of the left hand on the skull, and it was no sooner laid than the first joint came off with a well-directed vigorous blow of the tomahawk. I never again saw the one who failed and do not know what indignities were heaped upon him. I thought of him much on my return to the Agency, and afterwards.

In this story the reader has the struggle which faced each young graduate returning to his people in those days. Ridicule was as hard for them to bear as that facing present day graduates who appear dressed *sans* "plus fours." With the Indian youth it became a question of deserting his own people, his only friends. This boy decided in favor of his people at a time when they must all change their ways to meet the growing demands of the hated "white man's road." This one had hardly failed in his attempt to become a brave before the white race was to encroach still further on their freedom. Only a few years were to elapse before our politicians yielded to the popular demand to open up their country for settlement in the "Rush of 1889."

One evening, as the sun went down in the west, George Bent and I lay on a hillock overlooking the main Indian villages in the bottom lands north of the Agency. Each of us lay on his stomach, with elbows for a rest, and from our vantage point beheld the hundreds of tepees below us in a valley, while on the ground, level with our eyes, we could see the black mass of the village pony herds a mile west. Like boys the world over, in every clime, we were taking in everything about us and discussing the why and wherefore of many things.

As the sun sank lower below the horizon, we were entranced into silence by the artistry which painted the sky before our eyes in all the colors never successfully copied by any artist, or assembled in just the same way. It was one of the gorgeous sunsets which have been painted at the end of every clear day since the beginning of time, no two of which are alike in detail.

As the light faded, the pony herd became a blur, then was blotted from view in gathering gloom. Tepees became silhouetted by the hearth fires within. Suddenly we became conscious of a stillness which held us breathless. Every dog, frog, animal, insect, and bird was hushed. In the camp there was not a sound. Back of us and overhead in an oak tree we heard the faint sound of two birds saying good night as they nestled together; even the wind seemed to stand still as man, animal, and the universe appeared to be listening for the first sound of the evening. We boys looked at each other and craned our necks as we endeavored to discover any sound. Has the reader ever noticed that dead silence as the sounds of day hush at twilight, just preceding the voices of the night?

Suddenly we raised our heads as a ghost of a sound reached us, so faint that it seemed not to exist. It had an eerie effect. We settled back in the grass as if to escape some strange visitation. Soon it came to us again, and this time we were sure of the sound, but not of the cause. Again we heard it, and then knew it to be the news crier for the villages, standing on the edge of the plateau near the pony herd. He was calling to the crier of the next village a mile beyond him, and the sound came to us in increasing volume as the atmosphere seemed to clear of interference.

The musical sound of the Indian crier, intoning words of interrogation and imparting news, rose and fell in regular rhythm, the sound volume varying as the speaker turned slightly from side to side. After an interval of speech came a rest of a few minutes and in turn we heard the sound of another crier who was receiving and sending from the further village. We could not distinguish the words of this man, but those of the nearer one, although a mile from us, would come clear and strong to our ears, and soon George was telling me the news, for his ears had been keyed to the receiving of such messages.

Back and forth the two men called news, each waiting at the end of his delivery to receive the word *"piva,"* which signified he had been heard. They called this word in a long-drawn-out intonation with emphasis on the last syllable, as *"P-e-e-e-e-VAHH."* Half an hour was spent in transmitting news.

After they had finished, crickets began to chirp; frogs told us "too deep," "too deep"; coyotes began to cry; and a near-by wolf found his voice in a deep bass bark. As village dogs returned defiance, tom-toms commenced to take up the invitation for the dance with a "bome, bome, bome, bome"; others joined in from all directions until there was life again. Every one was happy and serene. Above the noise of the drums were heard the calls of friends from one tepee to another and the shrill treble of children giving vent to their feelings. Those people were always happy in their own home towns, and there was no curfew bell.

Every evening at twilight the Indians exchanged news in this manner, each crier acting as announcer for all his people. The custom made another lasting impression on my mind, which is recalled almost every time I visit a theater. When the kettle drums boom through the room, it calls to my mind the picture of those far-away evenings in the land that was. So, to me, the kettle drum has the position of most importance in the orchestra.

I really had a bully time those days and evenings about Indian camps. We boys gathered our gang together and roamed about at will. Each armed with bow and arrows, no bird, rabbit or prairie dog was safe that crossed our trail.

No writer I have ever read has mentioned one weapon of the Indians, which was very common among the members of the bunch I ran with. This was the sling, like my idea of the weapon David used on the giant Goliath. These were made of a heavy piece of buffalo hide for the holder, with strings of leather strips. Most of us carried one. I have seen an Indian boy knock down a bird in flight with a stone thrown from one.

Blunt sticks were also used as weapons. These were slender, peeled shafts of wood, four or five feet long, and were thrown as a spear.

At times we would form two lines of boys armed with spears, standing about twenty-five feet apart, one line facing the other. Each side would choose a chief who would take turns throwing a hoop down between the lines, and every boy there took his turn in trying to impale this on his spear. The hoops were of varying diameters, from six to eighteen inches. They were of limber willow and criss-crossed in the manner of a tennis racket with strips of rawhide. Starting with the largest hoops, they were thrown as fast as the chief could propel them from him. Every boy was given the chance at each one. As the contestants succeeded in the test by bringing down the hoop, they would drop out of line. After all had speared the hoop a smaller size was used. The six-inch hoop got by many and defeated their efforts, but always there were one or two lads who could hit any of the hoops at any speed. A hit must always be through the mesh of the hoop.

Again we armed ourselves with long willow sticks and balls of clay, forming two opposing sides for a mud-ball battle. At a given word, we started a simultaneous attack with these weapons, and soon the air would be filled with flying balls of clay that smarted when they struck. We often were plastered over much of our bodies, and nursed not a few bruises. Contestants were their own umpires as to who won, and the arguments often waxed noisy, but I never saw one of these youths angered by the game.

Then there was the kicking game. Two lines of boys would line up back to back and at a given word would flail out with one foot while balancing on the other. One must stand poised on the one foot, for the point was to throw the opponent off his balance to the ground. To watch fifty or more boys kicking at each other all at once was to witness a scene of action. As with other boys, they grew excited and yelled in delight as each succeeded in putting an opponent out of the game. The last on their feet were winners, and the evening was not complete until a championship had been established by the most agile one there. I can feel some of those kicks to this day.

Another diversion was swimming during the summer months. Every Indian boy and girl could swim almost as soon as he could walk and ride. I learned my first strokes from them. The old Indian method of propelling through water was swimming dog fashion with the hands while they kicked out with both feet at once. Indian youths seemed to kick high, often striking the surface of the water with the feet in unison. There were times when boys and girls disported themselves together. Swimming recalls an experience in a pool left on a sand bar in the North Canadian River that summer.

Quite a large body of water remained in this sand bar's embrace. The river had gone down only a day or two before our invasion. At least a dozen of us jumped in and soon found the pool to be two or three feet deep, with enough water to paddle in and splash each other. We had hardly reached our depth and begun yelling and splashing when one boy let out a yell that exceeded all the rest and grabbed beneath the surface. A tremendous splashing told us he had found something of interest. So he had. I have never seen, before or since, a cat fish the size of the one we finally, working collectively, landed from this pool. Left by the receding waters, the fish had lain quiet until the boy had stumbled over him. The contact set the fish to threshing about in a formidable manner. All of us tried to take hold of him at once and were baffled by the strength and sleekness of the body. Again and again we rushed into the water and tried to overwhelm him, only to be thrown about, or to receive, as one or two of the boys did, gashes from the long horns. We threw rocks, belabored him with poles, but were not succeeding very well in the contest, when some older Indian youths came to our assistance. Finally we had the giant poled out on dry land and among us all kept it from water until it was exhausted. This fish weighed forty or fifty pounds and had a head as large as that of the boy who found him. We awarded the prize unanimously to its discoverer, an Indian youth of my age and size. When the fish was dead, the boy took it by the gills with his hands, and with our help hoisted it onto his back, holding it with both hands over one shoulder. As he trudged proudly away toward the village, the tail dragged on the ground. How is that for a fish story? Somewhere among the Cheyennes must be some one who can back me up in this. Friend George was not with us that time.

Thus I roamed about the Agency and Indian camps every time that I left Red Fork Ranch. In the process was accumulated my knowledge of Indian life in the home, a smattering of the Cheyenne tongue, and the sign language of the plains tribes. Everything seemed natural to me and my participation in affairs was as one of the family. The older Indians treated me with consideration, due, no doubt, to my relationship to those whites who had been with them so many years and had been adopted into the tribes. I had been adopted by

Red Lodge and was well considered by Little Robe and Powder Face.

It was interesting to note the attitude of the older Indian youths toward me. It was no different from that of white youths having the advantage of two or three years' seniority. They all snubbed me.

It is certain that this environment during my formative period made an impress on my whole life. One result has been to make me take new and strange happenings in silence, and to face the inevitable in the same way.

A young buck of perhaps twenty years neared me one day wrapped in his blanket, with something, it seemed, carried in one of its folds. As I passed him, he seized me by the neck and forced my face into this fold of the blanket and I found my nose nestled in the coils of a rattlesnake. The young man wanted to see my reaction, and, as no outcry came from me, repeated the dose two or three times. When he finally released me, I stepped back and grinned into his face. He gave a grunt of approval and answered my grin.

In the tepees I learned never to pass in front of the older people or between any seated person and the fire. As a guest my place was always on the north side of the circle. We youngsters never spoke to each other in the presence of elders or to them unless we were addressed first. Many hours were whiled away watching and listening to the older men as they smoked and talked of former days and of doings about the camps.

Babies never cried and I saw the reason why. When a papoose set up its first outcry, the mother silenced it at once by placing her hand over its mouth and grasping its nose between her thumb and finger. There she held them till the infant choked, when they were removed, but instantly re-applied if another outcry followed. So long as the infant attempted to cry, it received the same treatment until it was subdued. They soon learned to stifle their cries on a motion from the mother's hand, and finally gave up so futile a habit.

All youths were well treated by their elders. Fathers never spoke in admonition, mothers sometimes pushed recalcitrant girls so they fell, or possibly in a tantrum pulled a boy's hair. Never did I see an Indian parent whip or really maltreat a child in any manner. Yet the same father would pick up a two-year-old boy as he toddled about, place him on a pony's back and start the pony going. He would watch unmoved as the child screamed in terror and clutched at the mane, only to fall to the ground. Again and again the process would be repeated until the child learned to hold on. They were taught to swim by being thrown into the water. When almost suffocated, they would be pulled out long enough to get their breath and then thrown back in again until they learned to keep afloat. It sometimes took a few days to complete the education, but the child had no rest until he mastered both accomplishments. Boys and girls both were included in this education.

Indian women and men both smoked. They would fill a pipe, and after it was going well would take a deep inhalation which filled the lungs with smoke, after which the pipe was passed to the next. The smoke was allowed to pass slowly from the lungs through the nose and mouth. Children learned the accomplishment before they were five years of age.

Indian boys of my own age were boon companions. I found them as sociable as any other group of boys could be. Tramping about the country together, we found all things of mutual interest. I was interested in them; they noted every action of mine which was new or strange. They were no more polite than the average boy, and commented on any feature of my deportment that struck them as objectionable.

Darlington Agency

While in school at Corning, Iowa, I had learned a song, the words of which were set to the tune of "Old Uncle Ned." The title of this was "Lazy Bill." The words ran something like this:

"I once knew a boy, and his name was Lazy Bill,
But he's dead, long ago, . . . long ago.
The last time I saw him he lay behind the mill,
I said, 'Are you going to school, Bill, to-day,'
Then he saw the teacher coming, kicked up his heels,
And ran like a woodchuck away.

Chorus:

"Then pack all his books in a r-o-o-o-w
Fix all his trinkets for a show.
There's no more work for poor Lazy Bill,
He's gone where all truant boys go."

There were other verses now forgotten, each telling some part of a very complete story, and ending in the line, "He ran like a woodchuck away."

In our forays I regaled my companions with this song, and on its first rendition discovered that its popularity lay in the last two words of the last line, which were intelligible to them. To their ears the last line sounded like this ". . . Chuckaway," and it meant something to eat. They had noticed cooks of cattle outfits calling "Chuckaway, Chuckaway," at meal times. The Indians afterward adopted the combined word to designate any kind of food.

As I rounded out each verse of my song, my auditors applauded with cries of "Ho-ho, Chuckaway Nevaw, Chuckaway." Thus I knew they enjoyed the song and repeated it as many times as I had breath for. It has been the only occasion of my life when I have been urged to give encores. My own family have been known to implore me to an opposite end. I have even been informed that my vocal efforts put every one else out of tune, by reason of resemblance to the famed "Rocky Mountain Canary." The Rocky Mountain Canary is known otherwise to westerners as the burro; to present crossword puzzlers as half a jackass.

One can understand my lasting affection for those who applauded my efforts in days gone by.

My time at Darlington Agency was busily occupied with accumulating events which were rapidly forming that first ring of experience. When the squaws began to bring in great bundles of brush and build windbreaks with them about groups of tepees, preparing for the winter storms, I returned to Red Fork Ranch. The cattle driving season was over, and aside from the stage coach arrival and departure, and groups of Indian hunters, there was not much to occupy our time except for the incidents outlined in the following chapters.

Chapter XXI

SKI-O-MAH of the Cheyenne, known all over the plains as Little Robe, came often and remained for a week at a time during the winter of 1883-84 while I was there. Thus I was thrown in close contact with one of my Indian idols.

During the cold evenings we three sat about the stove in the store or cook house and conversed on many subjects, mostly those having to do with the past life of the War Chief of the Fighting Cheyennes. I drank in all these conversations, as Little Robe talked with the mellow voice of the Indian and graceful movements of the sign language. Through these mediums I heard and memorized much of Indian history, customs and thoughts.

As I now recall and piece together all that he told us, he stands revealed as a veteran fighter of over thirty years of almost constant warfare. At times he would bare his body to show his scars, and then tell the incidents in which they were received. His form was of medium height; his muscles had the contraction of age. Ordinarily he spoke in even tones, dispassionately, as a philosopher would. Truly he had gone through enough to make him revert to the rôle as a protection, a partial solace to his sorely puzzled, troubled spirit. One could not associate with the man and not recognize the patriot and friend of his people.

Sometimes his eyes would flash, so that, boy as I was, I thought fire actually darted from his dark, deep-set orbs as he related some indignity put upon him, some instance of treachery on the part of the white man. Those flashed signals depicted his unbroken spirit, what he would like to do to avenge the wrongs of his people.

From him I gathered most of my knowledge of the Cheyenne tongue and what I know of the universal sign language of all the plains tribes. Almost every word he spoke was accompanied by a sign for it. If asked, he would pause to explain the sign and literal meaning.

In his young manhood he had stood the torture of the yearly medicine dance which made him a brave. He showed me the scars on both breasts where binding thongs had torn through the muscles. These had healed nicely, showing the efficacy of Indian surgery. He said that he had been about the camp within two days of the time of his torture, which had lasted over one sun before he could tear loose. Other scars on his arms attracted my curiosity and he told of the times he had cut pieces of skin from his arms as some special, savage penance.

He related many of his early exploits, the gathering in of enemy scalps (I saw over fifty of these at his home tepee), his many "coups," times when he cut the heart from a fallen foe and took a bite therefrom to gain some of the courage that had been there. One can see that he did this, not for the purpose of mutilation, but as a tribute to a fallen hero. Yet Little Robe often ended such a story with the statement, "It was when my heart was bad." His words would be accompanied by touching his heart with his right hand, then flipping the fingers from him in the sign for bad (get away from me).

Reverent, kind, courteous, this man never let any little service of mine pass without rolling out a hearty "Ha ho. Ha ho. Thank you. Thank you." At the ranch and in his home tepee he built up in me an admiration, trust, and adoration which has endured through the years and will last till "The long, long trail a-winding."

He had learned to like Ralph (we both came within the blood-tie regard which he extended to all our kin), and discussed his problems with him as an equal. That he respected Ralph's judgment was evidenced time and again by an emphatic nod of the head and flip of the forefinger for the sign of "yes," and a deep, throaty ejaculation of "Hah." This was given in such a manner as to remind me of my own father at home when he expressed his approval with a fervent "Amen."

Speaking one time of the association of Indians with the white race, he told of first contacts in the time of his father while the tribe was still on the Missouri River (Big Muddy). He said that his people had recognized the newcomers as superior in attainment, in fact, they knew so many things new and strange to his people that they had named them Spider People; *i.e.,* very wise.

One of the chiefs had shown wisdom at the time by voicing a prescient view. This man told his people that the strangers would eventually bring trouble to them. This dire foreboding had not been believed, for a generation, while the few whites lived among the Indians in peace, traded with them, and brought them many new things of use. Our friend had lived through those days of the mutual contentment of both races, but he had seen the fulfillment of the prophecy. He knew that the seer had spoken wisely. Little Robe and his people reverenced that man's memory.

Said he, "I remember the white traders who lived among us and married our women, who lived as members of our tribe. They were *piva tan,* good men. I sat one day with others on a hill and we beheld strange things passing along the valley of the Platte River, toward the West. We knew they were strangers, for they had the first wagons I ever saw, drawn by animals I did not know. These animals were the size of the buffalo, and when we drew close to them on our ponies we heard white men saying, 'Whoa Haw,' 'Whoa Haw,' and 'Gee.' We then knew the animals were called *'Wohaw,'* you call them cattle also. We crowded around the strangers when they made camp and one of our traders told us they were headed for the shore of the big waters far away in the land of the setting sun. We did not see harm in these people passing through our country, so we told them where to find water and grass many days ahead of them.

"Not long after we saw these strange people, soldiers came, and their chiefs asked us to make an agreement with them to always allow white people to make a trail through our land to the land of the setting sun. We saw no harm in that, the country was large enough for us all, and they agreed not to tarry in our country and to pass through. These soldier chiefs brought others who said they were sons of a Great White Father who lived many weeks, travel to the East. We went into conference with them while the soldiers looked on, they gave us presents and our hearts felt good. When they asked us to press our thumbs on a piece of paper to show we made friends with them, we did so, and told all our people to be good to the strangers, and not to molest them.

"Soon after the first, we saw many more coming along the trail. We watched them, for they were new to us and we were always curious. When we had the pow-wow with the soldier chiefs and the sons of The Great White Father, we had invited them all to sit in the lodge we had put up. We sat in a circle and The Whirlwind had lit the pipe and passed it to each man on his left. All had smoked, and we always knew that when any one smoked in the circle under cover of the lodge he agreed to whatever was spoken of. The Indians felt that way; it was their custom; no one had ever broken such an agreement.

"Another day, white soldiers came, who stopped at a point on the new trail. Without explaining, they simply told us they had come to 'sit down' at that spot in our country. We had not known they would do this, else we would not have agreed. When we told the soldier chief he said the Great White Father had sent them. Our people talked it over and agreed there was some mistake. These soldiers cut down many trees and built a big corral with wooden tepees inside. They had many guns. Then we knew they were going to stay, and we began to worry. We asked for another council to talk it over and find why our first treaty had been broken. There was not much explanation; they said we must make a new treaty. They asked us to give them some land along the Platte River to the Big Muddy East, and as far as we owned the hunting ground rights up to the Big Mountains, and a day's travel toward the up-hill side of the World.

"We were worried and sent runners to the villages of our friends and cousins in the Indian family, the Cut-Throats, Sioux, Cut-Noses, Arapahoe, and called them to a pow-wow. Many days we thought of our problem, while we chiefs retired apart and prayed to The Great One Above and listened for his voice in the grass. We decided not to fight yet, but to agree to another treaty. We sat in conference again and smoked the pipe, then placed our thumbs on a new paper, agreeing to give the land which was asked of us. From that day we knew no peace. More white people came and sat down where we had not agreed. Our hearts were bad, we painted our ponies for war, took our women, children, and old people away where they were safe, and fought for our land. The One Below seemed to work his will against us. The Great

One Above did not send us any good signs. We were beaten, and signed new treaties because we hoped the whites would become satisfied each time. We had to save our people. But we were at war all the time; our people could not stay in one spot for a home, even for seven suns. The snows of twenty winters had fallen on us before we came to Sand Creek with our lodges. We had gone to a pow-wow at Fort Bent just before that, they asked us to leave all our new guns and go into camp for the winter. We believed the first Agent, Wyncoop, and did as they said. Black Kettle quieted our young men.

"You know what happened. Our camp was attacked and hundreds of our unarmed people were killed, and they did not spare our women and children."

At this point in his tales the Chief's eyes burned with murderous fire, his voice rose to a thunderous volume as he shouted, "The white men lied to us, they were dogs, who called us savages."

After Sand Creek, the Cheyenne, Arapahoe, and Sioux divided, for there was fighting in the Dakotas and Wyoming, while other bands decided to hide away, if they could, where they could not be found. These bands never again joined the others of the tribes and have since been designated as Northern and Southern branches of the tribes named. The Southerns went into camp with Comanche, Kiowa, and Plains Apache, deep in the Indian Territory on the banks of the Washita River. There they set up villages which extended miles up and down the valley, where all were sheltered from the winter winds in deep woods, where fire and water were easy to secure. There they made winter camp with lodges in groups where a wind break of brush could be erected. The parfleche trunks were full of dried meats, and wild cherry, with roots enough to keep all in plenty until the next summer. Some felt safe, others had grown suspicious. The latter sent some chiefs to

Ski-o-mah, In-mut-too-yah-lat-lat

Fort Cobb to tell the commander there of their location for the winter. He approved of their action and told the chiefs to return to their people with assurances of safety. They did not feel any danger when they had reached their camps and there was unrestrained jollity.

Then came the attack of Custer's troops in the first light of a cold winter morning, the morning after the return from Fort Cobb. Little Robe was bitter over the memory of that terrible night and morning. Raiding troopers drove through the villages, applied the torch to the brush wind breaks, and destroyed all supplies of food, clothing, and shelters from the winter's blast. Naked women and children were killed by hundreds; the loved Chief Black Kettle fell as bullets cut him down. Little Robe's bands were with Black Kettle's; they took the brunt of the massacre. Little Robe had rallied his men and finally made the vicinity too hot for Custer's men. All this he told, and his bitterness at the apparent treachery shown him and his people led him to start fighting with all the savagery in him. He raided over the plains the next summer, killing and destroying wherever he rode. It was a terrible time for frontier whites and Indians as well. No quarter was asked or given on either side.

All this was told us at Red Fork Ranch by the principal Chief who had survived those former troublous days. His was a tale which revealed the real pathos of a proud people's gallant fight against great odds, overwhelming odds. They had only asked to be left alone, to be given a "square deal." They were fighting their worst enemy, avarice rampant in the American people. The winter following Washita, they were called to another conference. The great pow-wow at Camp Supply followed. There they met the army chiefs and agreed to "sit down" on reservations. There Little Robe had met Brinton Darlington and accepted him as their white chief.

This man had impressed Little Robe as being a man of his word, and he promised him to forsake the warpath.

After the death of Black Kettle, all the Cheyenne had agreed that if there was to be further warfare, they would want Little Robe to lead them. This made him the ranking chief of the Southern Cheyenne.

He stated that he did not feel any love for the white race as such. In fact he felt the isolation of his people by this time, and that they were looked upon by most of the whites as savages. He also felt that he had been treated unfairly. Nevertheless, he saw that it was useless to fight any longer, and because of his love for his own, gave his word to forsake the warpath.

When the Indians agreed to remain on reservations, the buffalo still roamed the land as they chose, and Little Robe had hoped that his people might still remain independent in their ability to obtain their living. The Indians saw that the buffalo were going to be exterminated if the slaughter was not stopped. They insisted that if they were to remain within the bounds of certain territory, the white men should be excluded from it, and that no white hunters should come south of the Arkansas River. This was agreed to by the United States Army officials.

This understanding made the Indians content and they had lived three or four years in peace and comparative quiet. Yet the white men kept encroaching on their land and slaying the buffalo for hides. Carcasses strewed the plains. This was done under their eyes and against their oft-repeated protests. While this was worrying them, a bunch of white traders had made away with the ponies of Little Robe's village, and his son had been seriously wounded in the ensuing fight.

Altogether, the Indians were rendered desperate at this

time, and some of the bands under Stone Calf and other leaders went on the warpath. Little Robe felt as they did, but saw the uselessness of revolt and held his own followers quiet while his authority as war chief was usurped by others.

Not only did he refrain from war, but during the ensuing trouble he protected the whites at Darlington Agency in person. Through his efforts, hostile war parties were kept away from the Agency. In the following years of sporadic fighting he remained steadfast and many times by personal persuasion or action saved the lives of the race that had brought woe to his people. While he would not lead his people in war, they respected him and would not harm him.

Now the government was insisting that he give away more of their lands. True it was that they were to be paid, and already they had realized on the leasing of the land to the cattlemen, yet he could not see how his people were to live. They had been reduced to beggars when the buffalo went and he resented this fact. The warrior spirit within him made him fight on when expedient; he had gladly welcomed every attempt to teach his people the "white man's road." For this reason he had recruited his young men at every call from the whites for their service. With a sigh he would say, "I have done my best for my people." He never lost hope and with the sigh would come a gleam in his eye which betokened the will to fight on.

While he had lost faith in the larger number of the white race, he acknowledged there were individuals who were to be trusted and revered. He claimed the same distinction for the Indian.

He knew that Wyncoop had not sanctioned the massacre at Sand Creek, nor had the Commandant at Fort Cobb agreed to the holocaust and killings at the Washita. Brinton Darlington had impressed him from the first day of their acquaintance as a man of his word. He was a friend of the Indian as well as a Friend in his faith.

Little Robe had also taken my Uncle Ben to his heart and under his protection in the troublous days when his young men would not differentiate between whites when some injustice had aroused murderous fury. Knowing that Ben Williams, known as Black Beard to the Cheyenne, was a "Dog Soldier" appointed by the Great White Father to keep bad whites from his country, he told him of a beautiful spot in the Panhandle country where he would be centrally located for his work. It was then in the buffalo and Indian country where raiding Indians often passed. The war chief told his friend to move to the spot and there would be protection for his family. (Uncle Ben told this story.) The protection never failed. Often, when raiding parties of enraged Indians broke the bounds of the reservation, Little Robe arrived in advance, pitched his tepee by the side of his white friends' cabin, and remained there until the danger was over. (I had learned all this and knew I was under his protection by reason of blood ties with his friends. My heart was good toward him.)

In his talks he also told us of the raid into Texas to steal horses from Mexicans, when he had taken his wife and daughter along at their insistence. He told of the fight in which he and his men sought to escape and did so, but his wife and daughter were both killed. He related how he had gone back and recovered the bodies of his loved ones and brought them with him to the Honneo River. There he selected a beautiful spot in a clearing on the north bank and reverently buried them under ground. In my time at Red Fork, Little Robe had often moved his village near the burial place, to be near them in spirit. Whenever this wild warrior told of the death of his wife and daughter Issenon, his eyes would fill and tears run down his cheeks in unrestrained grief. Again he would explain his feeling of grief when he believed his son was dead on the bank of the Ho-to-oa-oa and his reactive joy when he knew the boy lived. I knew this man was a fond, affectionate father such as I had back in Iowa.

When he told of the raid on the Mexicans to steal ponies my mind reverted to the cow-boys' viewpoint on horse stealing, and I asked, "Ain't it wrong to do that?"

Little Robe replied with an explanation of the Indian way of looking at it. "We have always thought it right to raid the camps of our enemies and take what ponies we could. It is an honor to bring back ponies. When we return from a raid for them, we count a 'coup' ever after and can place another stick in the pile when we are telling the story of our life."

As I had been raised in a religious atmosphere at home, I once said to him, "Do you believe in God, Little Robe?" He answered, "There is a Good God up above, we call him He-am-ma-wihio, which means The Wise One Above. He brings us good, and speaks to you when you listen. We go aside from the camp to hear his voice in the grass, or in the trees. There is also a bad God who lives under the ground, we call him Ah-tunk-a-wihio, The Bad Wise Man Below. He brings us bad things. We pray to him to leave us alone, and ask the one above to bring us good. Yes, there is also Mother Earth who gives us all our strength of body. The two Gods give us signs of their will, in the sky, on the ground, all about us. Mother Earth always gives us good." Thus I learned of the Indian Trilogy. Little Robe also spoke of all animals having souls which went to the Happy Hunting Ground. "That is why we ask the spirit of an animal to forgive the killing of it and Mother Earth to give us strength from the meat, before we eat."

Thus I spent glorious days that winter sitting with this old warrior, the ranking War Chief of the Fighting Cheyenne, learning of the history of his people, their customs, thoughts, past and present ambitions, loves, likes, and dislikes. The scenes of our gatherings are engraved on my mind forever.

At the ranch we would dispense with boxes for seats. If we gathered for an evening in the store, we spread blankets over the wood floor. We did the same thing over the dirt of the cook house. On the blankets we sat cross legged, in a triangle, where each faced the other. As the stories proceeded, we noted the innate grace of the raconteur as his hands moved in continuous action of the sign talk. I also enjoyed watching his lips as they barely parted to emit the spoken word and the expression in his eyes. There were also days when we three rode about our ranch. Little Robe was graceful on his pony as well as seated. The only time he was not so graceful was when afoot, then he waddled somewhat from slightly bowed legs. His motions were always quick. I have mentioned the sign language. Most of it which I still retain I learned from this teacher. I will mention what I still remember from those distant days and nights and tell as nearly as I can how to make the signs.

> FRIEND—Hold both hands in front of body waist high, fingers open, backs of hand to front, revolve the two hands about each other rapidly two or three times, end by bringing closed fists together with a resounding whack and hold for an instant.
> RUN—Hold both hands in front, palms open and facing together, rapidly move first one then the other forward, past each other in succession.
> WALK—Both hands in front, palms down side by side, move one then other forward with easy motion, as of walking.
> YES—Hold right hand waist high in front of body, back up, fingers folded. Flick index finger up and down.

Ski-o-mah, In-mut-too-yah-lat-lat

No—Hold right hand waist high in front of body, back of hand out, fingers folded. Flip first and second finger together, out and away from body.

Good—With right hand make motion waist high, as though stroking fur of house cat, two or three times. Literally, "good" means "smooth" to the Indian.

Bad—Hold right hand waist high in front of body, back up, thumb grasping finger ends. Flip fingers outward two or three times. Let fingers be extended fully with each flip.

Hungry—Hold the right hand open flat, with extended fingers and thumb joined, palm up. Bring the hand to the middle of the body, and slowly saw back and forth. Literally "it cuts across." Present, past and future tense.

Eat—With right hand open, fingers and thumb joined, make motion from the mouth down the throat. Literally "puts it down." Also sign for food. Present, past and future tense.

Enough—Holding right hand three fingers closed, thumb and forefinger forming crescent. Point crescent toward body at stomach line and raise it slowly to the mouth along the throat line. Literally, "I am full up to there." This is used in any tense relating to food.

Talk—Fold three fingers of right hand, back up, thumb and forefinger forming letter O. Bring to lips with O pointing to front. Flip forefinger away from mouth. Literally, "throws out words." Used in all tenses.

Stop Talk—Make sign for talk, then with both hands held one in front of the other, backs to front, fingers and thumbs extended and joined, make motion of cutting, one hand moving up, the other down. Literally, "cut off talk." This sign is also made with the right hand only, slashing down in front of the lips. The sign made with one or two hands may also be used to cease or "cut off" any action.

Tell Truth—Make sign for talk ending with all fingers and thumb extended together in straight line with thumb up. Literally, "talk straight." Used in all tenses.

UNTRUTH—Touch tongue with first finger of right hand, then hold up two fingers. Literally, "two tongues." Signifies the short and ugly word. Used in any tense.

COME—Make a crook of the first finger of the right hand, three fingers and thumb folded in. Hold crook away from body, then draw toward the same. Used in any tense.

GO—With right hand thumb and two fingers folded, first and second fingers extended, back of hand up, make motion away from body to height of shoulder, flipping the two fingers outward. Means to go, go, depart, will go, will depart,—past, present and future. Also indicates journey.

HEAR—Cup right hand and hold under or beside the ear, palm up or to front.

DO NOT HEAR—Sign "No" and "Hear."

SEE—Hold first and second fingers of right hand extended straight out, tips far apart, back of hand up with two fingers and thumb folded in. Bring to level of eyes and point ahead.

DO NOT SEE—Sign "No" and "See."

PEACE—Hold right hand up as high as arm length, palm to front, thumb and fingers joined. Literally, "open hand with no weapon in it."

WAR, FIGHT—Extend all fingers and thumbs of each hand, holding them wide apart. Bring two hands to front at face level and rapidly jab with each in unison, one toward the other. Used in all tenses.

DIE—With both hands open, all fingers and thumbs extended and joined, backs up. Hold right hand flat, thumb next body, with left hand make motion down and under right. Literally, "goes under." Used in any tense. Also use the sign for "Cut off" in place of the above.

WATER—With open right palm, rub over the belly as if washing oneself.

Ski-o-mah, In-mut-too-yah-lat-lat

FIRE—Hold right hand back down, all fingers and thumb extended. Bring close to ground and flip fingers and thumb at same time making slight upward motion.

WHAT?—With right hand extended waist high, thumb and fingers slightly separated as though holding a ball, back of hand out. Twist wrist a few times.

WHY, WHICH—Same as above.

DAY—Extend both arms to front, hands open, fingers and thumbs lightly joined, palms up. Bring both hands back shoulder high in line with body, and hold there. Literally, "all open."

NIGHT—From sign for day bring hands to front turning backs up. Hold right over left and hold for instant. Literally, "under cover."

SUN—Right hand extended upward, thumb and forefinger forming crescent, other fingers closed. This gesture held toward the east at level of horizon, signifies "sunrise" or "early morning." This gesture toward the west signifies "sunset" or "end of day." Intermediate time of day between the two extremes is indicated by making the sign toward the proper position of the sun.

MOON—Sign for sun, and night.

MAN—Right hand held in front of face, forefinger erect, other fingers and thumb folded in, back of hand to front. Make motion upward and outward.

WOMAN—Right hand held flat with fingers and thumb joined, extended. Make sweeping motion from crown of head, to right side and down to back, indicating flowing hair.

(NOTE)—The two above signs have been accepted for many years by Indians and whites, but are not the true originals. The Indians made a concession to the "modesty" of their white brothers. The real signs are a plain representation of hidden parts of the anatomy of each sex.

MAN RIDING—Hold right hand waist high, to front, fingers and thumb straight out, back of hand on side.

Straddle this with first two fingers of left hand and with the two make a motion like a horse trotting forward.

DEER—Hold the right hand up with the elbow crooked. Hand held with back up, fingers and thumb extended. Flip the fingers all together up and forward, imitating hurdling objects.

RAILROAD TRAIN—With right hand held waist high, all fingers and thumb extended flat, back up. Make gentle motion up and down and forward in imitation of train riding along on springs.

SPRING OF YEAR—Holding right hand near ground back down, thumb and fingers extended upward, raise the hand two or three times to illustrate grass growing.

SUMMERTIME—Hold both hands above head in front and on each side, with all fingers and thumbs pointing downward, to represent rays of the sun.

AUTUMN—Right hand held up with fingers and thumb separately extended up, back of hand to front. With left hand make motion of leaves falling from points of digits.

WINTER—Both fists doubled, backs up, right one above left in front of body. Make shivery motion of both hands, to indicate cold. This also indicates cold. As the passage of time was mostly spoken of in yearly periods as "winters," this sign was also used to indicate year.

TIME?—Both hands held up with backs out, fingers closed with both thumbs and first fingers closed as though holding the ends of a string. Hold the supposed ends close together to ask the question of "how long a time" such and such an event takes place or happened.

ANSWER TO ABOVE—With the hands held as above, start a series of jerks to part them, stop for a "short time" or extend to length of arms to indicate "long time."

HOW MANY—Hold left hand up to elbow height in front of body, palm up, fingers partly open. With right hand, rapidly flip back successive fingers of the left one after the other.

MARRIAGE—Forefingers of both hands joined together side by side in front of the body, thumbs and other fingers closed.

HUSBAND—Sign for marriage, then man.

WIFE—Sign for marriage, then woman.

PARENT—Hold right hand bowl shaped over right nipple.

FATHER—Sign for parent, then man.

MOTHER—Sign for parent, then woman.

YOUR CHILDREN—Hold right hand with forefinger pointing down, other fingers and thumb closed. Make motion down in front of crotch, then for sex.

BROTHER—Place first two fingers of right hand in mouth, back of hand up, other digits closed, then sign for man.

SISTER—Sign as above, then for woman.

To Count:

ONE—Right hand held up in front of the face, back to front. Close all fingers but the first, which is left standing.

TWO—To the above, add the little finger erect.

THREE—From the above fold the little finger down, add second and third to first.

FOUR—To the above, add the little finger again.

FIVE—To the above, add the thumb.

SIX—Holding the right hand in the sign of five, add the erect thumb of the left hand held close to the five, fingers of left hand folded, back to front. Make slight forward movement of six digits.

SEVEN—Holding both hands as above, add the first finger of left hand to the number erect, making the forward motion again.

EIGHT—To the above, second finger of the left, making forward motion again.

NINE—To the above, add little finger as the left thumb is folded in. Make forward motion.

TEN—Turn both hands palms up, all fingers and thumbs extended. Make same forward motion.

TWENTY—Hold right hand up and to side of face, fold thumb and fingers leaving little and third fingers erect, back of hand to front. Make circular motion to left and down by twist of wrist.

ONE HUNDRED—With both hands held erect in front of face, fingers and thumbs erect and joined, palms outward. Make circular motion to left.

ONE THOUSAND—Make sign for ten, then for hundred.

SIGN FOR INDIAN—To the Indian any race was of one skin texture and general color. Thus they indicated they were Indian by touching the skin on back of left hand with forefinger of right.

WHITE MAN—With the right hand held flat, back up, fingers and thumb joined extended in straight line, the hand was drawn across forehead from left to right, signifying "hat wearer."

NEGRO—With the fingers of right hand, touch the nearest black or darkest object, then make sign for "hat wearer."

Indian Tribes:

CHEYENNE—With extended index finger of right hand make cutting motion across first joint of left index finger. Literally, "cut finger." Older Cheyenne ended their trial tests in the Sun Dance by laying the left forefinger on a chopping block where the Medicine Man took off the first joint at the knuckle.

ARAPAHOE—Extend index finger of right hand with thumb and other fingers folded in. Raise hand with palm outward and lay first finger alongside nose. Literally, "cut nose."

SIOUX—With right hand held flat, back up, fingers and thumb extended and joined, make motion of cutting throat. Literally, "cut throat."

PAWNEE—Extend first two fingers of right hand sepa-

242

rated. Hold behind right ear and motion forward.
Repeat. Literally, "Wolf."

COMANCHE—Extend right hand to left and front of
body, first finger extended, others closed. Draw hand
backward making wriggling motion as of snake crawling on ground. Literally, "Snake."

KIOWA—Hold the right hand to right and close to face,
bowl shape. Make circular motion several times.

UTE—Hold left hand extended with fingers straight,
thumb folded in, edge of hand down. With extended
fingers of right hand, rub gently along the left forefinger and hand toward the wrist.

APACHE—Hold left hand for sign of Ute. With extended fingers of the right, flip back and forth along
the left as a barber stropping a razor blade.

This is the extent of my recollection of the teachings of
Little Robe.

Listening to this great warrior, gathering his knowledge
and ideas, one became convinced that he was intensely human,
a man who had done the best he could with his talents, who
tried at all times to do what was best for the good of his people. In this I claim for him the name of a true patriot. All
honor to Little Robe, Chieftain of The Fighting Cheyenne.

Early in the eighties, another Indian Chief of wide renown
began to make Red Fork Ranch a stopping place as he passed
to and fro on visits to other tribes. This was Chief Joseph of
the Nez Perce (In-mut-too-yah-lat-lat).

Ralph knew him before I arrived at the ranch; I met him
first a few weeks after my arrival. He came up the trail one
day driving a team which drew a wagon in which he carried
his camp gear. His son, an Indian lad of my own age, accompanied him.

Joseph was on his way to the village of Little Robe where

he talked over affairs of mutual interest. He had also learned to class Ralph as a friend, and at our first meeting he gave me his cordial greeting. (He was a silent man, brooding over the position his people were in at the time, prisoners in a country where he and they were not at home.) Soon he brought his boy forward and told us two to be friends. (This boy grew into a man and succeeded his grandfather and father to chieftainship in the tribe. He is still alive in the state of Washington.)

After our introduction we two looked each other over in a sizing up such as all boys indulge in. I felt it incumbent upon myself to act as host. I asked if my guest could shoot; I had not learned very well. We decided to try our skill and Ralph let me have his Winchester and a handful of cartridges. Going out on the bottom land west of our ranch buildings we took turns shooting at prairie dogs. We both were so small that it was hard for us to hold the man-size gun out straight, so we lay on our bellies and shot from that position. This is not a record of skillful marksmanship, for my memory tells me we missed every shot, but I can still see long marked paths of bullets, where they skimmed the surface and seared their way toward the mounds of the cheerful marmots. We almost did hit some of them, but not quite. We two boys had a good time and were entertained with the noise we were making, and the antics of our almost victims as they turned handsprings backward into the safety of their burrows.

Chief Joseph came to us and said that his boy had never shot a gun before. He had been too young when they were still in their old home. He also said, "Soldier Chiefs will not let us have guns." Guns were still needed. I think he carried a rifle in the wagon, for an Indian was not safe without one as he traveled about. The acquaintance started then was further improved when Joseph showed us how the gun should be handled, and by subsequent visits of the pair to Red Fork.

I saw them several times, and also sat in as Ralph and Joseph talked. He spoke mostly of his hope to be allowed to return with his people to their old home. His spirit was far from subdued, for a murderous gleam showed in his eyes as in Little Robe's when he told of certain happenings in his life. He seemed to have a high regard for General Nelson A. Miles, and voiced the opinion that this man would get them back to Idaho. (This subsequently proved true. Miles persisted, cut red tape, and secured the release of the Nez Perce from the confinement which was so fatal to hundreds of them. They returned to a changed country.)

This man impressed his personality on my memory. I have always had an affectionate regard for the red warrior who was also a gentleman and patriot for his people. He also learned to address me as Nevaw.

Of both these warriors it can be said that it was an honor to know them. They were warriors brave and true. SKI-O-MAH, IN-MUT-TOO-YAH-LAT-LAT, NEVAW has spoken. I cut their story here.

Chapter XXII

INDIAN FENCE BUILDERS

WHEN Ralph was first faced with the problem of fencing in the range of Red Fork in conformity with government requirements, he rebelled at the idea. No one had ever fenced in that country of unlimited range, why should he? Calm thought told him to meet the issue and order the work.

He finally hired white men to cut fence posts. Texas John worked deep in the woods, others worked near the ranch buildings on Turkey Creek. Among these were Pike, Baughman, a giant woodsman from Wisconsin, and two or three others whose names I never knew. Spring came early and he set about securing help to set the posts. He finally went to Little Robe and told the Chief of the chance for his young men to learn to walk on one white man's road. Criers called and tom-toms were beaten calling them all to a pow-wow. Many volunteered, ten were selected. I had more company to investigate, other entertainment.

Ten young bucks rode up in front of the store one morning in late February. Each was mounted on his pony and carried either a rifle or a sixshooter. Each wore an eagle feather of the initiated, buckskin or blanket leggings, gee-string, moccasins, knife in leather scabbard, beaded tobacco pouch and stone-bowled pipe. Of course I was on the reception committee with Ralph as the other Westerners hung back. As the Indians sat their ponies I dodged about among the restive steeds, while each rider drummed his pony's ribs in an incessant tattoo. They all wore expectant grins, and I grinned in return. Ralph welcomed them in words.

Then Ralph mounted his pony and led the band of six footers to a spot at the edge of the black-jack woods, some two miles north of the buildings, and there selected a camp site where they could live their own life, apart from the whites, who would not live with them.

They did not bring tepees or women with them. Ralph furnished army tents which were brought up later in the day. They were to live as Indians on the war trail, letting the apprentices prepare the meals. The apprentices, four in number, were Indian boys who had yet to win their eagle feathers.

I had ridden along, stayed all day, and noted all they did. Ralph had expected them and a well-filled wagon came along with supplies. He brought the articles which any cow camp had, and in this case there were also superfluous luxuries.

Their commissary was well stocked from the ranch stores with beef, pork, beans, coffee, sugar, syrup, and flour for bread, which Ralph had to show them how to make. I soon learned that they did not care for much to eat in the morning nor at noon when the white men ate at regular hours. They conformed to the hours, and at the first two meals of the day ate only hot bread and coffee. But they did prepare and eat heartily of an evening meal. That was really the only meal they enjoyed.

After the first day, fresh beef was killed for their use as they needed it. In the absence of buffalo meat beef satisfied them. The evening meal would consume hours in the preparation and eating. I watched many meals and partook of my share.

Those meal times stand out in memory now with the crowd of laughing Indian workmen enjoying every moment.

A fire was started on the ground and the beef, cut in sizable lots, would be laid on each side of it. They would drive stakes through it into the ground so that the side of beef would lean slightly toward the fire. In this manner it was roasted by reflected heat.

While the meal was being prepared, the men sat about on the ground Indian fashion and recounted the stories of the day's doings, or their own past history. The meal at night was the social hour of the day and often dragged along till midnight.

Many of them preferred the meat to be only hot, and not cooked, others liked it fairly well done. As soon as one of them saw that the meat was to his taste, he would go up and cut off a strip with his knife and return to his place with it. There he would consume his portion by setting his teeth in a mouthful and cutting it off in front of his lips with a sweep of his knife.

The work that these men were doing was of the hardest manual type. Cutting post holes, setting the posts, and stretching barbed wire called into play many muscles they had never used before and made sore hands. Until they were hardened, every man was the sorest he had ever been in his life. But they never shirked or loafed. They made of the work a contest in which each tried to outdo the others. Their aches and pains were the subject of good-natured raillery around the camp fires. Many were the descriptions of the new sensations of pain. On the other hand there was comfort in the knowledge that they were getting exercise which they needed and had missed.

Indian Fence Builders

Ralph spent much of his time directing the Indians in person, and while they were on distant portions of the range he camped with two white men, assisting in the work. One of these was of French extraction and the other from the Emerald Isle. It was a lonely job for them, and in time their own company palled on both. One day the strain became so great that they fell to fighting. It was a free-for-all-no-hold-barred type of contest. Blows with fists, kicking, gouging, and biting all were a part of it. The boss was away and they had the whole wide prairie for their battle ground.

Now the Indian warriors had never fought an enemy except as race against race or tribe against tribe. For the members of one race or tribe to fight was unusual. To them all whites were of one race. They were told that the whites were those on whom they were to pattern. Also it was naughty for them to fight at all. Here were two white men doing all the damage they could to each other.

The real warriors looked at each other in silence. Then it dawned on them that here was a fight with nature's weapons with no death to result. It was the best show they had ever seen—two white men trying to damage each other, while they were not implicated in any way.

When the true understanding of the affair dawned on them, they broke into yells of approval, formed a ring about the contestants and urged them on. Each blow and kick, each bite and gouge, was greeted with pleased shouts. They did a war dance about the two men and added their war cries to the noise of the conflict. It was great fun, but finally came to an end when the Irishman was licked.

That evening a number of visiting Indians came into camp and all were feasting in their usual style, when Ralph arrived from headquarters. It was late and he immediately retired to the tent with the other two whites without knowing of the day's events. He had fallen asleep when he was awakened by yells and cries that led him to believe his red friends had broken loose on the warpath for some reason.

Looking out from his tent he beheld a crowd of the Indians yelling, fighting, and dancing the war-step. Two of them had started to illustrate the day's fight. They struck at each other, threw each other down, and when down would bite and gouge. The other spectators who had witnessed the day's battle, seeing where the actors were leaving out something, would dash in and supply the missing act.

Ralph was mystified and worried to see the Indians resolving themselves into what seemed a mass of fighting, yelling demons, but was enlightened as to its cause by the Irishman, who, to his chagrin, saw the performance brought to an end with an imitation of his admission that he had had enough.

It was a great day and night. The Indians were greatly enlightened as to the way of the white man. Who ever said that these people do not appreciate humor?

A few weeks later Ralph was alone with his Indians carrying on operations at the edge of the cedar grove. The two white men had left so that he lived with the red men in their camp and took part in their meals and evening conversations.

Sitting around the fire one evening after the meal was well advanced, the Indians suddenly sprang to their feet and ran into the darkness of the woods, leaving him alone. Thinking that they had heard some animal and had gone in pursuit of it, he paid no attention to their absence for some time. After he had finished his meal, however, he took up their trail. Some of them had grabbed up sticks from the fire and soon he was guided by the lights to a clearing where they were all assembled.

Two strange Indians were there, seated on the ground and stripped of every vestige of clothing. The Cheyenne boys were engaged in dividing the belongings of these strangers, including their ponies. Walking up to the leader of the Cheyennes, Ralph asked for an explanation. Flipping his thumb in the direction of the captives, he uttered the one word, P-a-w-n-e-e," with scorn and contempt in his look.

The manner of uttering the word, the inflection of the voice, showed just what he thought of these ancient enemies of his tribe. To a Cheyenne, a Pawnee was just a dog, even worse—a *theik* (ghost). The Pawnees had been hunted and killed for years by the stronger tribe, and whenever they fell into the latter's hands they were robbed of all they had as a matter of course.

These two had been passing by when the keen ears of their enemies had detected them. They were soon overtaken and despoiled of their belongings. Even their lives were awaiting the decision of the majority, when the white man came on the scene. One man against a band of vengeful Indians would seem to furnish material for drama. Not so. The young ranchman merely gave his Indians a talk. He told them that he was their friend in all things, but would not be unless he pointed them to the right road. They were not on the war-path now, and all Indians were going to "sit down" together in the country. Each must help the other. Pawnees were now brothers, and there must be no killing or seizing of each other's property. This was not a "gift dance." [1] After listening to

[1] While technically at peace with enemies a band of Cheyennes would pay a surprise visit to a Pawnee camp. Racing into the village with war cries, each Cheyenne would embrace every Pawnee he met. Custom then demanded of every embraced one all his possessions which could be carried away. Then came a dance with all participating.

him, the Indians threw the strangers' property at them, and turning around, they ran laughing back to their neglected evening meal. Ralph saw the Pawnees gather up their property, don their clothes, and ride away.

Chapter XXIII

WHILE at Red Fork that winter, word was brought to us of a practical joke which had been played on two greenhorn tenderfeet at Pond Creek ranch during the fall.

Two young fellows had been there hunting. They were filled with stories of prowling Indians, until they were continually on the watch for possible ambush by Redskins. Every tree, every tuft of grass on the prairie, seemed to hide bloodthirsty scalp raisers. They were good shots; the country yielded them much game.

The story ran that they became separated one day while hunting on Wild Horse Creek. Each started to find his partner, while bearing in mind the fact that Indians were also hunting them.

Each stepped from tree to tree in the woods, or crawled from one tuft of grass to another in the open. While proceeding in this manner, one of them discovered a tuft of grass in front of him which appeared suspicious. He had seen it move. Lying as still as an inanimate object he watched. Soon he noted a head appear cautiously in view and then duck from sight. Here must be an Indian; the friend was forgotten. Watching closer, more intently, with rifle cocked and pointed, the man fired at the next appearance of the head. It ducked from sight, to be followed by a shot from its vicinity. Several times shots were exchanged but neither scored a hit. Then ranchmen came who hailed the first man and told him it was his friend he was firing at. Then the joke was explained.

This story fired our crew at Red Fork to emulation. Baughman had an idea.

His idea resulted in a long-drawn-out period of hazing, masquerading under the name of a joke. Ralph seemed to be away with his Indians or at the Agency most of the time. I was the only witness of proceedings.

The giant woodsman from Wisconsin was the victim, and young as I was I still was forced to wonder at his gullibility. He was a six-foot, broad-shouldered, bearded specimen of manhood with the mentality of a child, but no one could equal him in skill as a woodsman. He knew his work so well that he could drop a tree to an inch of the spot selected for its fall, and he could split logs with his ax without the aid of a wedge.

Baughman and Pike took this man's measure, gave him all the information he asked for about the country and surroundings, and added hundreds of per cent more of misinformation. All winter long they filled the days with this work of getting the sucker ready for the killing.

Soon it was announced that the Indians had heard we were going to build a fence at Red Fork, on their land, and they were opposed to the improvement. In fact they were going on the warpath about it. Not only the Cheyenne and Arapahoe, but all tribes were combining to exterminate all whites in the country. The war trail would be followed by thousands upon thousands of redskins. Red Fork Ranch was to be wiped off first, because the first fence would be built there. Baughman was their worst enemy. He had killed so many in fights that wagons were used to carry the scalps alone which he had taken. He was bad medicine, and with him out of the way the rest of the country would be easy to wipe clear of the hated white men. All winter long this story was repeated and enlarged upon. It was dinned into the ears of the greenhorn days and evenings.

The Great Joke

The methods of the savages on the warpath were related for his enlightenment. Indians could conceal themselves on approach so that they could never be seen until they wished to be. In the open country, without a stick of wood to hide behind, they had been known to materialize apparently out of clear air. When they killed a white man they cut up his body in horrible ways. The least they did was to skin the whole body and eat the heart. If they captured you alive, there were many favorite ways of torturing you. Staking one out by an ant hill to be eaten piece-meal until only polished bones were left was a favorite with them. Building a fire on the stomach of the prone victim was a close second.

Ways and means by which to defeat the Indians in their dastardly designs were discussed. It was decided to form a little company of brave and devoted fighters right there on Red Fork Ranch. They would place themselves in the way of the whelming tide of destruction and turn it from its fell purpose. Pike, the oldest man, was elected Captain. Baughman was the brave, fearless scout. Chape and three or four others were included in the nucleus of a company which was to rally at Red Fork on the first alarm, or when the scout sent for aid.

It was unanimously decided that the choice position in the brave company was to be that of cook. Not that it would be the best by reason of work, but because Indians were amenable to reason only when faced by such a dignitary as camp cook. When no other white could control wild red men bent on destruction, if the cook came to the front at the right moment he could stop the most impetuous charge. By majority vote of the company, the coveted honor was conferred on the big woodsman from Wisconsin.

In order to fit him for his position he must be given instruction in the rudiments of the sign language, and be properly dressed to impress the red men. This was very important and much time was put in on the uniform to be worn by the cook mediator.

He wore a large black Stetson on his head, and a full black beard covered his face and chest. His black and red checked woodsman's shirt was worn with the tail out. Rough trousers were loosely tucked into the tops of cow-hide boots. He was given spurs to wear and he kept them on at all times. About his waist, in addition to his cartridge belt and holster, was another leather belt to which was strung a collection of dried animal hoofs in such quantity that one struck against the other as the wearer walked or moved. A leather thong was placed about his neck, strung through a dried buffalo hoof. This was smeared with a generous portion of asafetida, and was spoken of as a potent charm which would influence any savage to docility. It certainly was potent and very influential on any one near. To the crown of the hat was affixed a whole wild turkey tail adornment, with the end of the tail standing erect, making a striking headdress that would be the envy of any Indian. On each shoulder and each elbow was fastened a turkey wing.

A harness was made and placed about the man's chest to support a deer head on the back between the shoulders. This head was full antlered and held upright by a leather arrangement. To the prongs of the head, attached by thongs, was a cook's outfit, consisting of a coffee pot, frying pan, several tin cups, and tin plates perforated for the thong. When this man was dressed in his full regalia, he was a sight to draw the attention of any Indians, stir their envy, and possibly put some of them to flight.

After Texas John came in from his winter camp he joined the company and took part in periodical drills which were to help in proper military maneuvers in the face of the enemy. Even I was part of every drill up to a certain point.

With the cook in full regalia the company was put through a formation drill in front of the store building by Captain Pike. At the head of the single file marched the Indian-charmer, and at a certain point the others dropped out and he became the whole show as he practiced his peace sign. This was very important and he was put through his paces until he had it perfect.

At the command of the captain he would advance toward him, and coming to a halt, would salute his superior officer. Then would come the command, "Make the peace sign." At this command, he would right about and go down on all fours in the dirt. Then reaching down, he would make a mark some three or four feet long in the dust with his nose. Wheeling about on all fours until he was at right angles with the first line, he would root out another with his nose that crossed the first.

The attainment of speed was the object of frequent drills, and the man needed the assistance of the whole company to keep the pots and pans attached to the deer head from coming about his ears and crabbing his action. Many times was this ludicrous performance gone through with. The big simpleton had swallowed the whole story and really felt that he was perfecting himself in action that would probably save the lives of all of them at a critical moment. What a sight he was as he capered around on the ground. A small troop of cavalry from Fort Reno were present one morning and witnessed the show. Baughman was in his glory and took all the credit.

While they were still practicing and with perfection still some distance ahead, there came an incipient Indian raid one Sunday evening that almost spoiled the final show. The crowd of post-choppers had gathered in the store, and were augmented by one lone freighter who was camping there that night and was not in the know. The freighter's pal was put wise to the fun and he and Baughman decided to give a little demonstration unknown to the rest.

The one in the secret lined up eight of his mules abreast and he and Baughman mounted the two animals on the outside ends of the line. When they were ready, they trotted briskly up the trail from the direction of the cattle corral. Nearing the buildings they loosed their six-shooters and fired shots into the air, at the same time letting out blood-curdling yells. Sounding like a troop of Comanches, they rode in the bright moonlight until they were abreast of the cabins, then, executing a right-about with their mules, advanced toward the waiting crowd inside.

With the first shots and yells, every one prepared in his own way for an attack. All but the woodsman and the one freighter inside realized that this was an impromptu affair and waited to see what would happen. So it was that the advancing line of the enemy out in the moonlight was not met with shots.

The cook mediator had sprung to his feet at the first alarm and looked about for some one to tell him what to do. The lone freighter ran to his side. With drawn guns they stood looking through the front windows as the file came into sight. When the line wheeled to come toward the waiting men, the woodsman leaped for the south doorway, knocking me down, incidentally, and brushing aside all other interference. He reached the door, and sprang into the open, closely followed by the freighter. They eluded all pursuit, and reaching the Chisholm Trail, were soon lost in the night and did not return.

When the next morning's stage drove in from Bull Foot, the two frightened men were on it. They had reached the stage station early in the morning and told of an Indian attack on Red Fork. They felt sure that they were the only survivors of a massacre. The man at Bull Foot had known of the whole affair, and told them that he had word that the Indian attack had been repulsed and the enemy scattered. He persuaded them to return to their comrades at Red Fork with him.

This first affair made the woodsman so uneasy that it was decided to stage the finale within the next few days after his return. Accordingly he was paid his wages, and furnished with a pony on which to get away if he escaped the savages, for the news was that they would return in full force within a few days. Each day Baughman scouted, and finally brought news that the plains were covered with Indians south of the Cimarron. They were camped for the night and would attack without doubt the very next morning at daybreak.

In the early morning light all the brave company of defenders were routed out for a final drill. The cook went through his performance of the peace sign with alacrity and perfection. Then he was told to mount his pony with others and ride forth to meet the enemy. He was assisted into his saddle with all his equipment intact. At this moment, shots and yells were heard down the trail. Over toward Turkey Creek two blanketed figures could be seen riding from the woods into the open and giving their war cries.

Evidently the Indians were attacking from two sides. The ones toward Turkey Creek were riding north toward the trails, as if to cut off escape in that direction. With the first shots in the distance, the woodsman had drawn his gun and waited for word from the captain. He noted the actions of the blanketed figures and sensed the fact that, if one got ahead of him, escape would be cut off.

Heading his pony up the trail, he spurred it into a gallop.

As soon as he did this, every man behind him opened up with guns and there was the sound of a lively battle in the rear.

Not waiting for further orders, nor pausing to put his well-drilled peace sign to the test, he galloped away, pots and pans rattling about his ears and flying off the deer horns in every direction. Soon he was clear of these impedimenta, and then bent his energies to the work in hand. He spurred and whipped his pony until he was flying over the trail. The blanketed riders did their best to head him off, but he outstripped all competitors by the time he had topped the rise toward Bull Foot Ranch. He escaped, never to return.

As he advanced up the trail, he alarmed many freighters with a story of his escape from an Indian massacre at Red Fork. Ranchmen knew better, but many others were frightened into going into camp and preparing for an attack. It was two or three days before the usual number of freighters began to come into Red Fork, where they heard the story of the great joke.

This whole affair exemplified a certain class of western humor. To terrorize such a simple-minded person in this manner was considered a wonderful accomplishment. The whole winter was given over to this joke, as it progressed from day to day; yet it was not out of the bounds of possibility that the Indians might cause trouble. Hardly four years had passed since Dull Knife made his memorable march through the country to his old Dakota home. Events were crowding on the Indians in such exasperating volume that they were in a continuous state of uneasiness and chagrin at their own impotence.

So it was that when this poor victim of the joke reached Caldwell and told his story, he gave publicity to another of the numerous stories of "uprisings" on the part of the Indians, and added to the total of unfounded tales of the ferocity of our

The Great Joke

red brothers. It was perfectly lawful to use their names as the perpetrators of any villainy that came into the minds of the white jokers. Many another tale of Indian uprisings and misdeeds had just as much foundation as this one—no more.

Chapter XXIV

DAN JONES, who owned Red Fork Ranch at an earlier time, left his home in Kansas and paid us a few days' visit that winter. While there he related one of his early experiences on the site. As it was an illustration of the hardihood of frontiersmen such as he, I will repeat it as my recollection dictates.

During one winter soon after he had taken ownership, he was called down the Chisholm Trail on business. He traveled alone, and was on his way back to the ranch when he reached the ford of the Cimarron. The river was low, but it had been cold the night before and a rim of ice bordered the water. The sand at the river's border was also frozen enough to make it crusty.

As he guided his pony to the ford, the animal broke through the crust of sand at one place, stumbled, and threw Dan to the ground so violently as to break one of his legs, and then ran away. It was the off season for the cattle drives and this accident left the man in a helpless predicament, with almost no chance of being found. After weighing his chances for help, Dan dragged himself through the water of the river, reached the north bank, and with much effort, proceeded painfully to pull himself over the trail by his hands until he reached a point where he was in sight of the ranch cabin.

At this point he fired his six-shooter and waved a handkerchief until attention was drawn to him and he was rescued.

Sunset

Injured as he had been, exhausted, and almost frozen, his constitution pulled him through and he made a quick recovery.

Spring had come, grass was covering the plains with fresh green color, when I was one day forced to make way on the Chisholm Trail above the ranch buildings for a cavalcade which spread across the trail breadth and extended for a mile or two down its length.

A troop of cavalry from Fort Reno led the van. Following it came one wagon after another, each drawn by horses or mules. Some of the wagon covers bore legends such as "Oklahoma or Bust." Lad that I was, I could see that these vehicles were poorly equipped. It was a parade of poverty. Wagon seats held most woe-begone people, poorly dressed men, and dejected women,—not a smile in the whole caravan. Silently they passed along, closely guarded by troopers who rode along each side of the column and brought up the rear. Thus I met my first Oklahoma Boomers. This crowd had endeavored to become "Sooners" under the leadership of "Cap" Payne, and had reached the vicinity of the cedar grove on Red Fork Ranch, there to be corralled by troopers and turned back to Kansas.

The troops were there to enforce the law, and protect the boomers from possible attack by cattlemen. It was "dog eat dog," for the cattlemen wanted the land for themselves, both they and the boomers wanted it from the Indians. Poor Lo.

During the spring of 1884, brother Ralph received a special appointment as Cattle Commissioner for the Cheyenne and Arapahoe Indians at Darlington Agency. In fulfilling this commission he was absent from Red Fork much of the time, as he purchased cattle down the trail and drove them to the Agency for beef issue. He took a room in the Cheyenne

Indian School building at Caddo Spring, to use when he was in that vicinity. I shared this with him or occupied it alone while he was away. It was here that I spent my last weeks in the old Indian Territory.

I became acquainted with Mr. Coggshall, the School Superintendent, and his force of teachers. Ralph was "waiting on" a teacher named Amelia Kable. Her sister Elizabeth was also a teacher there. I was the younger brother in parties of an evening, when Ralph, George Maffet, and "Lafe" Merritt called. George and Ralph later married the sisters; "Lafe" is still traveling alone. "Lafe" and George were conducting a newspaper at the Agency, named the *Cheyenne Transporter.*

These young newswriters were an enterprising pair, a distinct social asset on that frontier. I have no doubt of this, but at that time I was not interested in older boys any more than they were in me. My sole interests lay in the Indian camps, even to the exclusion of my own relatives in the Agency. My time was spent roaming about with my Indian boy companions or alone if they were otherwise occupied. George Bent and I became well acquainted by reason of this close contact, for he was then attending school in the same building where I resided.

My room became a store house of everything of interest to a boy. Many land turtles crawled about the country and at one time I had a full half dozen in my room. The last sound I would hear at night was made by their claws as they ambled about and tried to mount the side walls. They often disappeared mysteriously, but it was no trouble to keep my herd at full quota. Bows and arrows, slings, spears, and moccasins littered the place, making a veritable paradise for me. I am not so sure of the teachers who gave me attention when Ralph was not there.

I ran as wild as my Indian companions. I witnessed the Sun Dance that year and also found some excitement about the

Agency. Cattle men were crowding onto Indian land and there were frequent fights between them and Indians. Often I witnessed the Indian police starting out on an expedition, or their return with prisoners. Uncle Ben Williams also seemed busy and came to the Agency with prisoners or to get a posse of Indian deputies to make some arrest.

One day, Miss Lizzie Kable asked me to take her riding pony and place it in the Indian village herd. It proved to be a little, white, wiry, fiery-eyed Indian pony once owned and trained by Bear Robe.

Now I was no different from most boys. Boys are labor-saving experts. The avoidance of useless effort comes naturally. I had no sooner taken the commission than I instinctively planned to avoid unnecessary effort. I knew that the herd might prove to be miles away; and that if I rode out properly equipped, I must walk back carrying said equipment. I had no such intention. Accordingly, I mounted the pony bare-back, passed a leather thong about its neck near the shoulders in lieu of a bridle, and set forth.

I rode down the trail toward the Agency, keeping a look-out to the west through the black-jack woods for the pony herd. A ride of several miles having failed to reveal them, I became convinced that I must have passed them, and so wheeled the pony to retrace the route. It so happened that Indian ponies are always wheeled about in this manner at the start of a race. My mount assumed that he had received a signal and set out to win. He covered the ground like an antelope, while I, taken completely by surprise, could only cling for life to the futile leather thong.

After a mile or two, I determined to forestall the inevitable and take the initiative in the matter of dismounting. I had seen Clyde Bear Robe and his companions vault from their seats while at a full gallop—why not I? Scared as I was, the idea appealed to the theatrical instinct that is so rarely lacking in any of us. Taking hold of the pony's withers for a purchase, I threw my legs up, over and forward in order to strike the ground standing. But, alas! the performance had been insufficiently rehearsed. My hands slipped at just the critical moment, and as I fell, the pony's knee caught me in the face. I was thrown to the ground senseless and badly lacerated about my head and face.

Before I had fully recovered my senses I struggled to my feet and staggered aimlessly about as some of my Indian friends reached me. Several of my teeth were loosened and hanging by the gums. Mrs. Bear Robe took a hand and pushed these teeth back into their gum sockets while I was still bleeding profusely. These remained where they were put, but the count revealed one missing. Before I was taken away, every Indian there made a diligent search for the missing tooth. It was never found, and I had the discomforting suspicion that my person concealed the missing molar.

The following day I felt shooting pains at the back of my head and along the spine. I crawled to my room in the school building, went to bed and lost consciousness. The injury had resulted in a bad case of spinal meningitis.

Ralph returned from the cattle trail to our room that night and found me delirious. He had me removed to the Agency and called Doctor DeBrae from Fort Reno and Doctor Le-Garde of the Agency force. These two men pulled me through as severe a case as ever existed with this dread malady. There were no refinements of the sick room there; no ice. I was unconscious many days and the doctors disagreed at all times as to the final outcome. DeBrae said there was no hope; Le-Garde said the constitution would pull the boy through. I am writing this more than forty-three years afterward.

Sunset

When I first regained consciousness, I found myself on a cot placed near a window on the first floor of Uncle John's house, with Aunt Sally in charge. In the first moment of my return to life, I became aware of Indian cries and a great hubbub of voices. Looking out I beheld a mob of several hundred Cheyenne warriors milling around and around a squad of Indian police, with Bill Darlington leading them; a group of badly scared cow-boys riding in the center. Warriors rode yelling and cursing on all sides of the police, and the crowd almost knocked down the little picket fence bounding the lot on which the house stood. Here a six-shooter was aimed, there a rifle was pulled down for a shot at the men in the center whenever an opening showed in the protecting cordon. But always the opening was closed by the body of some Indian officer before the shot was taken, and Bill rode with never a look to right or left as he sucked on his pipe with bowl turned down, the most unconcerned man in that wild mob.

The Indians had been roused by the killing of White Buffalo a few weeks before. He was a very popular young man in the tribe, and his murderers had been brought in by troops from Fort Reno. This excitement had barely cooled when another Cheyenne had also been shot. This time several braves had gone on the warpath, surrounded the bunch of cattlemen, and were on the point of annihilating them, when Bill Darlington and his dusky police rode up and saved them. I witnessed from my bed the finale of this affair.

As the crowd rode by I plainly saw Indian police drive their ponies into breaches that drew the body of the rider into the line of fire, literally protecting with their bodies the lives of those who would shoot them without compunction, were positions reversed. I like to remember that first glimpse into the world again, showing me a band of "savages" teaching white citizens a lesson in self-restraint and obedience to law which too often failed them.

I think the stage coach must have arrived from Caldwell during the excitement in the Agency, for almost my next sensation was of seeing my father come rushing in the front door. He then took charge of me.

His first job was to clip my matted hair. It had grown as long as my Indian companions'. My ventures into Indian camps and homes had resulted in a full crop of what we call cooties. Nursing me along in the torrid climate, father soon saw that I must be taken away from there and set about it before I could sit up to ride.

I made a fuss over losing my hair and the cooties, but soon learned of a more serious calamity. The disease had robbed me of hearing in one ear for life, and impaired that of the other.

I started the trip back to Iowa stretched on a pile of buffalo robes filling the back spaces of a two-seated surrey, and with only occasional glimpses of consciousness. I do not recall leaving the Agency or any of the trip to Caldwell, with two exceptions. I opened my eyes once and beheld Old Chape framed in the doorway of the log store building at Red Fork Ranch, waving his last good-by. I also recall Miner at Pond Creek showing us to the loft as father took me up and put me to bed for a night there. Of Caldwell I have no recollection on that trip, but I do recall the arrival at home in Corning. I was more dead than alive, and had a relapse right there. A constitution framed in the open endured well. In a few months I was in school again; before three years more had elapsed, I was riding the range in another section of the West.

Contemplating the experiences outlined in these pages, I feel that I had grown my first ring of experience by the time I was brought back to Corning, Iowa, after being away over

INDIAN POLICE PROTECTING WHITE MURDERERS

fifteen months obtaining an intensive training which no one can get to-day.

Memories of those days are cherished by the writer, but the sun has set forever on the conditions which made them possible. My Empire has been blotted out by a settled Commonwealth.

Chapter XXV

AT the time when Emerson Hough was running the story "North of 36" in the *Saturday Evening Post,* he appended a note to one of his chapters stating that he had traveled the old Chisholm Trail from end to end and across its length many times; yet at the time of writing, he could not tell the reader where it lay in terms of present day localities. He asked whether any reader could tell him. I wrote him of what I knew, but my letter reached him in the hospital where he was confined with a fatal illness, too late for him to see.

It is likely that the cattle drive which he mentioned in the story had reached the point just above the Cimarron when they first met Jesse Chisholm, and from that point on, they followed close to the lines laid out in my story.

The present line of the Chicago, Rock Island, and Pacific Railroad from Caldwell south follows closely the lines of the old Chisholm and Reno Trails, described here. This holds true from Caldwell, Kansas, down to El Reno, Oklahoma. South of this point, I was not familiar.

I thought the present city of Jefferson, Oklahoma, must be on the site of the Pond Creek Ranch. The present town of Pond Creek occupies former open spaces of the Chisholm Trail. Being certain of the location of Pond Creek Ranch north of the Salt Fork of the Arkansas, I was puzzled to find the maps placing the town of Pond Creek, Oklahoma, south of that river. I wrote to Mr. Joseph Thoburn, Secretary of the Oklahoma Historical Society, of my dilemma. He replied:

In After Years

"You are right as to the location of Pond Creek Ranch. It was north of the Salt Fork, near the present village of Jefferson. When the Cherokee Outlet lands were opened in September, 1893, the government had laid out a town-site on the south side of Salt Fork and named it Pond Creek. The railroad company laid out the town north of Salt Fork and named it Round Pond. There was great rivalry between the two, and the railway company refused to build a station and stop trains at the town on the south side. Exasperated residents wrecked one or two trains and finally Congress passed an act requiring railways to build and maintain stations and stop all trains at all government town-site locations. Pond Creek was the county seat throughout the territorial period, but since statehood, that honor has passed to Medford, which is the next town north of Jefferson."

I was complacent to find my memory of it substantiated.

Again I tested my knowledge of old locations with the author of "Tumbleweeds." The story interested me greatly, for it pictures scenes in my old empire at about the time it was opened for settlement in 1889,—does it well and quite true to detail. After reading the novel, I sat down and wrote the author, Hal G. Evarts, as follows:

"After thinking over 'Tumbleweeds,' it seems to me that most of the story was located along the line my reminiscences cover. It is interesting.

"The way I dope it out, the town of Casa in the story was the location of the original Pond Creek Ranch. Sulphur Springs is the present town of Pond Creek, while Casa is the present town of Jefferson. The Half Diamond H home ranch location (of the story) looks to me as though it were near to, possibly somewhat south of the Old Bull Foot Ranch Stage Station, and Alvin (of the story) is the present town of Dover, on the location of our old Red Fork Ranch houses.

273

"This is the way I dope it out. Would be interested to hear from you, now that you have my description of the old place locations, as to how near I check up."

With the letter, I sent an outline of my chapter on "The Chisholm Trail." I received the following reply from Mr. Evarts:

"Your letter and articles on the early life in the strip have been exceptionally interesting to me, and I thank you for sending them on. Your doping out of the towns, even though I had them camouflaged, is exactly correct. As to the old Bull Foot Ranch Stage Station, I cannot say, as you know I told you I was not down in that particular country until long after it was settled."

In this and other ways, I have verified the memories implanted in my mind before I had reached my thirteenth birthday, and can tell you pretty much what a trip down from Caldwell, Kansas, would do to bring them back.

I do not know how large a city now goes under the name of the old cow town of my memory, but arriving there I would have some old resident pick out the location of the first, and in my time, the only street. Once that is located, and with the points of the compass as a guide, I could people the town again with residents of forty-five years ago.

Around the old railroad station, I should see scores of blanketed Indian men, women, and children standing about muffled in their wrappings as they watched the arrival of the "iron horse." These people would be watching silently, with immobile faces, which would not betray the surprise, even terror, that they really felt at the wonders of the white man.

I should see long, lean cattle-men, squatted down on their heels, also there to see what was to them an oddity. Many of these cattle-men had never ridden on the steam "kyars."

In After Years

As I walked down the street I should see graceful centaurs galloping by on cow-ponies, or ungainly, waddling, bow-legged men entering saloons, or places of trade. In a cloud of dust from the street would appear a pitching, lumbering vehicle propelled by four horses, all under the guidance of Dobe, the stage driver. I should see no shade trees in the town, and, as a bright star against a black night, my eye would come to rest on a lilac bush in full bloom in the yard of Cousin Sarah.

Again I should picture Lord Wilson as he "did the town" on that far-away day, attended by a score or more of waddling, spur-clanking companions. At one time the only occupant of the street would be this member of the British nobility as he bade defiance to the natives. He would fade from the picture to the accompaniment of a roar of voices punctured by scores of pistol shots as the men bade good-by to this doughty Briton.

I should see a man step into the street with hand on his belted gun and advance after a man ahead of him. The man in front turns by instinct and beats the would-be murderer to the draw, and I see my "killer" bite the dust.

I should see arriving freighters and cattle outfits from the south bent on doing the town. Indian freight trains in charge of some chief would be setting out down the trail as I started with Dobe on this journey of fancy.

Leaving the town on the Chicago, Rock Island and Pacific Railroad going south, I might make out the crossing of Bluff Creek and there picture my crossings of the dry bed, and Lord Wilson immured in the darkness of night on the no-longer treeless spaces as he watched for the "run of snipe." After leaving the city of Medford my eyes would strain for some indication which would tell me where I first looked forward to Pond Creek Ranch. Crossing the Salt Fork I would contrast my comfort with the bedraggled, water-soaked group thrown from the stage coach one night forty-three years ago. As we

275

reached the present town of Pond Creek I would feel again the misery I felt as I passed along on the inside of the sodden stage coach the same night.

Enid would mean nothing to me, unless I could gaze off to the east and see Pete being thrown from his cabin at Skeleton by Long Nine.

At Hennessey I should strain to find some familiar feature of the landscape as we approach Dover (Red Fork Ranch). Would it be as I had known it in even one aspect. At Dover I should look for something familiar, but in vain, and should fall back on memories. Could I call up the dash of the Son of Little Robe and his companions with pursuing cattle-men and United States troopers as they passed to the west of the present station? Could I again picture Uncle Ben in the strength of his manhood, facing Wild Bill's gang there alone? Where are the two lone graves on the sand hill south of the station? Do I hear the bull-whackers' early morning fusillade of whips, the cry of the Indian freighters; can I see Dobe making his grand flourish across the tracks? Is that Dan Jones waving a handkerchief and firing shots to attract attention toward the river? Go and see what has happened to him. Do I see a young man and a boy racing up from the south? The boy has just learned to ride and is proud of himself.

I know I could picture good Old Chape as he bustled about, preparing biscuits "like mother used to make" and hear him scraping the old tunes for me again, or his mellow voice raised in the songs I loved to hear, or giving me the parting salute of "So long, see you later."

Brother Ralph's face would appear everywhere about, as he was showing me the pony he gave me, teaching me how to eat chicken, or telling me of the country and its ways.

The roar of the cattle stampede in the night, the sand storm by day, wild deer, turkeys and other denizens, would scamper about. My old friends, the saucy prairie dogs, would bark their greetings. Oh! there are memories clustered about the prosaic station of the town of Dover, Oklahoma.

Boarding the train we would reach the crossing of the Cimarron and there my thoughts would stand as I pictured the Indian youth holding off his pursuers from the south bank, lying wounded unto death through a night, and his father's joyful coming in the morning.

Texas John and I would watch the discomfited officer wade from a sand bar to the south bank to join Dobe, waiting to take him on. Thousands of Indian freighters would be dashing through the water, other thousands of cattle with the cow-men will be swimming through to the north bank.

Journeying on toward Kingfisher I would see the prairie fire trying to overtake Pike and me as we dash for life at a speed which must equal that of the train. We would reach Phil Block's, and there I picture many welcomes and my first and only meal of "bow-wows," the original hot dog.

Toward the east I would look across the Kingfisher Creek and try to see our old cow-camp there, and a great stampede of cattle in a summer storm with a boy tagging along in the rear, uncomfortably soaked to the skin.

In the city of Kingfisher, it would be hard to locate the old stage station, but once there I could picture many happenings, with brother Ralph fighting off his vengeful negro trooper pursuers, as told in connection with the negro officer.

Setting out for the south from Kingfisher, I could relieve many lonely rides to reach Darlington Agency, with the red Stony Hills as the only landmark to the west. There I could picture myself with the team plodding north as I conveyed Old Chape home.

As we neared the old Caddo Spring site, I should need directions to find it, and from that point on to the crossing of the North Canadian River memories would well-nigh overwhelm me.

Reaching the edge of the bottom lands, I should look for the hundreds of tepees, as I heard the far-away, musical voice of the crier calling his news at the close of day; the myriad of tom-toms; dogs barking, wolves howling, the rush of runners through the camp, the cry of children, the speech of their elders, "the voice of the Indian camp."

Looking southward over the North Canadian, I should think of the life that once was there, especially on Beef Issue Days; then would come the fading of this vision of my mythical Empire of yesteryear.

With such surroundings in my most impressionistic years, a dyed-in-the-wool westerner of the United States of America was created. Subsequent experiences in other sections of the West up to my nineteenth birthday still further accentuated my western character. My first trip away from my West into the foreign East took me to Chicago, thence on to the Hub. Clothed in a double-breasted reefer, never having worn an overcoat, I ventured into the strange land with a forty-five six-shooter belted on under my coat and vest. Swearing I would never be guilty of wearing a "biled" shirt, I arrived in Boston.

Leaving the West behind me, becoming a "foreign" Easterner, I thought never to cross reminders of my old life after leaving it. Some one has said "this world is pretty small after all." So it has proved in my case.

When General Grant's tomb was dedicated, there was a great parade, as many will recall. I stood with my wife in the crowd on the side lines to witness the military display. At the head of the procession rode General Nelson A. Miles.

In After Years

Next to him in the rear rode an Indian arrayed in full native dress topped with a gorgeous war-bonnet. The two men rode single-file, and I was not over a hundred feet from them, so I recognized in the Indian my old friend of Red Fork Ranch—Little Joseph, the Nez Perce.

He had come on to Washington to press a claim for his people to be allowed to return to their old land in Idaho, whence they had been removed to Washington state. The bitter warrior was prevailed upon to come to New York for the express purpose of paying tribute to his White Father. The man who rode in front of him in that parade was he who had captured him in the Montana wilds in 1879.

I was greatly moved to behold my friend that day, but was fated never to talk with or see him again.

One year I was employed as expert witness in a suit against the Waring Hat Company of Yonkers. It was an accident case and the attorney for the plaintiff was Karl Miner, Assistant District Attorney, under William Travers Jerome. During a recess one day, Miner spoke of having lived on Pond Creek Ranch. He is the son of the older man I knew at that place. We two, the younger Miner and myself, had never met before.

Through Mr. Joseph Thoburn I learn that Phil Block was still living in the year 1925. Block was an emigrant from Germany, who was stolen by the Cheyenne as he was crossing the plains in the '60s. He was adopted into the tribe, grew up and married Indian fashion. He led a hardy and eventful life.

After the Indian Territory days, he had removed his family to Illinois. From there he communicated with German relatives in the old country. While visiting them in the year 1914, he was caught by the war and not allowed to return to this country for several years.

George Bent still lives, and we two keep tabs on each other after a fashion. The girl he called his "white mother" married my brother Ralph. I joined the newly married couple on their ranch south of the Spanish Peaks, Colorado, and spent many days with them. Amelia was always proud of George and of the fact that he gave her credit for redeeming him from the life of the red man. Thus I kept track of George as he journeyed the "white man's trail" during all his early years. Again I learned of him from Amelia while on a visit to Colorado some fifteen years ago. He always wrote to her. During the past four years I have heard from him frequently.

He writes an excellent hand, discusses various subjects, and seems altogether happy in keeping alive old memories. I wish to present an outline of this man's record, another example of the adaptability of Indian character to present day environment.

He was too young to remember his mother, who lost her life while saving his during a raid of the United States troops on their camp.

Carlisle, Pennsylvania, Haskell Institute, Lawrence, Kansas, and a Quaker College at Wabash, Indiana, all saw the young man as he advanced in education for his life work.

For several years he has given his time to the education of fellow Indians, and is now on location with the government school at Chemawa, Oregon State. This is one of the largest Indian schools in the country. There George acts in the capacity of Athletic Instructor, Band Master and School Disciplinarian, a good enough record for any man.

My last letter from George tells of his having married an Indian girl of the Mission Indians. His services are in great

In After Years

demand during summer months, by the Boy Scouts of America. He is engaged by them to accompany the boys as instructor in camp life, to give them of his Indian lore.

As an example of the quality and character of this man, let me quote the first letter from him after our many years of separation.

CHEMAWA ATHLETIC ASSOCIATION

CHEMAWA, OREGON, AUGUST 25, 1921

Dear Hubert:

Your letter came to me as a pleasant surprise, and it brings back many fond recollections. I hope the opportunity presents itself sometime when we can meet. We could relate some of the old times—the happiest days of our lives.

I have tried to live as Mrs. Collins taught me, to her belongs all the credit of what I am to-day. I have grown up away from home and the environment of the Indian. I have forgotten my Indian and it is rather embarrassing when I go down to visit, to have them talk Indian to me and I cannot reply.

The country has changed so that you would not recognize it. It is all settled up and towns have sprung up here and there. The old Agency site you would not find for the large brick building that served as an office, and the Commissary burnt down some years ago. A few of the dwellings remain and one of the traders' stores. The old Arapahoe School site was turned over to the Masons for a mere price and they established a home there, remodeling the buildings. Nothing will be there in a few years as a land mark,—only the name. The Cheyenne School has also gone under reconstruction. The large frame building where I received my early training also burnt down. Modern buildings have been built and you will probably remember where the spring house stood.

Just east of that on the hill is located the Agency buildings and Hospital. So time has wrought great changes.

I have just returned from camp in the Cascade Mountains. I was Camp Director for the Boy Scouts of America of Salem. We had an ideal camp, took hikes, some of these were for three days. At the camp fire in the evenings I gave them Indian Legends.

Last summer I spent two months in Alaska. Two thirds of our students are Alaskans. Some came from as far north as the Arctic Circle, many coming from the interior where travel to the coast is made by dog team. They told me such wonderful tales of the North-land I was convinced that I must go and see for myself. I found it worth the trip, scenery beautiful and primitive. Had many thrilling experiences that will always remain with me. I found all nationalities and some places where there was little regard for law. The first post I stopped at was a fishing base. Hundreds of men there for the season—gambling and drinking galore. The first night I spent there, there was a shooting fray, between a Filipino and a Chinaman—both died. As Robert Service, who writes so much about Alaska, calls it, "The Land God Forgot." I have begun to think he was correct.

The Indians are called natives there, and they live by fishing and trapping. Their features—a great many of them resemble Japs, we find a goodly number of Russian descent. Many of the early prospectors have left children there. Their educational facilities are poor. I learned a great deal on the trip.

I hope I can hear occasionally from you. I am going to send you under separate cover a photo, so you can see what an Indian looks like. You will see by my button that I am a "Bill." I suppose you are? Aside from being everything else, I am a musician—play the cornet. I occupied first chair in the cornet section in the Salem Symphony Orchestra last winter. Would you ever think of a wild Indian, who was your playmate, getting along that far. Perhaps I am out of place, but it appears I have been the "Dark Horse" of our family.

In After Years

I am real glad to have heard from you, and if ever I get into your section of the country, I shall certainly call around and see you.

Wishing you the very best, I am,
Sincerely your friend,
GEORGE W. BENT.

I was proud to receive that first letter, proud for George's sake, and to know he still cherished the friendship of so long ago.

How many white people can write as interesting a letter couched in the same language and diction?

That first letter has been followed by others, all of which display the same degree of intelligence. It is not surprising to me, as I have known these people so long, but this sample is offered to the consideration of those who still picture the Indian as an untutored savage, or attaining to the limit of "pidgin English" vocabulary.

My blood often boils when I note the persistent picturization of the Indian as a savage who delights in gore and more gore, riding onto the stage with a whoop and going down to inevitable defeat. Would that some genius would come forward and plan a picture on the scale of the "Birth of a Nation," depicting the monumental struggle, physical and moral, which has faced these people in America. These tales picture much of the Indian side of the story while only touching the border of the whole. The great struggle they passed through, the patriotism they showed, their continued efforts to survive against prejudice and misguided philanthropy, deserve telling in their true light, void of maudlin sentimentality.

Dr. Grinnell has done a great work in picturing the Indian as he was. Hamlin Garland is an understanding interpreter of their character. Both of these men have done much for the Indian which will stand more clearly defined as time passes.

283

My feeble effort in these pages is to verify them in my small way.

Looking back on life for the Indian as I knew him, and his struggle to keep his head above water as an independent citizen, one is led to many bald truths which are not pleasant to contemplate.

In our dominance as the white race, have we not always been selfish, as the Indians charge? Greed alone dictated the actions of the old time westerner. It was at the bottom of all prejudice against the Indian. "The Book of the American Indian," written by Hamlin Garland, gives true accounts of various phases of the struggles of these people to maintain their independence against odds.

Add to these my own few tales, and multiply the sum by thousands to get the sum total of individual stories of these people.

Greed of the white man has dictated every move made toward the subjugation of the Indians. Reservations were the first move, which opened up great areas of our domain to settlement. These tales cover the last of old reservation days. Soon after, even the original reservations were too large for the Indians, so said their covetous white neighbors. More of their land was taken from them, they were crowded closer. This was not enough; what land was left to them was portioned to them in severalty, quarter sections, every other one of which was given a white man. Everything was done to break the spirit and morale of a people.

Wholesale cheating has accompanied every move, the whites taking the rôle of cheater. Should an Indian resort to the courts of justice, he did not find redress there. Left with an unassailable title to a portion of their former holdings, we now see conspiracies against individual holders of Osage land, as witness the murder of several of that tribe in Oklahoma.

In After Years

The case is now in the courts, and it is doubtful if the victims of white man's greed will find redress for a single wrong. So the story has gone all over the United States. Even the Hopi cannot feel safe in the possession of their few miserable acres in Arizona, by reason of the discovery of coal there. The Navajo kept much of their territory from invasion of white prospectors for years, and knew what they were doing. Some slipped by them, and now their canyons and hills are to give up their wealth to the dominant race.

It will be said that they are paid for this land, they even can go in and choose what they want to keep. When the plains Indians were given such a choice, as when the division of the land into quarter sections faced them, the old time warrior spirit bid them choose the hills for theirs. Thus they took up the land which would not return them a living, prompted by the instinct to remain where they could see their enemies coming. But they had first choice. If one of them should choose a desirable bottom land, every agency of intimidation was brought to bear to compel him to move. So it has been in every section of our country.

Beaten in war, held prisoners, arriving at the stage where they dare not even show a temper under provocation, for fear of the cry of "Wild Indian," cursed for "Damned Indians," classed with "Dagoes" and "Squareheads" by those who boast of the "Square Deal" as their slogan, how could these men do else but lose spirit? With this breaking down of their morale, the men lost their assertiveness in the family.

Women and girls witnessed the humiliation of their fathers and brothers, and fell easy prey to any temptation placed in their paths. Every reservation has seen the coming of some white cur to their village who cast the first white smile on some comely Indian maid. She interpreted this as a sign of real favor from the dominant race, and fell easy prey to foul accomplishment. Thus was a formerly self-sustaining, capable, self-reliant race of people debauched.

Any other race with the record of sires fighting bravely as these did, with native arts developed to a point never excelled, with records of unselfish generosity, love of truth, reverent living, would have a Hall of Fame filled with mementoes of their heroes, records of their deeds and accomplishments. Our government took the stand that everything Indian must be pounded out of these people. In the early reservation days, the Indian was held a prisoner of war on his land, must not leave its environs without leave or an accompanying escort of soldiers. At the same time, official red tape often held back supplies of food when it was sorely needed. The people starved. Every agent was an autocrat with the entire keeping of these people subject to his caprice. Did the proud spirits hold out on a point of principle as they saw it, the agent would hold back the life-sustaining food, and whole families starved during the dispute. Many outbreaks were fostered and started by men who were starved animals, grieving that their families were suffering. With fanatical desperation they would try to break through the cordon and reach life where they could find it. In those days they were surrounded by whites who looked upon them merely as savages, to be shot on sight as were wolves. These people had always taken care of themselves and only wanted the same opportunity again. They readily took up anything which offered the way to the white man's road. They believed they could hold their own with any race. Many shining examples are now extant of such a change from Stone Age training to that of skilled artisans, professional men without peer. After such training they were expected to be self-sustaining, but the road led back to old scenes because of prejudice, jealousy, anything except the Golden Rule.

In After Years

Another factor has been the destruction of whatever beliefs they ever had. Creedists ever jealous of their own special tenets to the point of excluding all others sought to teach them a new faith. Their special way of approaching God, insistence on the recognition of the Savior or be damned, was offered to these reverent people as the only means of reaching the Hereafter. The pagan was told to forget all he knew of communing with The Great One Above in meditation and supplication. He was told to follow the one teacher who in turn vilified all workers of other creeds. The Indian soon learned the white man had a hundred different Jesus Roads. In that emergency the Indian craftily adhered to the one who came among them with the most presents. One minister of the gospel reached Darlington filled with zeal and the optimism of the thought that he would convert every Indian to his way of thinking. He spoke of that possibility and Ralph said, "If you have enough presents to go around, you can convert the whole tribe." It was true in the sense that all would have rallied to a first service knowing they were to receive some honorarium. But they noted the cool looks one worker gave the laborer in another field of thought, and knew there was anything but the spirit of Christ in their feelings for one another.

Thus the Indians soon divided the creeds they met into classes, named with the descriptive clearness of their customs. They have always revered the Quakers as true friends of theirs and call them Friends. Methodists are Shouters; Baptists, Duck under Water; Episcopalians, White Shirts; Catholic, Drags his Shirt on the Ground. Some of the definitions are not complimentary, to say the least. Their whole attitude is of scoffing at those who insist on creed, in preference to living a general faith. They feel that their own was not so bad, they believed in a Great Being and while not understanding him fully, followed his voice whenever they could. Not so bad.

Charles Godfrey Leland was a close student of Gypsy life in all parts of the world. He was their understanding friend. Commenting on the ostracism of the race, he makes the following statement:

"When a race is greatly looked down upon by another from the standpoint of mere color, as in America, or mere religion, as in Mohammedan lands, it always contains proportionately a larger number of decent people than are to be found among those who immediately oppress it.

"It is when a man realizes that he is superior in nothing else, save race, color, religion, family, inherited fortune, and other contingent advantages, that he develops into a prig and a snob."

This applies to the attitude of the whites toward the Indians of these United States of America. It were better that we acknowledge dealing with fellow beings who possess many redeeming qualities, and that we repent in sackcloth and ashes for man's inhumanity to man.

NOTES

My brother Ralph had spent all his days on one disappearing frontier after another. This trail led to a ranch in the Spanish Peaks country of Southern Colorado, after Indian Territory. Again entering the government service, he was made the first School Superintendent over the Hopi Indians in Arizona. He went there in 1889 and remained four years, after which he returned to his mountain ranch. Again he served in Keams Canyon during the Nineties, then he was sent to the Sioux at the new school established in Rapid City, South Dakota. There he served for several years, going thence to Pawhuska, Oklahoma, as agent to the Osage. Later on he returned to his home in Rocky Ford, Colorado, and there acted as special agent for Indians of all tribes coming to the beet fields to harvest the crops. His work at home was varied with stock raising, and irrigating projects among the Hopi, Navajo, Zunis and others in New Mexico and Arizona. To this day he is an intensely practical friend of all Indians, and is visited at his home by his red friends.

Crane, in his "Indians of the Enchanted Desert," has words of praise for my brother Ralph and his work among the Hopi of Arizona. He states the fact that only two white men ever won the confidence of that tribe, and brother Ralph is the only one living.

CHAPTER IV

After Agencies had been established at Darlington and Fort Sill, a new route was laid out, off the cattle trail, but near by and parallel with it, known as the Reno Trail. This was used by freighters and travelers who wished to avoid the big cattle herds on the Chisholm Trail. Later it was used also by the stage company.

The two trails ran close together from Kansas to the Cimarron. At the Salt Fork, the Reno Trail forded several miles further up the river, but ran back close to the other near the headwaters of Hackberry Creek. Again, as the trails came toward the Cimarron, the Reno followed a natural opening through the timber straight south, from the point where the Chisholm turned east by south in its opening to the river ford. The Reno followed its own course here to the river bank, and forded it more than a mile farther up the stream than the other ford of the Cimarron. This Reno ford was also much used by the Cheyenne and Arapahoe, for they could soon reach their villages on the North Canadian by turning southwest from it. The Reno Trail bore due south from this ford, and over the prairie to Kingfisher Creek, where another ford was made before continuing over the high plains to Darlington Agency. Coming down into the bottom land where the Agency lay, the trail turned to the west along the river bank to reach its station, and then with a sharp turn to the south, forded the North Canadian and continued on to Fort Reno. From here, it went straight on to Fort Sill. This Reno Trail lay always to the west of the Chisholm Trail, but never were they separated by more than a mile at any point, except at the crossing of the Salt Fork and Cimarron rivers.

With the inauguration of the stage line, change stations were established at Pond Creek, Bull Foot Ranch, Kingfisher Crossing, Fort Reno and Fort Sill. Red Fork Ranch and Darlington Agency became only points of call.

Pond Creek Ranch, Bull Foot Ranch, and Kingfisher Crossing came into being because of the stage line. Skeleton Ranch on the Salt Fork was an occasional point of call and eating place for stage passengers, but was off the regular route. Along the entire trail, except at Caldwell, Darlington and the two forts, all buildings were of logs.

Meals were served regularly to passengers at Pond Creek, Bull Foot, and at Fort Reno. At times they were to be had at Skeleton, Red Fork, and Kingfisher. These meals were alike along the line—salt horse (sow-belly), biscuit, and coffee. The latter was served without milk or cream, and often without sugar.

The stages were Concord Coaches drawn by four-horse teams of mules or horses. They were swung on leather straps, and seated six people inside and many on the roof with the driver. Baggage was carried in a "boot" in the rear. All U. S. Mail was carried both ways by this route.

The stage stations were manned as a rule by employees who proved trustworthy, but it was a lonely life, and frequent changes occurred. For this reason, men who were known to be either outlaws or in league with them were sometimes placed in charge of the stations. The drivers were mostly reliable old frontiersmen, and were, of course, the aristocrats among the company employees.

At the time of the taking over of Red Fork Ranch, there was no hint of the changes that were to come in the next few years. The owners were progressive enough to see the value of a store placed on the great trails where there was no competition outside of Caldwell and Darlington. They prepared for this, and maintained quite a trading business from the start.

In 1883 it became clear that their range must be restricted to boundaries and the surviving member of the firm set about fencing in the leased range. He hired many cow-boys out of work to cut posts during the winter and the following summer, and with the aid of his Indian friends succeeded in erecting over eighty miles of wire fence.

This giant task had hardly been finished before the government decided to open the country for settlement. The leases were taken from the cattlemen, and they were forced to abandon all the improvements they had made. Later, these fences were all taken down at the orders of the government. It meant the ruin of many, among them the remaining partner. He left the country, where he had built up and lost a fortune, with all his possessions in one covered wagon, and joined the tide toward the setting sun. Eventually he became a nester (farmer).

The Chisholm Trail was followed continuously for twenty-two years by cattlemen. This route bore almost due north from Texas to Kansas, deviating only at fords of streams or to find openings through obstructing woods. A course free from such natural barriers could have been laid out a few miles west of where it was, but that would have been through the heart of hostile Indian country.

In the last years of its use as a highway, its appearance was that of a wide beaten path, devoid of any growth.

Its old course is only a vision now, and this record can merely tell where it lay north of the Cimarron River. Its general direction in the vicinity of Red Fork Ranch is shown on the map printed in the forepart of this book, which is drawn from the author's memory of it. Thence it went due north to Abilene, later only to Wichita, and still later, as the railroad terminals were moved nearer the Indian Territory, to Caldwell, which was on the borderland, and was the Chisholm Trail terminal for over half of the trail's life.

One might as well ask a native New Yorker if he knows where the New York Central Railroad is, as to have asked an old time Westerner the location of the old Chisholm Trail. Yet who can place it now?

CHAPTER IX

The many so-called bad men of the West came by their reputations for reasons as varied as their number.

Men of the Wild-Bill-horse-thief type were not vicious to the extent of murdering for the sake of killing only. Let him follow his choice of horse-stealing unmolested, he was most amiable, with no thought of otherwise harming his fellow men. The stolen stock was taken when the owners were unaware of the proximity of thieves. If there was a chance of a fight to secure the horses, there would be no theft. Once a herd was made away with, the only killings liable to occur in connection therewith would be of officers of the law who interfered, or members of the gang who might quarrel among themselves. With this type of men, killings were generally the last resort in self-defense, or in avoidance of arrest, which amounted to the same thing. Otherwise they were a genial crowd of reprobates. In cities they might have made second-rate sneak thieves.

Cattle rustlers were of the same class as horse thieves, and all were bad men according to the degree in which they killed to follow their chosen bent. Other bad men were not thieves, but killers alone. The more notches on the individual's gun, the more dangerous he was reputed to be.

One man who gained a reputation as an all-around horse thief, cattle thief, and general bad man in the old Indian Nation was Cherokee Bill, as described in Chapter IX.

I had never known of the magnitude of his doings until I came across a series of articles in *The Saturday Evening Post* under the name of Fred E. Sutton.

Sutton charges thirteen murders, one of a brother-in-law, to Cherokee Bill. He tells of this criminal fighting his way out of the court room as he was being tried for his crimes, only to be dissuaded from his purpose by his fellow outlaw, Henry Starr.

His mother witnessed his death. As they were preparing the body for burial, a photograph of his mother was found on his breast, together with a piece of poetry dedicated to her.

In this verse he expressed his hope of meeting his mother in heaven. When the poem was shown to Starr, he said, "Bury it with him. When God sees it, maybe He'll take him in." Knowing what I do of his youth, I cannot help but think, "Another good boy went wrong."

CHAPTER XI

There is a section foreman on the Chicago, Rock Island, and Pacific Railroad line from Caldwell, Kansas, to Kingfisher, Oklahoma, named William Ray. This man spent some time on Red Fork Ranch the year they were building the fences. He remained in the country and became a resident of Dover after its settlement. From him I learned of the fate of my old friend, John G. Chapin (Old Chape). Chape saw the formation of a new town on the site of Red Fork Ranch and remained as a citizen of the new community for a number of years until he was too old to care for himself. He then was taken to the Old Soldiers' Home at Fort Leavenworth, Kansas, where he died and is buried.

CHAPTER XIII

In a letter from Charles A. Siringo, we have the following statement in reference to Baughman (Boffman):

Notes

"Will say that Theodore Baughman is the same man you mention. I was in Chicago, and used to see him often at the time he run a 'Blazer' on those railroad strikers."

CHAPTER XIV

"Riata and Spurs," by Charles A. Siringo, appeared in print in the spring of 1927. Through the publishers I was placed in communication with Charlie and wrote him of the incident of his saving my life, asking if he recalled it. This is his reply.

"The incident of my running the longhorn steer back into the herd seems like a dream. The chances are I did pull off the stunt, as I was in that part of the territory at the time."

CHAPTER XV

The name Tosimeea, in the Cheyenne tongue, means the-one-who-takes-out-his-teeth. At the council of United States Commissioners with all the tribes at Medicine Lodge, in 1868, Brinton Darlington had astounded the Indians by removing an upper plate of teeth which he wore. Darlington was made the first agent to settle these people on a reservation and accompanied the Cheyenne and Arapahoe to the site of the first agency. The Indians applied this name to him. It signified what it literally meant and also was used by these tribes to describe an Indian agent. When John D. Miles succeeded Darlington on the death of the latter, it seemed natural to the Indians when they noted that the new man also removed his teeth. After that, all Indian agents were each the-one-who-takes-out-his-teeth to these people.

Darlington won the very highest regard of the wildest Indians, and Little Robe was absolutely loyal to him, even after Darlington died in 1873.

Noting the white men as they drove oxen across the plains, the Indians had heard the newcomers calling out—"Whoahaw! Whoa-haw" and "Gee!" From this they took the word Woha. As oxen were of the same species of bovine which soon came to cover the plains country, these Indians applied the name to all cattle.

The plains Indians had a legend that the buffalo hordes of the old days came-up-out-of-the-ground at a spot somewhere in the Staked Plains region of the Texas Panhandle country. This belief was at the bottom of their insistence that all white buffalo hunters be kept from the Panhandle of Texas.